PROTECTING
PHARAOH'S
TREASURES

PROTECTING PHARAOH'S TREASURES

MY LIFE IN EGYPTOLOGY

Wafaa El Saddik

with
Rüdiger Heimlich

The American University in Cairo Press
Cairo New York

The author and the publisher are grateful to the Sawiris Foundation for Social Development for the generous support that made this translation and its publication possible.

First published in English in 2017 by
The American University in Cairo Press
113 Sharia Kasr el Aini, Cairo, Egypt
420 Fifth Avenue, New York, NY 10018
www.aucpress.com

First published in German as *Es gibt nur den geraden Weg: Mein Leben als Schatzhüterin Ägyptens*, copyright © 2013 by Verlag Kiepenheuer & Witsch GmbH & Co. KG, Cologne, Germany

Translated by Russell Stockman

Exclusive distribution outside Egypt and North America by I.B.Tauris & Co Ltd., 6 Salem Road, London, W4 2BU

Dar el Kutub No. 14247/16
ISBN 978 977 416 825 3

Dar el Kutub Cataloging-in-Publication Data

El Saddik, Wafaa
    Protecting Pharaoh's Treasures: My Life in Egyptology / Wafaa El Saddik.—Cairo: The American University in Cairo Press, 2017
        p.   cm.
        ISBN 978 977 416 825 3
        1. Egypt — Antiquities
        932

1 2 3 4 5   21 20 19 18 17

Designed by Sally Boylan
Printed in the United States of America

For Hadi, Tarek, and Azmy

CONTENTS

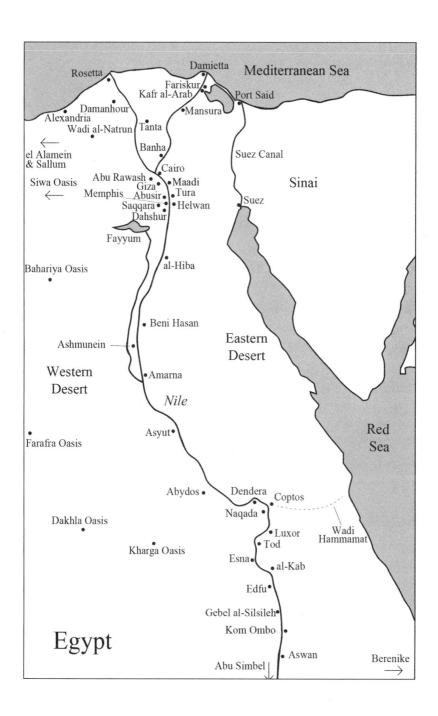

Rosetta
Damietta
Mediterranean Sea
Fariskur
Kafr al-Arab
Port Said
Damanhour
•Mansura
Alexandria
Wadi al-Natrun
Tanta
el Alamein
& Sallum
Banha
Suez Canal
Sinai
Siwa Oasis
Abu Rawash
•Maadi
Cairo
Memphis
Giza
Abusir
•Tura
Saqqara
•Helwan
Dahshur
Suez
Fayyum
Bahariya Oasis
al-Hiba
Beni Hasan
Eastern
Desert
Ashmunein
Amarna
Western
Desert
Nile
Red
Sea
Asyut•
Farafra Oasis
Abydos •
Dendera
Coptos
Dakhla Oasis
Naqada
Wadi
Hammamat
•Luxor
Tod
Kharga Oasis
Esna•
•al-Kab
Edfu•
Egypt
Gebel al-Silsileh•
Kom Ombo
• Aswan
Berenike
Abu Simbel

PREFACE

S abah is back, and I can't tell you how happy that makes me. Since the days of the plundering, Sabah had not set foot in the Egyptian Museum. Dark, lost years. The shattered vitrines, the damaged objects, and the artifacts missing to this day—with that despicable break-in and unspeakable theft, to Sabah the integrity of the building had been violated. It was as if an ultimate taboo had been broken, and she could no longer feel right in the museum.

How many years we spent side by side in the 'treasury of the pharaohs'! I remember our first days in the cellar, when we fought our way through the cobwebs for the first time, through stacks of crates and boxes that turned the depot into a giant labyrinth. Sabah even screwed in the lightbulbs herself in order to shine light into forgotten corners. For years we worked in the cellar and tried to reorganize the building on Tahrir Square from top to bottom. We labored as if it were possible to do such a thing in the tenure of a single director. Presumptuous of us!

Of course it was presumptuous, but we did what we could: arranged and listed, documented and repositioned, and where possible sent works of art to the country's new regional museums. We did what generations of our predecessors had not even attempted. We often sat at the computer until late at night, made it possible to look up finds from long-forgotten excavations, and combined artifacts into new exhibits. We worked in opposition to self-important bureaucratic inanities, to corruption and ignorance. All that is described in the present book. But nothing depressed me over the long term more than Sabah's absence all those months since the plundering of the museum. Sabah stands for tomorrow, for the future, for hope. And she is precisely what we need in the museum and in the entire country.

Five years have passed since the 'Revolution.' And where do we stand today? Prices are rising higher and higher, and incomes don't keep up with them. In Luxor the hotels are empty. In many faces I read sadness and despair. Many families are going into debt merely to survive. I find it altogether incomprehensible how millions of poor and unemployed people manage their everyday lives. I travel to Luxor, where I know many people: the families of my former excavation teams, colleagues, and friends. Many of the city's people are starving. Many lack the money to send their children to school. There is so little work in the hotels and restaurants that their employees alternate shifts so as to earn at least a little something. One man I know is paid LE200 a month (about $25), of which he spends LE120 on his son's medications. Since the Revolution revenues from tourism have dropped by LE66 billion; 275 hotel ships stand empty, and a mere 5 percent of the hotels remain open. More than four thousand tour guides have left the country.

Luxor, that beautiful, restful city—"hundred-gated Thebes," *Diospolis magna*, as the Greek writer Herodotus called it, that picturesque landscape with its wonderful climate—and not a single smile on its people's faces. I look at the Nile, to Egyptians the eternal river. It is the same river that created Egypt's high culture. Since the beginning, people have drunk its water, and they still drink it today. The river hasn't changed, but the Egyptians have. They were always thought of as the Mediterranean's easy-going, humorous people—but their jokes have become cruel, and there's no more laughter.

Barely a year after Mubarak's fall, people were perplexed, faced with a choice between plague and cholera, between the old regime and Morsi. After the military, the Muslim Brotherhood was the best-organized political force in the country. But like Mubarak, it had no practical experience with democracy. Morsi's Freedom and Justice Party won the first free elections, then—following the pattern of Mubarak and his predecessors—grabbed more and more power to itself. Women, especially, had to fear for the rights and entitlements they had attained in the past sixty years. For women it was a year of profound depression. The Egyptians said, "we've given Morsi a driver's license, but he doesn't even know how to drive."

Egypt seemed to be sinking into chaos. People were afraid to go out at night. My friend Azza's husband was kidnapped. When her son tried to pay the ransom, he too was snatched. Then came terrible news from Luxor. Mariam, my Coptic friend, called me in tears on January 7, 2013: Two friends of mine, the daughters of Tawfik Pasha Andraus, a member of the Wafd Party in King Farouk's time, had been murdered in their home in Luxor. Laudy, seventy-nine, and Sofi, eighty-two, were found dead in their rooms. To this day there has been no explanation of the crime. I was shocked and speechless. I had known the two aristocratic women since my excavations in Luxor in the 1980s. I often visited them for afternoon coffee. We would talk about the history of their home, a venerable palace that has stood on the bank of the Nile near the Luxor temple for more than 150 years. In it hung paintings by Italian masters, and it was filled with precious antiques and fine old furniture. The former governor of Luxor, Samir Farag, wanted to raze the house, but Laudy and Sofi defied his attempts to condemn it. In their wills they specified that the house was to be given to the state so that it might be used for a museum. Police investigations determined that the palace's contents had been untouched. So the murderer's motive wasn't robbery.

Perhaps it will later be determined why criminality shot up precisely under the rule of the Muslim Brotherhood: kidnappings, murders, plunderings. For that reason, on June 30, 2013, millions of people took to the streets demanding that the army intervene. For them el-Sisi was Egypt's savior. At the time I was working on a book about the Amarna period, about the intolerance of Akhenaten's religious revolution. It seemed that history was repeating itself. Then too Egypt was facing collapse, and it was only the army general Horemheb's seizure of power that brought stability.

Five years have passed since the Revolution. We have experienced violence, assassinations, arrests. I read the Egyptian news columns in foreign newspapers. I speak with worried and politically discouraged friends and acquaintances who gaze at the Nile filled with anxiety, who in fact know only the media's negative headlines. I see their skeptical responses when I remind them that the streets are safe, that social conditions are precarious, to be sure, but by no means chaotic; we no longer have to fear being robbed or kidnapped. The historic sites are secure, archaeologists are at work again. There are many signs of hope.

It was a bitter blow for me when the children's museum within the Egyptian Museum was closed. I had invested so much work and love in the creation of that gift to Egypt's children. In the face of the plundering and illegal excavations of the past few years, I have deliberately devoted all my time to my museum education efforts. To my mind it is the only effective way to counter the threat to our ancient heritage by our own people. Only when our children take the protection of ancient sites into their own hands will we be able to save them—our children are our legacy. For they need history and identity. With the support of all my undaunted and faithful colleagues in European and American museums, I organize workshops for children and young people. Among them are more and more children from Syria, traumatized and apathetic. But I manage to make them happy, if only for a few hours.

Sabah is back. She is working with the young curators. She is as committed as ever, and perhaps with that commitment hope will return to the museum. I have been there often—and each time come back despondent. The building is dark, there is not even money for lightbulbs. In the intervening five years there have been seven directors, none of whom stayed long. The same has been the case in politics, with ministers and prime ministers.

So I continue to give lectures, organize workshops, intervene in the cause of the children's museum, and I am proud of the group of committed young people who support and encourage me in this. I see the blind Ahmed Nagi, who makes extraordinary paintings; the deaf and dumb Nesma, who dances to melodies she can't hear. Both were still children when I began scheduling events for blind and hearing-impaired children in the Egyptian Museum under the supervision of museum educators Tahany Noah and Fatima Khawasik. I look at this young generation and know that despondency is not an option. It never was and never will be. And as I write these lines, the news has reached me that the children's museum is indeed being reopened. And that two-thirds of Mubarak's ugly National Democratic Party high-rise HQ has been razed and the rest is to go soon. Now it is again possible to see the Nile from the museum. It is a wonderful feeling.

Cairo, January 2016

1

DAYS OF RAGE

riday, January 28, 2011. Nothing is working. Since late morning we have tried again and again, but there's nothing to be done: The mobile phone is dead, there has been no Internet connection for three days, ever since Eid al-Shurta, the 'Day of the Police.' January 25 is their annual holiday. Children have no school, stores and markets are closed, and people relax in parks or along the Nile. The nation commemorates the group of policemen shot by British soldiers at a police station in Ismailia during the occupation. On television Mubarak gave one of his speeches, as irrelevant as it was boring. The president conveyed holiday best wishes to high-ranking policemen, army generals, and the heads of his seven secret services, assuring them of his highest esteem. In Egypt everyone knew who was congratulating whom: The pharaoh was flattering the people who prop up his regime.

Three days later everything is altogether different. In Tahrir Square and in many Cairo neighborhoods, crowds of people are milling about in memory of Khaled Said, the twenty-eight-year-old blogger from Alexandria whom civil security forces dragged out of an Internet café on June 5, 2010, and beat to death in the entrance to a nearby building. The crowds are chanting his name—and "Down with Mubarak!"

1

Since Eid al-Shurta the security forces have been doing what Mubarak expects of them: beating people. But people are standing up to their attacks. It is magnificent. Wherever they are driven back they regroup. A huge demonstration in the city center is announced for this Friday afternoon.

The tension can be felt even in our suburban district, Nasr City. In the afternoon we do a little extra shopping. People look at each other with unsteady glances. Then in the evening we are told that scores of major criminals have escaped from the prisons. Of course everyone knows that this is an attempt at intimidation on the part of the security agencies. They want people to stay home. "That won't help these criminals," my husband Azmy growls, referring to the thugs in the government. He gazes from a window down at the street. Below, volunteers have gathered in front of the entrances to the buildings, patrolling with sticks. "The people won't let themselves be intimidated anymore."

Since this morning columns of vehicles have been heading for the city center. On pickups and in vans people sit shoulder to shoulder, women as well as men. They know what awaits them in Tahrir Square. The police have been instructed to be brutal, to use tear gas, clubs, rubber bullets, if necessary even live ammunition. Some demonstrators have already been killed and wounded. Nobody knows how many have been hauled away by secret service people. But the people's rage is far greater than their fear. "Yesterday Tunis, today Cairo," they chant. They know that it's now or never. They've had enough of poverty, corruption, phony elections, and police brutality. The military behaves the way Egyptians expect it to: guardedly, not aggressively. It is mainly Mubarak's police and secret services that people are afraid of.

For days—like everyone else in Egypt—we have kept the television on. The state channels keep broadcasting the president's conciliatory speeches over and over.

*

The last time I had met Hosni Mubarak was in October 2010 in Rome. It was another of the Ministry of Culture's smoke-and-mirrors maneuvers. Only a few weeks before Mubarak's state visit to Italy, the ministry had instructed me to put together a list of 190 treasures from Cairo's museums. Mubarak wanted to take something along for then-Italian prime minister Silvio Berlusconi: an exhibition of treasures from Egyptian history. But my selection was not approved. The minister of culture found it not spectacular enough. A new selection was ordered—this time put together by the office of the antiquities chief, Zahi Hawass, and my assistant at the museum, Said Hassan—and this one was considered to be appropriate. I couldn't believe my eyes: a large sandstone bust of Akhenaten, a granite statue of Sekhmet, various gold artifacts from Tutankhamun's tomb, Egypt's oldest copy of the Qur'an from Dar al-Kutub, and pieces from the Coptic and Islamic museums that were never allowed to leave the country. Furious, I called Zahi Hawass to protest. To no avail. I told him, "You'll have to say no!"

But Hawass explained, "This is what the president wants."

"But the president has no idea what he'd be taking out of the country!"

"It is how it is," Hawass replied.

"I won't sign such a list of loans."

Instead, it was signed by my assistant.

A few days before Mubarak's state visit, Hawass called me from the Supreme Council of Antiquities, Egypt's antiquities administration. He was unable to attend the opening of the exhibition in Rome; he had a scheduling problem. I would have to set up the exhibition at the Egyptian Academy of Arts in Rome in his place and then guide Mubarak and Berlusconi through it. I declined, but Hawass ignored my protest. "The minister insists on it."

Now everything had to be done very quickly. A few days before they were to leave, the loan items weren't even insured yet and transport had not even been chartered. My coworkers had no visas. There was no exhibition catalog. We were told that the labels for the display cases would be sent along by the ministry. In my years as director of the Egyptian Museum I had learned one thing: If it has anything to do with the president, everything possible will be done; money is no object. So we booked a special flight with Egyptair—at double the usual fare, of course. On Sunday we flew to Rome, and the crates were to follow by midday on Monday. The opening was scheduled for Wednesday. I hadn't signed a thing, no freight documents, no transfer receipts. Yet if something were to be missing or damaged on arrival in Rome, or worse yet, if an object failed to return to Cairo after the exhibition, I would be the one called to account. That's another thing I had learned in my past seven years as director: Whatever I did and whatever I signed, I had to be constantly mindful of the lurking federal prosecutor. Again and again the ministry and the Supreme Council of Antiquities had tried to entangle me in various suicide missions.

I traveled with my three closest coworkers. We had two days and a night to put it all together. We were constantly being watched by Mubarak's security people, and I, in turn, didn't let them out of my sight. I knew I couldn't trust anyone. We worked with virtually no time for sleep. The exhibition spaces were in the Academy's basement, down a narrow flight of steps. As soon as I had seen the large Akhenaten bust on Zahi's list, I suspected what we would be facing. It took us hours of sweat-drenched effort to inch it down the stairs. Just don't let it tip, no scratches, I prayed. These pieces have survived for three thousand years, we surely don't want to destroy them in a Roman stairwell.

The display cases had already been arranged; there was no chance of changing the nonsensical way the objects were to be presented. The labels were filled with errors, some of them simply wrong, so I phoned to order new ones. The ministry people assured me that Mubarak didn't read display case labels anyway. "Leave them as they are!" We worked like dogs to meet the Tuesday evening deadline. Yet I knew that Mubarak still had appointments in Berlin on Wednesday. They were only placing additional time pressure on us.

On Thursday morning Mubarak and Berlusconi appeared. Their entourages and security people flooded the building. Farouk Hosni, the minister of culture, admonished me, "No more than fifteen minutes." Mubarak was obviously tired, his handshake limp, his gaze unsteady, and he was having trouble standing up. Two or three times during the tour he leaned heavily on my shoulder. Silvio Berlusconi was obviously uninterested. In the background people kept motioning to me, "Faster! Faster!"

I tried to draw the two gentlemen's attention to the Egyptian Book of the Dead, the scene in the judgment of the deceased in which his heart is weighed against the feather of truth and morality, and Anubis checks the balance on the scale. Next to him crouches the Devourer, a monster with the head of a crocodile and the body of a lion. "All those who have flouted the laws and offended those nearest them," I explained to them, "are gobbled up by the Devourer."

That was the only time during the entire tour that Mubarak took notice and briefly smiled. All around us the photographers snapped pictures. That was the moment that the Egyptian television news programs would show over and over: a smiling Mubarak. Back in Cairo people asked me about those pictures in amazement. In the antiquities service many of my colleagues now saw me as destined for the highest offices—Mubarak had smiled. Once Berlusconi had gone, Mubarak sank down onto a sofa, his entourage arrayed in a semicircle around him. No one spoke to him. He simply stared straight ahead, exhausted. That is the picture I remember.

*

The Rome incident had been only a few months before. It was now the beginning of 2011, and for five weeks I had officially been the director emerita. Yet the telephone never stopped ringing. I could hardly abandon the antiquities service, the Egyptian Museum, and all the people I had encouraged for seven years. I was able to reassure the callers that I would be staying in Egypt. But Azmy and I were exhausted. After the harried days of my departure we needed rest; we first had to adjust to the new daily schedule. Previously Ashraf, my driver, would have been waiting outside the door by 8:30; now we could watch Al Jazeera in the early morning. Previously we would have been stuck in rush-hour traffic on the elevated highway, with me reading files, Ashraf talking about his family, his daughters, and what he had just picked up on the grapevine from other drivers from the antiquities service. Frequently it included veiled warnings. There had been telephone conversations, so-and-so had spoken about me . . . . In the seven years I was director I had been prepared for a great deal, thanks to dear and loyal friends who saw to it that I didn't walk into any traps.

The revolutionary events in the streets of Tunis in December 2010 caught us by surprise, most of us at least. Azmy and I were certain that something would happen in Egypt as well. We had lived in Germany for more than sixteen years but had visited Egypt a number of times every year, often for weeks. Perhaps it is easier to observe changes in a country and its people from a distance: how the poor grow poorer and poorer and the rich even richer; the ever more brazen self-confidence with which the powerful help

themselves; the virus of corruption that infects every segment of the population; the emigration of intellectuals; the resort to Islam on the part of those
with no opportunities; the encapsulation of the monied elite and the frustration of the losers. We knew that the social gap could not continue to widen
forever. It was only a question of time before something had to happen. Yet
now, when in fact something had happened, we were both surprised.

On those January days in 2011, we followed Egypt's 'turnaround' on
television with great excitement—just as before, in 1989, when we witnessed
the fall of the Wall in Germany. We watched as Berliners attacked the Wall
with picks and people fell into each other's arms sobbing with happiness.
Azmy and I had understood: We were living in a country where a lot of things
were about to change. And we thought, it was also a new beginning for our
children and for ourselves. Now here we were standing in front of the television again, and we understood: We're living in a country where much has
to change—and much will change, *in sha' Allah*. But will it also be a new
beginning for the two of us? Azmy and I were not out on the square with
the young people. Our sons were where they had grown up, in Germany and
America. But we had no doubt where we would have had to look for them
that day. They would have been out in Tahrir Square with the crowds, screaming "Peacefully! Peacefully!"

Hour by hour more people crowded into the square. No one was attacking
any walls with picks, but Egyptians were tearing down the symbols of power:
Mubarak posters. I couldn't help but summon up images from my childhood,
of Gamal Abdel Nasser. Wherever he appeared there were massive crowds,
there was euphoria. The people loved him and idolized him. Now once again
tens of thousands were streaming across the Nile bridges and into Tahrir and
Abdel Moneim Riad Squares. Once again the people were euphoric—in their
repudiation. There was no new Nasser; this time the charisma of revolution
radiated from the people gathered on the square themselves. Foreign wire
services reported that the situation was growing increasingly critical. Finally,
the battle between state authority and the people came to a head. We watched
on the screen as the police violently dispersed the crowds. Policemen in civilian clothes were beating and kicking unarmed young people, the television
showed blood-streaked faces and bodies. I thanked God that I did not have
to fear for my two sons, but I was enraged, disgusted—and at the same time

helpless. Had I been twenty years younger, I would have been out on the square, I would have been standing in front of 'my' museum.

Suddenly we saw flames. The television showed the Egyptian National Democratic Party building on fire. I had always hated the ugly structure. Built under Nasser in the 1960s in the ubiquitous Soviet style of the time, it stood on the grounds of the Egyptian Museum, whose garden still extended to the bank of the Nile at the time. The site had originally been set aside for future extensions to the building, storage depots, and workshops. But at the time no one was consulted. While still a student I had watched the hideous structure being built. Not only did it spoil the view of the Nile, it was a brazen, lawless land grab.

Now the building was burning, and at first I felt a certain satisfaction. Maybe the ruin could finally be torn down. I had always wanted to expand the old museum, just as its founders had envisioned when they erected the structure on the British army's expansive drill grounds. The idea of building a new Egyptian museum far from the city center, Mubarak's 'Grand Museum,' still strikes me today as utterly absurd, far-fetched in the truest sense of the word. I love the old museum structure. It stands in the heart of the city. With the $600 million projected for the new building in Giza, the venerable old building could finally have been fully upgraded.

But as the flames rose higher I began to fear that the fire could leap over onto the museum itself. I tried to calm myself with the thought that in 2008—against resistance from the antiquities administration—it had been given a new coat of nonflammable paint. In 2002, for the centennial jubilee, the ministry had the museum painted a somewhat garish red, the same shade, as it happens, the minister of culture's private home was painted. I had discovered that it was not a nonflammable paint, but one that was astonishingly expensive and impractical. On an inspection tour I collected chunks of the thickly crusted pigment and had them analyzed in the laboratory. The result: The paint was damaging the stone. I sent the report to the ministry and demanded new and environment-friendly paint for the façade. The thick crust had to be scraped off laboriously. Although the new nonflammable paint was far less expensive than the one the ministry had applied, no additional paint was approved for the museum's interior. It was declined by the same people who had turned down my previous proposal about the museum's security. But what if there were cars burning behind the museum, and the heat shattered the windowpanes and the flames penetrated the building's interior? It would be a catastrophe. And what if the new paint was not in fact nonflammable, if it was only rated fire-resistant? That would be unsurprising, given the usual pattern of corruption.

But the fire was only the beginning. The telephone rang, and on the line was a journalist from the newspaper *Rose el-Youssef* I had known for several years. He asked anxiously whether the museum was secured.

"Perfectly safe if the security people are still there." At that moment I was unaware that the police had already withdrawn from the area and left it unguarded. I attempted to reach our security firm by landline, but no one answered. Instead, I again spoke with the journalist from *Rose el-Youssef.*

"Doctor Wafaa, the Egyptian Museum, the Mit Rahina Museum in Memphis, and the storerooms of historic sites are being plundered! I beg you, do something!" He had already tried to reach secretary general Zahi Hawass and Sabri Abdel Aziz, the director of archaeological sites in the antiquities administration, but without success. I assured him that I too would try to phone the secretary general. But I was equally unsuccessful.

Destruction and plundering—I refused to believe it. The museum, together with the presidential palace, is one of the most secure buildings in Egypt. There are guards, cameras. How can it be that so many responsible people are failing to do anything? Then came the first reports on television. I felt rage and bitterness. They had robbed 'my' museum! Was it the so-called mob?

Finally I reached Sabri Abdel Aziz. He told me that he too had heard of the incidents, but in view of the problematic situation there was nothing he could do. The police had withdrawn, and the ancient sites were left to themselves. I then called a high-ranking police officer I had known for years. He tried to calm me, but he too sounded somewhat uneasy: The museum and the excavation sites were secure. But I no longer believed any of it. An archaeologist phoned and confirmed the journalist's report. I called a general I knew and begged him to call up the army to protect the cultural sites. He also tried to placate me: Soldiers had been stationed in Tahrir Square around the museum. Young people had long since formed a human chain circling the building. The army was sending out units to protect historic sites.

I hung up and wondered whether behind all this there were really only a few daring plunderers taking advantage of the situation. Despite the wars and revolutions of the twentieth century, Egypt's historic sites had never been vandalized. At times like that you imagine all sorts of things. You speculate, make assumptions. Is this sabotage? Are the break-ins being instigated by the very people who are creating chaos in the country by pulling back the police and opening the prisons?

Down on the street we heard pistol shots. The local residents—among them students, professors, doctors, engineers—were standing guard in front of doorways and at intersections to protect the suburb from marauding convicts. The streets were dark, and residents were asked to keep bright lights on in every room so there would be enough light below.

I got a call from Luxor. On that day of all days we were expecting the return from an exhibition in New York of a precious object from Tutankhamun's tomb: the pharaoh's chariot. But just as it arrived at the Luxor airport demonstrations had begun in downtown Luxor as well. People were demanding not only the fall of Mubarak but also that of Samir Farag, the city's hated governor. In cahoots with the antiquities administration, Farag had cut a swath straight through the old town. The ancient alley of sphinxes between the Luxor and Karnak temples was being excavated for tourists. Thousands of people had been forced to abandon their apartments, hundreds of buildings razed, properties requisitioned without compensation. Farag was showing off his power as Mubarak's governor. But because of all his machinations and repression, the city was a smoldering volcano. That night and for the next few, people attacked every building bearing Mubarak's name or that of his wife, police stations, the house Farag had only recently built on the east bank of the Nile—on a beautifully situated tract but one that had formerly been used for agriculture. He had simply ignored the law forbidding construction on arable land. Farag could afford to. He was very close to Mubarak, a member of his powerful inner circle.

At the Luxor airport the police were having to decide whether they should really take the chariot back to the museum, given the explosive situation in the city. Since I had been responsible for organizing the New York exhibition six weeks before and no one else in Cairo could be reached by telephone, the museum's director had turned to me. The head of the German transportation firm, Hans Ewald Schneider, wanted to stay in Luxor in any case. We immediately agreed that it should wait until dawn, when the chariot could be transported through what we hoped would then be empty streets. It was a long, sleepless night. In the morning a call came telling me that the chariot was safely back in its special display case.

Transmission by the broadcaster Al Jazeera was forbidden. The TV screen was black. A friend phoned to tell me to turn on Al Arabiya, there you could see pictures from the Egyptian Museum. My heart was pounding when I saw that the glass in several showcases was smashed, objects were lying on the floor, two mummy heads were separated from their bodies. I was stunned. What about the surveillance cameras mounted in all the galleries and corridors, also guarding the museum's grounds day and night, around the clock? Where were the videocasettes on which the break-ins must have been recorded? Then, in response to reports about the museum, Zahi Hawass, secretary general of the antiquities administration, explained that no artifacts had been stolen. The hooligans had been heading for the new museum shop, from which jewelry had been taken. The burglars had entered the building by way of the fire escape at the back of the museum. But I had had the bottom section of that fire escape removed! According to Hawass, the intruders had smashed thirteen display cases and seventy historic objects. They had not managed to take anything away, for they had been captured and turned over to army personnel. Now the museum was sealed. There was a group picture for use by the world press: Zahi Hawass on the steps of the museum surrounded by heavily armed soldiers, to show that the museum was safe after the difficult hours of the night of January 28. I felt some reassurance, but I wanted to be more certain, so I called my museum colleagues, and their stories were altogether different. They reported major losses and the removal of important objects.

The announcement of the plundering of the museum was not made until February 12, after Hosni Mubarak's resignation. But still the statements were opaque, based apparently on the time needed to check the holdings against our database. That was very difficult for me to understand: Our curators could have reported immediately what was missing from their display cases. When I asked why they had not done so they explained, "We weren't allowed access." There could be no justification for this prohibition.

Later Zahi wrote on his personal website explaining his reluctance to announce the thefts directly: "I had to speak to the media. What should I say? … I announced that the masterpieces were there, safe in the museum. The Egyptian Museum was safe, and that meant Egypt was safe."

He also explained that he could not announce that the museum had been robbed because with such a vast number of objects on display, it would have been irresponsible to speak out before an inventory could be taken—and that would have taken time.

Finally he said that "if I had said that the museum had been robbed, the Revolution would have been held responsible and the world might not have supported the young people."

The next day's news and rumors made me increasingly worried.

Colleagues sent me a copy of an internal communication from the antiquities administration in which it was said that the museum was safe and sound, the seventy damaged objects would be restored within five days, and the damage was not so very bad. Seventy objects restored in only five days? I had to ask myself who in the world might be able to restore seventy objects in such a short time? What if objects had been stolen after all? Then photos and descriptions of them needed to be provided immediately to airport and customs people and to Interpol. It would be a terrible dereliction not to, for that would make it easier for fences to spirit the pieces out of the country. The thefts continued to be denied up until February 11. The government formed after Mubarak's resignation appointed Zahi Hawass a cabinet minister responsible for antiquities. It was now officially said that eighteen objects had been stolen, including gilt wooden figures from the tomb of Tutankhamun. Moreover, it was clear that excavation sites and magazines had been looted. Explanation followed explanation. It was obvious that the authorities should have gotten to work much earlier. We now know that some seventy pieces were spirited away that night. Half of them would resurface later, including a small limestone statuette of the pharaoh Akhenaten and a gilt wooden statue of Tutankhamun that was found in a bag on a subway platform. To this day ten display pieces are still missing.

On January 28, I determined to write this book. I could see the people on the street and admired their courage. I knew many intellectuals who had long since openly expressed their opinions orally or in writing. The regime had slandered them, tried to silence them; it arrested, tortured, and murdered people like the young Khaled Said.

It is possible to divide the Egyptian people under Mubarak into four groups. First there were the corrupt ones: They were pragmatists of power, to whom morality was as alien as the desire for a functioning state under the rule of law. The second group was composed of opportunists: They didn't like the corrupt ones, but took advantage of every opportunity to advance themselves into higher, better-paying offices through connections. The third group was the Egyptian majority: They had no connections, no money, and were exclusively concerned with making a paltry living, sending their children to school, and obtaining needed medicines. Many had long ago given up hope for a better future. Some 80 percent of young people wanted to leave the country.

We belonged to the fourth group: They could afford to leave the country, sent their children abroad, and tried to stay out of the way of the corrupt and unscrupulous ones. When I returned to Egypt from Germany in 2003 to assume a management position in the antiquities service, I was fully aware that sooner or later I would have to deal with corruption. That became obvious in February 2004. I was sitting in the office of the Egyptian Museum's director watching my predecessor, Mamdouh Eldamaty, calmly packing documents into a fairly thick file box. He gave me a friendly smile, then suddenly turned serious. "That's my life insurance. And I advise you to do the same. Stay alert. Make copies of all important procedures. You understand what I mean."

In the seven years that I was the director I was alert. I protected myself and kept a journal about all the important and the many questionable internal procedures and directives from the antiquities administration. It helped me to keep my head in what was often a suffocating atmosphere—to stay my own course and not simply chuck the whole thing.

The most dangerous challenges were the ones presented with cordiality and charm, with praise and flattery—in the person of Suzanne Mubarak, the most powerful woman in Egypt. Only a few days before my retirement in December 2010, I received an invitation to the president's villa. It had to do with the Suzanne Mubarak Foundation's new children's museum, a formidable new building in Heliopolis that was still in need of a director. For more than twenty years I had worked on museum educational programs for Egyptian children, especially those of the poorer classes. And to that end a circle of friends and supporters had founded Children's Alliance for Tradition and Social Engagement (CATS), an association registered in Germany that, thanks to the donations and the engagement of volunteers, introduced Egyptian children to handicrafts and art, to Egypt's cultural heritage in our museums, and to our ancient sites. And of course at precisely that time the press had reported the ceremonial opening by Prince Henrik of Denmark of the children's museum I had set up in the cellar storerooms of the Egyptian Museum. For her new chic museum, Suzanne Mubarak was looking for someone who also enjoyed a reputation for integrity abroad. Her museum was to be financed by sponsors' donations, and the director's spotless reputation would assure donors that their money would actually benefit the private museum.

Suzanne Mubarak's villa lay in a well-guarded district far from everyday Egyptian life, far from the dirt, noise, and corruption of the metropolis. There even power had its cordial aspects. Suzanne Mubarak was charming, attentive, and outgoing. We had often met before, when I would guide her through ancient sites at the side of state visitors and other prominent figures. She asked me to tell her about my educational projects for children in the Cairo Museum and pretended that she had never heard of them. That couldn't be, for at the request of a German foundation I had put together a study on the adoption of educational programs in Egypt's museums of which she had had a copy for years. Without saying so directly, the first lady simply assumed that I would be interested in becoming the director of her new museum and opening it as soon as possible. She then let me go without requiring a binding acceptance. Days later I once again had an evening phone call from the president's office. My contract was now ready. I was told of the high salary it already specified. When could I come to sign it? I knew that you didn't openly deny Suzanne Mubarak anything; that would be a dangerous affront. So I explained that I was just leaving on a trip abroad. But the gentleman in the president's office insisted. To finalize the contract it would be sufficient if I were to give him my ID card number, and that I could do over the phone. I declined; I don't negotiate contracts on the telephone.

How absurd is it? The January 28 on which the Egyptian Museum was plundered was, at the same time, a day of deliverance for me. In the previous weeks I had been at a loss. I had no idea how to escape the clutches of the president's office without damage to myself. Now I was determined: I would be betraying myself, but above all betraying the youth of Egypt if I were become the director of a museum founded by people who torture young people and beat them to death. At the same time, my mind was racing with other thoughts. I was not standing out there with the people who at risk of their lives wanted to free our country from a corrupt clique. Did I have to reproach myself for staying home at a crucial time? Was I finally failing to act?

I had left my homeland when I married my husband in Germany. We had established a family in Cologne, where we were able to lead *our own* lives. But we had never turned our backs on Egypt. We had always been there. With the means at our disposal we had tried to do what we could for the people unable to leave. When in 2002 I was offered a chance to actually accomplish something in a responsible position in the antiquities service, I had to think about it a long time, wondering whether I should accept the offer and impose a return to Cairo on my family. It was a difficult time, out of which a visit from a friend of my father's helped me in May 2003. Dr. Diab Refai was from Syria and a longtime family friend. I had always greatly valued his advice but hesitated to tell him about the offer from Cairo. He sensed the ambivalence I was feeling, even though I hadn't said a word about it. But Diab Refai had heard about the Cairo offer long before; it was the reason for his visit.

"Wafaa, when the moment comes when your country needs you—and it will come—you'll make the right decision, won't you? I know it and you know it too. *In sha'Allah.*"

I explained to him that I was worried. "I'll have to work for a corrupt regime."

Diab shook his head. "You won't be working for the government. You'll be putting yourself in the service of Egypt's cultural heritage, and of people who are counting on you. You'll know how to deal with the corrupt ones. You'll find a way."

I had to think of the saying my mother used to repeat to me in such situations: "The straight and narrow is the only way."

No, on that 'day of rage' I did not feel that I was failing all the courageous people in Tahrir Square. Instead it was a marvelous confirmation: I had been in the right place at the right time. I would stay, and I would continue to make my contribution for the people I am able to help. On that day I determined to do no more work that had any connection to Mubarak, his wife, and the regime. I would continue on the path I had set for myself many years before.

I went across to my workroom, where a heavy case filled with files stood behind the desk. My 'life insurance.' In the desk drawers lay my journals. They go back to my childhood, to my time with my family, my student years, and my first excavations. They led me to Vienna, to Cologne, and finally back to Cairo. It was time to retrace that path and ask myself: What is it that has so changed this country and its people since the days of my childhood, since the Nasser years? I remember a time when the cancer of corruption had not yet grown out of control, I remember a spirit that protected us from the seductions of radical Islamism and from our own self-contempt. I could see my father before me, my mother, the uncles and aunts. I could see our house in Fariskur, in the Nile Delta, my grandfather's library, in which as a child I discovered so many things that would be of importance in my life. That too was a time of upheaval. At what point did we stray onto the wrong track? When and why did we betray ourselves? What changed us, and where do we go now?

There is no way that the old cliques should stay in power and continue to pull their strings. The people who have worked toward a different Egypt for so long—decent, hardworking people of integrity—finally have to be given a chance. There have been and still are such people in Egypt, even among us Egyptologists in the antiquities service. They have distinct notions about a different Egypt. It was high time to open the drawers and lay on the table all the things that had had to wait too long.

2

WIND IN THE REEDS

By coincidence I was born in Busat Karim el-Din—which translates as "the carpet of Karim el-Din." Who this Karim el-Din might have been, I don't know. Perhaps a sheikh, a holy man, some scholar who in the Middle Ages arrived in the Nile Delta like one of my ancestors and left nothing behind but his name for a village no larger than a prayer rug, so tiny that you won't find it on any map to this day. Perhaps something is known about him in Busat Karim el-Din, but I have never been back there. Once I did see the place from afar. I was already a young girl. We were driving from Fariskur to Cairo when my father pointed out between the cotton and rice fields a few simple thatched mud houses. "Over there is Busat Karim el-Din," he shouted. "That's where you were born." As I stared out of the window I thought to myself, Couldn't I have been born in Mansura? It is a big, beautiful city on the river, the 'Bride of the Nile.' That's the sort of name your birthplace ought to have, not some old carpet of Karim el-Din, whoever he was.

Where have we come from, and how did we become what we are today? Time and place play a major role, of course—they stamp our personality as indelibly as the impression on our birth certificate. But isn't there a whole

17

world hidden behind those brief notations about our lineage? My father, Taha El Saddik, was an engineer. In the late 1940s and early 1950s he worked for the government, building small water and power plants that for the first time supplied the villages of the Delta with clean drinking water and electricity. He would move from village to village, taking his family with him. So on December 12 or 13, 1950—later, no one could remember exactly—I first glimpsed the light of the world in not-yet-electrified Busat Karim el-Din. There was no doctor, no hospital, only a midwife. The next day, December 14, father drove into the small town of Fariskur to officially register the birth of his fourth child. The family then continued to live in Busat Karim el-Din for a further two years.

In fact it was by no means happenstance that I was born there on the Damietta arm of the Nile, a few kilometers from the coast and Lake Manzala. Two of my older siblings, my brother Mohamed and my sister Nur, were born in Cairo, to be sure, but my sister Safaa, two years older than I, had been born in Fariskur, and my younger brother Kamel in Kafr al-Arab. That small town and nearby village were the twin poles of my childhood, as they had been for my parents, grandparents, and great-grandparents. For as far back as my family can remember, it has lived and worked there, built its houses and worked its fields. I feel I must tell you something about this family, its houses, its fields, and those of its members I knew as a child, for they all helped to influence my thinking and later career.

You can occasionally read in western travel guides to this day that the vast majority of Egyptians are still fellaheen at heart, children of the Nile, reared within the rhythm of the river's seasonal changes. Simple people, frugal and good-natured, who require only a patch of land beneath their feet to be content. That may have been the case for thousands of years, but no longer—not for a long time now. I think the turning point occurred in the final years of my childhood. Presumably I could even look up the date in the military records for October 1956—the day that didn't change everything, but still so very much.

I experienced the following events the way one perceives things as a child: from the faces and gestures of the grown-ups, from the excitement in the villages, my parents' troubled expressions. I did not understand what happened in 1956 in the same way that my siblings did, but it was perfectly clear that something had changed for all of us. The events are captured in pictures and film sequences, in scraps of conversations and surges of emotion I can still recall today. When I ask myself what changed us, why we became who we are today, those pictures and memories of my childhood, of dear people and confusing events, begin to provide the answer. I'll describe them the way I still see them in my mind's eye.

My father married young, at twenty-two, immediately after finishing his studies. My mother wanted to let marriage wait awhile, although according to the conventions of the time, at twenty-two an attractive and well-educated woman was already a virtual spinster. But fate would have it that her sister married a man who had an appealing brother. Work led the Cairo University graduate and his wife who had grown up in Alexandria, the 'White City,' to the very region of the Delta from which their families had come.

Grandfather would have liked for all of us to live in his big house in Kafr al-Arab, but Father declined. An engineer needs to be free and mobile, he said. Perhaps there was more to it than that—perhaps he needed to distance himself from his father's house. For Grandfather el-Sayed El Saddik was Kafr al-Arab's *omda*, or mayor. He was a landowner, a member of parliament, and a figure of respect. He wore the traditional *omda*'s costume: a white gallabiya, over it a black shawl and a turban. Whenever he wished to cross the street, men would rein in their donkeys and dismount to let him pass. No one crossed the street before him. He was a strict man, but a cordial one. Whenever we children would visit him in his big house, we would usually find him seated on the ground floor, where the farmers consulted him or the chief of police paid visits. He was always extremely busy, frequently driving to Cairo to attend sessions of parliament. He had little to say to us, but whenever he saw us and we would reverently call him Papa Sidi, he would be pleased, gather us in his arms, and give us hugs.

I have no memories of Grandmother Nur, for she died early. Mother told us that Grandmother had loved our father very much. He was the first of her children not to die in childbirth. For that reason the village women advised her to protect the boy by dressing him in girl's clothing and having him wear earrings. The birth was even kept a secret from the authorities for two years, so officially my father was always two years younger than he actually was. His whole life he suffered from the fact that he had a pierced earlobe. Boys at school would tease him, saying he must be a girl. I wonder what he would have said about the fact that today men wear earrings as a matter of course. Father was a good-looking man with a dark complexion, thick black hair, and brownish-green eyes. At thirty he looked a lot like Gamal Abdel Nasser. Umm Ahmed, our housekeeper, would always exclaim whenever she saw Nasser's picture in the newspaper, "My God, that's Sidi Taha." In everything related to work Father was extremely conscientious, a perfectionist, just like Grandfather, but at home he was gentle, indulgent, and full of fun. He had a wonderful smile.

Father also had a much older half-brother whose children were even older than he was. The half-brother was also an *omda* and member of parliament, and like Grandfather he was named el-Sayed El Saddik. We children were always deliciously amused when the half-brother's children would visit and address our much younger father as "uncle." My siblings and I were "the *omda*'s grandchildren" and "the engineer's children." Because we wore modern, citified clothes, we were also treated with respect by the local farmers, but it was mainly because we were the children of the man who was bringing clean water to the villages.

We lived in a fenced-off area on the edge of Kafr al-Arab. The bungalows of the coworkers and their families stood in the square around the chief engineer's house. Our house was the largest, with a front garden, in the middle of which was a pool with water lilies and other aquatic plants, ringed with date palms and sycamores. I now know that our front garden was patterned after gardens I later studied in the pharaonic precinct at Karnak. Our house was fully modernized, with electricity and running water. Father's office and an entrance hall were on the first (ground) floor, and we lived upstairs in six rooms with a large kitchen. The balcony and roof we had all to ourselves. From there we could see far across the village into the Nile Valley. In the large garden behind the house Mother grew fruit, vegetables, and herbs. It seems as if I spent half my childhood in the fruit trees, the other half on the swing Father had hung from the guava tree.

And then there was the water tower, the tallest structure between Mansura and Damietta. We children were forbidden to climb its two hundred steps unless Mother first prepared a picnic and took us up with her. Below us Kafr al-Arab lay like a toy village. A strong breeze brought delicious air from the sea. Despite all the admonitions, we would later climb up alone, for we were curious to know what was behind the forbidden door. We lifted the iron hatch and a loud echo rumbled inside, the sunlight sparkling across the surface of the water. With fright we could see why our parents had so insistently warned us not to go inside the tank—if we had fallen in we would surely have drowned, for we couldn't swim. But how proud we were of our father, over in the plant where the big machines were housed, who had provided this huge quantity of clean water for thousands of people.

I can still see the view from the water tower. Around us there was nothing but fields: cotton, wheat, and rice—an endless tricolor of snow-white, yellow-gold, and deep green with the broad Nile between them, seemingly flowing lazily. But Mother had also urgently warned us about the river. Lurking beneath the still surface was a dangerous current. In July and August the Nile would flood the Delta, and I remember how the river advanced to become a reddish-brown sea. Since the late 1960s and the completion of the Aswan High Dam, there are no longer such summer floods. The age-old seasonal changes have been interrupted; the fertile soils from the highlands of Ethiopia no longer reach the Delta.

We were allowed to fish only along the canals. In no circumstances were we to wash our hands in the Nile water, for in it were the tiny worms that cause bilharzia. We would stroll along the watercourses with a net attached to a bamboo pole, the reeds waving high above our heads. Sometimes we would follow the monotonous sound of the saqya, a kind of waterwheel introduced into Egypt by the Greeks. The wheel that lifted water from the Nile in large clay jars and poured it into the irrigation canals was driven by an ox plodding in a circle on the trampled ground. The farmers would stand in the mud barefoot, and we had to think of the bilharzia worms. Sometimes we were allowed to sit behind the ox in place of the farmer, who would goad the tired beast for us with a stick. That was our merry-go-round, and great fun. Many years later, on the walls of tombs in Thebes, I would again see the oxcart, where beneath the wheels the grain was separated from the husks, and the shadoof, the long, counterweighted pole used by the fellaheen to raise water or heavy stones.

How happy we were when in the late afternoon we would race home with a small eel or a Nile perch. "We caught a fish! We caught a fish!" we would scream. Umm Ahmed and Umm Ali, our old housekeepers, would then have to inspect the fish and properly praise it, assuring us, "The fish you catch yourself is the most delicious of all!" In a corner of the garden, next to the enclosure for chickens, ducks, and doves, they would slide the fish into the clay oven in which the two of them baked the most delicious bread every day.

But most wonderful were the days of the cotton harvest. I can still see us children tumbling in a tall, soft mountain. Father told us that European children played the same way. But they didn't jump into a white mound of cotton, but instead into a white mound of snow. Even if their snow was as white as our cotton, we countered, at least ours isn't disgustingly wet and cold, but heavenly soft and warm.

At the end of the cotton harvest the farmers of Kafr al-Arab held a festival, and we would be invited. In the center of the village the men would sing and dance to the sound of a flute, a lute, and drums. Once I also saw a *ghaziya*, or belly dancer; she wasn't half naked—like those who entertain partygoers in Cairo—but wore a long dress. The villagers would clap and sing, "Today we celebrate a sacred festival, Lord, bless the harvest and let it increase from year to year." My parents wouldn't dance, but they would sing and clap along with the farmers.

Harvest festivals were also times for weddings. The evening before the ceremony the bride's hands and feet would be painted with beautiful henna designs, and a hairdresser would come over from Mansura. After the henna ceremony the bride was made up and she put on a lovely pink dress. The women were all adorned in long, colorful gallabiyas and head scarves. I can still hear the singing and the *zaghareet*, the women's joyous trilling. On the wedding day the bride appeared in successive dresses, pink, light blue, and finally white, while the women danced around her. The bridegroom sat outside with the men. Only when the bride stepped to the door in white would he receive her, accompany her to his carriage, and drive her home to his relatives. A week before, the couple's new furniture would have been welcomed with music and dancing. The entire village was intended to notice how richly the bride's family had set up the new couple. The number of arriving carts was very important: sometimes there would be more than twenty piled high with furnishings, and the villagers would continue to marvel about it for weeks. I don't want to get married, I would tell my sister. But she would only laugh.

Grandfather el-Sayed also had a carriage, drawn by a white horse. On Thursday evening he would send it for us children so that we could spend "a lovely day" with him. Grandfather's house stood right next to the Nile and was much roomier than ours. It was *al-dowar*, after all, the home of the *omda* where people gathered on the ground floor, village guests were received, and festivities were held.

My father's family had been rice growers for generations, and Grandfather's fields extended from the Nile all the way up to the Damietta–Cairo road. In the villages the mayoralty is reserved for the man of wealth, and traditionally he passes it on to his son. The office is entrusted to him on the assumption that he will be charitable. But in the final years of the King Farouk era, not every large landowner was openhanded and well-meaning. Under Farouk, 0.5 percent of the population owned roughly one-third of the land. This feudal system, supported by the British, was abolished only by Nasser's officers in 1952. And rightly so, for not only were many large landowners filthy rich, they were also skinflints who cared about nothing but their privileges.

Grandfather el-Sayed did not have to be forced by Nasser's land reforms to surrender a part of his property. He was among those who considered it a divine gift and a privilege to be able to help the needy and perform acts of charity. My father once told me how Grandfather el-Sayed responded to two fellaheen who had come to him lamenting about their rent and their crop by promptly presenting them with the piece of land they were farming. Neither of his two sons from his second marriage would become a rice farmer. Father studied mechanical engineering in Cairo, his brother Mohamed el-Said dentistry. Mohamed el-Said would later teach at Oxford as a professor, and he was president of an international society of dentists as well as the Egyptian Society of Dentists, and vice president of Cairo University.

Late Friday evening two of Grandfather's employees would drive us back home. The road ran through the fields, and if the moon wasn't shining the stars seemed impossibly bright. Sometimes we would see meteors, and the men would say they were the souls of the blessed returning to visit the earth. A kind of exquisite terror was always associated with those homeward journeys, for the men took delight in making the time pass quicker for us by telling scary stories. It was especially creepy during a full moon, for then, the two would whisper, hungry wolves and hyenas would streak through the fields searching for something to eat. I guarantee you that on such nights we could clearly hear the howling of wolves and hyenas and would hasten our steps. When we passed the cemetery it became even scarier, for the men told us that ghosts and djinns were sometimes seen hovering above the graves. At home Mother would first have to put our minds at rest. No, she would say, there are wolves and hyenas only in Upper Egypt, not where we live, and there simply are no such things as ghosts and djinns. Those are fairy tales that ignorant people have been telling for a long time. That reassured us, of course—but still I would lie awake and wonder whether people had told such fairy tales in the time of the pharaohs.

My mother, Tawhida al-Diasti, was a pretty woman, of medium height, with light skin, brown hair, and brown eyes. She radiated a profound internal calm and had a sharp intelligence. We called her our Sherlock Holmes. Mama came from a family of scholars and scientists, and I suspect that part of my heritage is strongest in me.

Fariskur lies only some three kilometers from Kafr al-Arab—yet at that time they were two different worlds. My mother's parents' house was stately and spacious and wonderfully situated in the midst of fields and a huge, park-like garden. Grandfather Mohamed Ibrahim al-Diasti had come to live in Fariskur again after he retired. He had been director of Alexandria's port authority and could afford a stately house. On each of its two floors there were eight rooms, and the roof was so large that there was space for the servants' apartment and rooms for baking, washing, threshing, and storing.

Although Father had brought electricity to the villages of the entire region, the house in Fariskur remained without power. It was my grandfather's wish, and after him my mother's, that the original atmosphere of the house, built in 1882, be preserved. It was in fact quite delightful to sit in the light of candles and oil lamps in the evening. It was even more festive in the month of Ramadan. After sunset and supper we would join up with the neighbor children. We would all carry little glass and tin lanterns and go from house to house—like German children do on Saint Martin's Day—singing Ramadan songs. Most of our songs went back to ancient Egyptian times, for example "Praise of the Moon," which was translated into Arabic and adopted by Islam. The louder we sang, the more lavish the people would be with their gifts. They would open their doors and fill our bags with sweets. In Kafr al-Arab the farmers were too poor to be so generous.

On the ground floor of the house was a large hall with a high ceiling, and all the walls were completely lined with books. That library was the true history of my family, put together by generations of scholars, and when I was still a child my mother would show me the writings of my ancestors. My siblings and I still have them to this day. This family history reaches far back almost to a time when there were as yet no written records. I relate it here the way my mother and my grandfather did.

The patriarch of my mother's family was a certain Sheikh Hassan al-Diasti. He is said to have arrived in Alexandria from Kufa, in southern Iraq, at the end of the thirteenth century. Since antiquity, the Egyptian metropolis on the Mediterranean had been a cosmopolitan center known throughout the East for its contributions to science, theology, and philosophy. At that time it had become a center for Islamic scholars coming from North Africa and Andalusia. Among these was the famous Sheikh al-Mursi Abu al-Abbas (1219–1286), above whose tomb one of Alexandria's most beautiful mosques has stood since the eighteenth century. Although Kufa was a center of Shiite Islam, Hassan al-Diasti was a Sunni. Whether he arrived in Alexandria as a Sunni or only became one under the influence of Sheikh Abu al-Abbas, we don't know. The pious Hassan traced his family back to that of the Prophet Muhammad, and thought of himself as one of the Ashraf, or so-called nobles, and so did his descendants.

After Hassan had devoted years to the study of the Qur'an, Sheikh Abu al-Abbas is said to have instructed his pupil not to remain in Alexandria, but to take Qur'an teaching to the country populace. He was to go from village to village, city to city, until he encountered people who were unwelcoming. There he was to stay, build a school, and teach the Qur'an. He did not go far. He now lies buried in his mosque in Fariskur. Qur'an study and a tempered Islamic faith would continue to be the family's calling.

My great-grandfather, Sheikh Ahmed al-Gedeli, was a graduate of and later theologian at al-Azhar University in Cairo—to this day virtually the Vatican of Islam on theological issues. My great-grandparents were both theologians and Mecca pilgrims. Like her husband, my great-grandmother, whom we called simply Nina el-Sheikha, taught at a mosque in Mecca. We still have a few of my great-grandfather's manuscripts written in a very beautiful hand, including truly significant writings on the interpretation of the Qur'an, on the Arabic language, and even on astronomy. He belonged to the Shafiite school, which professes a tempered Islam, and I feel that describes my faith as well.

In politics, Sheikh Ahmed supported the Wafd movement, which was founded at the end of the First World War and worked for Egyptian independence from Great Britain. Since 1882, British consul generals had ruled Egypt as a virtual colony. Egypt was required to supply the British textile industry with ever increasing quantities of first-class cotton—at the cost of declining grain harvests at home. This one-sided extortion reached a peak during the First World War: cotton prices were kept low, but prices for the greater and greater quantities of imported grain exploded. Impoverished farmers and city dwellers could no longer pay for food, and there were rebellions and violent protests against Britain's policies. Throughout the history of the British mandate in Egypt, there had been repeated uprisings, some of them very bloody—Egyptians were never particularly compliant pawns in Europe's 'Great Game.' Following the Urabi Revolt in the 1880s, "Egypt for Egyptians" had become the national slogan. When delegates of the Wafd Party sought to press Egypt's right to independence at the Paris Peace Conference in 1919, the British prevented them from attending, which led to still more vehement rebellions and protests in Egypt.

At that time every Egyptian nationalist was a Wafd supporter. My great-grandfather's political writings attest to his nationalist and anti-British stance, one that his son Abdel Rahman al-Gedeli would share. My great-uncle Abdel Rahman was close to Saad Zaghloul, leader of the Wafd Party. The British put down the mass protests with overwhelming force, killed some eight hundred Egyptians, sent Zaghloul into exile, and arrested thousands of Egyptians. Abdel Rahman was one of those thrown into prison and given a death sentence. But miraculously the papers incriminating him disappeared—apparently he had influential friends. The death sentence was withdrawn. In 1922 the British, forced to yield to growing political pressure, changed the protectorate into an allegedly independent monarchy. In reality, the British High Commissioner retained power. King Fuad was merely his puppet, and the large landowners continued to be favored by British policies with respect to raw materials. During his brief tenure as prime minister, Saad Zaghloul, having returned from exile, was unable to change anything. When Zaghloul finally attained that office in 1924, my great-uncle Abdel Rahman served as his secretary.

He also held important offices under King Farouk and later under Gamal Abdel Nasser, doubtless because he belonged to a respected family of theologians. He became the deputy al-Awqaf minister, responsible within the Ministry of Religion for questions of faith, review of sermon content, and the administration of religious endowments. I still remember my mother showing me a piece of black brocade woven with silver threads that we preserved with special care: a piece of the Kaaba's black covering, or *kiswa*. In the 1930s my great-uncle was Egypt's amir al-Hajj, an honorary office in which he was responsible for the ceremonial delivery of the huge curtain to Mecca. At that time, given Egypt's political and theological importance in the Muslim world, the *kiswa* was traditionallly produced in Cairo—now it is made in Mecca itself. Also, it was my great-uncle who saved the life of his best friend, Ibrahim Abdel Hadi, the last prime minister under Farouk. Under pressure from King Farouk and the British, Abdel Hadi had concluded a truce with the Israelis in 1948. After the Free Officers under Nasser seized power, he was sentenced to death as a traitor to his country. My mother told me that my great-uncle intervened with Nasser personally: "How could you dare want to execute such a man? He is a loyal Egyptian nationalist, and without men like him you wouldn't even be here!" Nasser commuted the death sentence to life in prison, from which Abdel Hadi was released after a relatively short time for health reasons. He died in 1981 at the age of eighty-two.

I must have still been very small when my mother and my grandmother Sakina Ahmed al-Gedeli took me to see my great-grandparents' old house in Fariskur. My great-grandparents had long been dead, and strangers were living in their house. I remember the iron knocker on the front door, the mashrabiyas (traditional oriel windows with wood latticework) and walls and ceilings of wood, and a high reception hall—where my great-grandparents received their Qur'an pupils—in the center of which a marble fountain cooled the hot summer air. Grandmother Sakina later told me that as the only daughter she always accompanied her mother, even when she was teaching in Mecca. So she knew the entire Qur'an by heart, and my mother, in turn, learned it from her. At that time Grandmother Sakina still dressed as women did at the beginning of the twentieth century. She wore a black dress and a head covering with a very fine white, or sometimes black, veil in front of her face as protection against the dust of the street and the sun. She was an affectionate, even-tempered woman, and very pious. It seems I most often saw her in prayer, and we thought of her as a saint, for she was very generous with the poor.

I never heard from Grandmother Sakina or my mother that as faithful Muslims my sisters and I should wear veils. I was brought up to be religious and conservative in terms of dress. I find it shameful that today girls wearing head scarves use flashy makeup and otherwise try to attract attention to themselves, how purveyors of Islamic clothing advertise that by wearing such-and-such a hijab you will capture the glances of all the men. I respect it when women wear the head scarf from religious conviction. But I do not accept that they should be forced to do so. I side with Sheikh Mustafa Mohamed Rashid, a man who earned his degree at al-Azhar University in sharia law, who asserted that the Qur'an nowhere mentions the head scarf as a religious injunction.

My faith is my personal affair. I pray, I fast, I pay zakat, and I have been to Mecca five times. I think of my work and the earnings I make from it as a privilege, one that allows me to be able to help the less fortunate. But I do not wear a head scarf, and consider any sort of social pressure to do so as an encroachment on my freedom and my faith, and I become defensive about it. In the Egyptian Museum I was the only woman who did not wear a head scarf. Many of my colleagues wore it only because they wanted to protect themselves from importunate men.

My family is far removed from such a petty Islam. The Qur'an, as I learned from my mother and grandmother, primarily provides us with the inner composure for prayer, for fasting, and for helping our fellow human beings—even if they're not Muslim. At that time the idea of exploiting the Qur'an for political purposes was as alien to my family as using force as a means to an end. That was why Grandmother disapproved of the Muslim Brotherhood. As a young man my father sympathized with the brotherhood but turned away from it because of its tolerance for violence. And I remember precisely what my grandmother said when she once saw Anwar Sadat on television. During the Second World War, before he became one of Nasser's Free Officers, Sadat was said to be involved in the assassinations of England-friendly Wafd politicians. "Anyone who kills will be killed!" Grandmother muttered. I recalled her words on October 6, 1981, when Sadat died at the hands of Islamist terrorists.

Today I think still about my great-grandfather's writings: If faith—any kind of faith—is to guide our actions, then that faith has to be lived as a principle of practical tolerance. The Wafd champion of 1919 wrote, "A nation is always only as moral as the majority of its citizens. People of faith live their faith for their own sakes and the sake of their fellow human beings—and do not misunderstand it as a dictate of the presumed orthodox over the presumed unorthodox. Faith works solely through the word, never through the sword." We were always a pious family, but religious fanaticism was and is foreign to us. How else could my faithful Muslim grandparents, of all people, have been able to send my mother to a school run by Catholic nuns?

My mother Tawhida grew up in Alexandria. It was a family tradition that after finishing middle school, daughters would leave school and prepare for marriage through courses in knitting and homemaking. But my mother wouldn't have it, and attended seminars in poetry and art instead. Later she was admired for her incredible memory, her ability to recite long poems and complicated passages from the Qur'an.

Unlike many young people of their generation, my parents married out of affection and love, and so far as I can judge, had a happy marriage. At least we children were never aware of any problems or differences of opinion between them. My mother greatly respected my father's work. I know it sounds old-fashioned to today's young generation, but in the little time he was able to spend at home she 'covered his back' as it were. At the same time, her working day seemed twice as long as ours, and I now know that women worked harder then, for housework was more laborious and time-consuming. I remember a scene I observed from the window of my grandfather's house: A farmer rode by on a donkey, followed by his wife on foot, carrying a heavy jar on her head and a child on her arm. Presumably she had been working for many long hours in the fields and would now have to prepare dinner for her family. Behind them came a big white ox, a powerful beast trotting along behind a small boy. I had to ask myself how this powerful animal knew that it had to obey the spindly little boy. I have always been in awe of country women's endurance.

Mother loved to tell about her time in beautiful, cosmopolitan Alexandria. She knew everything about the city's history. In her day Alexandria was still a vital international mix of Greeks, Armenians, Turks, British, French, Germans, and Italians. Greeks and Armenians also lived in my grandfather's house, and Mother told how the various families, regardless of nationality or religion, would honor their neighbors' holidays by bringing gifts on special occasions. I feel that that tolerant mix of Christians, Jews, and Muslims was as much an influence on my mother as the scholarly atmosphere in her parents' and grandparents' houses. I can still hear her Alexandrian vocabulary. In that multicultural polyglot babble there are words and phrases that are simply unknown in other Arabic vernaculars. Whenever I used one of them at school, my classmates would look at me in puzzlement.

When her sisters married and moved to Cairo, and her older brother Hassan left for France to study economics, my mother stayed behind with her parents in Alexandria. The port city was a British garrison town, and at the beginning of the Second World War more and more Australian and Indian soldiers could be seen on the streets. The British High Command for the entire Near Eastern Theater was headquartered in Cairo. Mother told us about Rommel, the 'Desert Fox,' who had a great number of Egyptian admirers who hoped that he might at last drive the hated British out of the country. Rommel advanced from Libya up to the Egyptian border at Sallum. Mother said that the rumble of artillery could even be heard in Alexandria, which the Germans also attacked from the air. More and more wounded soldiers and civilian refugees arrived in the city. As my grandfather reached retirement age at just that time, the three of them moved to Fariskur, where they occupied the beautiful old house in which I had felt so comfortable. Grandfather then devoted himself to his varied interests, his passion for learning and research. I can still see him in his red fez, with his round glasses, and behind them his twinkling, honey-colored eyes. He would sit in his library smoking his pipe and reading. But whenever he saw me he would set the book aside, for I was his favorite. I couldn't yet read, and Grandfather would reach for *Kalila wa Dimna*, the famous collection of ancient Persian animal fables. I still love those wise and humorous stories about talking animals, and whenever I read them I can hear Grandfather's voice, the voice that also taught me the first verses of the Qur'an. The house had a laboratory as well, a room in which Grandfather experimented with medicinal plants, which my mother also planted in her garden. If we caught a cold, had a scrape, a sprain, or a gastrointestinal complaint, she would treat us with her herbs.

It was 1955, and I was not yet five years old when I begged my mother to let me go to the school in Fariskur. I wanted to leave each morning with Nur and Safaa, and I cried so long that mother finally took me to the school's director. I was allowed to go along for a few days as a test, and then to stay. The teachers at the school were all pious Muslim women, but none of them wore a head scarf as is expected in schools today. If you look at pictures or films from the 1950s and '60s, you note with shock that in the streets of Cairo and Alexandria there are almost no women wearing head scarves, never mind a niqab.

When we wanted to swim—even after we had long been living in Cairo—we would drive to the Mediterranean, sometimes near the port city of Port Said, but mostly to Ras al-Bar, which is closer to Fariskur, and where the Nile's Damietta arm flows into the sea. The river's current continues out for a long distance, and it is amazing to see that the sea doesn't manage to subdue the Nile's flow.

In the late fall of 1956, Safaa, Nur, and I walked the three kilometers to school every morning. The bus to Fariskur ran only every three hours, and the train didn't stop in Kafr al-Arab. Sometimes a heavy shower would overtake us—in the Delta it rains much more than in Cairo or Upper Egypt. At the time there were still no weather forecasts, and if it was raining in the early morning we were allowed to stay at home. But if rain surprised us on our way to school, the farmers would wave us into their mud houses, where we would shed our school uniforms, sit in front of the stove, and wait until our clothes were dry and the rain had stopped. We were happy each time we were able to visit the farmers in their modest huts. The people were poor, but amazingly friendly. This early familiarity in contact with so-called fellaheen would be of great use to me later at excavations and in the museum.

On the way home again we would test our courage on the railway bridge. Who dared to cross the canal on the bridge? We would climb up the embankment and put our ears to the tracks to listen for an approaching train. Sometimes we would have to wait until one passed by. Then we would cross the canal by stepping on the ties. I wouldn't dare do it again for any amount of money. The water lay far below us. We must have had an indulgent guardian angel.

One day when we got home everything had changed. For several days Father had sat intently in front of the radio, and Mother had been more serious than usual. She told us that we wouldn't be going to school for the next few days. "There's a war." We asked what war was and who our enemy was. I can still see her painting the windowpanes with a dark blue paint. Suddenly we were no longer allowed to use any electric lights, only kerosene lamps. Outside, the workmen filled countless bags with sand and piled them high.

In a fiery speech, to the frenetic applause of a crowd in Alexandria, on July 26, 1956, Gamal Abdel Nasser declared that he was nationalizing the Suez Canal and would use the income from the canal's operations to finance the construction of the new dam at Aswan. The broadcast of the speech was the signal for the takeover of the canal office by an Egyptian military commando unit. Everyone in Egypt knew that we could expect the British and French to retaliate. The episode has gone into the history books as the Suez Crisis, a highly euphemistic term, for the 'crisis' was a proper war, with many dead, wounded, prisoners of war, and massive destruction. I have no idea whether it was really Nasser's intention to provoke such a violent reaction. It is possible that he felt it would lead to a crisis, but that in that Cold War period and with the colonial era a thing of the past it could be resolved diplomatically. Given the events of the previous years, it was obvious that sooner or later Egypt would claim ownership of the Suez Canal.

The years after the Second World War were frustrating for Great Britain. Even though it had been victorious, its economy had suffered disastrously. It lost one colony after another: India, Burma, Sri Lanka. It was no different for France, the 'Grande Nation.' In 1952, when the Free Officers forced King Farouk to abdicate and go into exile, the British had lost their last bridgehead in Egypt. My grandfather el-Sayed had been a supporter of the monarchy, but he was furious with the prime ministers appointed by King Fuad and his successor, who—some more, some less—permitted the British to assert their own interests. Father always said that Farouk was only a plaything of the British, a spoiled child who in exile in Italy transformed his ample pay-off into an ample corpulence.

With the Suez Canal, the two colonial countries still owned the artery through which oil flowed to the West, and thus a gushing source of income. To Egypt, now a socialist republic, the Suez Canal Company was a relic of the colonial era, and for that reason President Nasser forced the British to withdraw their eighty thousand soldiers from the Canal Zone in 1954. While the West was arming Israel, it refused to provide weapons to Egypt, as an enemy of Israel, so Nasser turned to Czechoslovakia. The United States was so angry about his appeal to the Eastern Bloc that it promptly retracted its promised loan for the building of the Aswan High Dam. So Egypt was in desperate need of money. What was more obvious than nationalizing the Suez Canal? Nasser offered the British and French financial compensation, and at first it appeared that a diplomatic solution might be possible through the United Nations. But in fact, in secret meetings the British, French, and Israelis had long since been planning a campaign with the goal of marching into Egypt and deposing Nasser. On October 29 the Israelis, claiming the need to secure their borders, invaded the Sinai all the way up to the canal. Two days later the French-British armada attacked, bombed Egyptian airports, and virtually leveled Port Said.

Kafr al-Arab is only a few kilometers from Port Said. I still remember the sirens howling over our village. We were given gas masks, which we found somewhat amusing, and we started to play with them. But Mama stopped us. She had experienced the war in Alexandria, and soon my sisters and I needed to learn the precautionary measures she still remembered from Alexandria. Papa was also worried: Our house was near the machinery plant with the water treatment system and pumps. Pilots could interpret the buildings as a military target or even bomb them intentionally. We could hear the distant rumble of artillery from Port Fuad and the enemy warplanes. And bombs did fall in the vicinity of Kafr al-Arab. Father became increasingly concerned. And then it happened: We could make out the plane on the west side of the Nile from afar. It was streaking in our direction, then suddenly it disappeared. There was a loud noise and smoke billowed up. An angel had protected us.

Refugees began arriving from the destroyed cities of the Canal Zone, especially the ruined Port Said. Thousands of homeless were quartered in schools, where families were separated only by hanging mats. I saw crying children and mothers who had lost everything. Many men and women had stayed in Port Said and were fighting in the ruins. I couldn't understand the violence. Egypt was no longer a colony, after all, but a free country. And now bombers were roaring over our heads. "We won't set you free! You're still under our control!"

On the radio we could hear incessant reports of victory, that Nasser had sunk a number of ships in the canal. My siblings and I rejoiced and sang what all Egyptian children were singing: "Eden has drowned in the canal. We're all your children, Gamal," or "Give us our sky. Our sky is a fiery signal for you! Our canal is your grave." The British prime minister, Anthony Eden, was enemy number one; Gamal Abdel Nasser, our almost mythical hero, the embodiment of our hopes for victory, freedom, and justice. I don't know what Father was thinking at the time, or my grandfather, the member of parliament. Were they too carried along by the surge of patriotism? My father, the engineer, was a cool, calculating man. Had he already guessed that Egypt would suffer a crushing defeat? That it was only thanks to the intervention of the United States and the threat of an atomic bomb from the Soviet Union that the three invaders had to withdraw after six weeks? Eden was forced to resign. The whole world condemned the military action of 1956 as a shameful relapse into colonial-imperial behavior on the part of the British and French. Nasser converted their international loss of face into a great national victory. It would interest me greatly to know what my grandfather Mohamed Ibrahim, the port director from multicultural Alexandria, would have thought about the laws passed a few months later, with which Nasser dispossessed Egypt's Jews, directed them to leave the country, and silenced disapproving opponents. But Grandfather Mohamed never had to learn of them. He had died in 1954.

Like the rest of the country, we were caught up in a wave of patriotism. I can still see myself waving the Egyptian flag in front of the entire school. That was in 1958, the year in which Egypt and Syria joined together to form the United Arab Republic. The day was celebrated with ceremonies in every school. My classmate Suheir, the daughter of Fariskur's police chief, and I were chosen to play the roles of the two countries in a dance on the school's stage. I carried the Egyptian flag, since I had long black hair that complemented the green flag with its white crescent and three stars. Suheir, with her long blond hair, carried the green, white, and black Syrian flag. Then finally, to the enthusiastic applause of the schoolchildren and their parents, we replaced the two flags with the new red, white, and black flag with two stars in the center. Even though the United Arab Republic survived for only three years, the two countries have kept that flag to this day, though Sadat had the two stars replaced with a falcon, and Mubarak, in turn, exchanged the falcon for an eagle. Now, since the Revolution, many people would like to return to the old green flag. In any case, back then I was very proud to be allowed to carry it.

My marvelous life in Kafr al-Arab and Fariskur suddenly ended in 1958. We had to move to Cairo. Quite unexpectedly, my father's brother and his wife both died, one shortly after the other, leaving behind eight children under the guardianship of my parents. I desperately missed my beloved little school, my teacher, the farmers on my way to school, our house, and the fields that had been my playground. From one day to the next we found ourselves in the crowded, noisy metropolis, and what was worse, we were living with our eight cousins in their apartment that was far too small for all of us. Father had still not found one for us nearby. But our cousins were anything but agreeable to having to share their rooms with us. They tried everything to get rid of us. For example, they once staged a seance that I can now remember only with laughter, but that at the time seemed by no means amusing. My cousins placed a white tablecloth over a small basket to which they had tied a pencil. Then with all sorts of magic spells they conjured the spirits of their parents, who were supposed to leave a "yes" on a slip of paper in the basket as proof of their presence. Of course they had fixed it so that there was in fact a scrap of paper with a shaky "yes" written on it in the basket—and needless to say the spirits let us know that we should disappear as soon as possible. We had seen through their tricks, but the message was clear: Get out!

We now joke about that episode, for as soon as we moved out our relationship improved. We were together a lot in our free time and during summer vacations, and today we are like siblings.

Father finally found us an apartment. It was right next to the Abdeen Palace, formerly a royal residence and at that time the official home of the president, which is surrounded by gardens and a beautiful park with tall trees and rare palms. We lived on the fifth floor, and since the area around the palace was not yet built up with high-rises, from our balcony we had a view to the west of the Pyramids in the distance and a strip of the Nile; to the east we could see the citadel of Salah al-Din and the famous Sultan Hassan and Ibn Tulun mosques. We were living in the heart of Cairo, in a quarter that still recalls the fact that Cairo was once thought of as the Paris of the East. It was only a few minutes' walk to the Nile and to Tahrir Square, to the Egyptian, Islamic, and Coptic museums, to the Khan al-Khalili market, or to the main railway station.

It is difficult to describe how I felt. From a tiny village I had suddenly been catapulted into the center of Cairo, Egypt's capital and the cultural and political center of the Arab world at the time. We lived in one of the four 'Belgian Buildings,' imposing structures built by a Belgian firm at the beginning of the twentieth century for high-level palace employees. The apartment had very high ceilings, and in one of the rooms Father had a second ceiling installed halfway up so we had a play space two meters high. He even built us a swing. And the hydraulic engineer also installed something very important: In Cairo at that time, drinking water was rationed during the day, and sometimes the higher floors didn't receive any at all. Father had a water tank built into the bathroom that automatically filled at night, so we were never short of water.

The apartment was right above the boulevard used for major parades. On July 23, Gamal Abdel Nasser rode by in an open car on his way to Abdeen Square to give his legendary speech on the anniversary of the Revolution. From our windows we could watch everything. Exotic birds from the palace garden would sometimes perch on our balcony in the morning. Below, the streets and broad sidewalks were scrubbed daily, and the city smelled so clean. And then there was our large roof. It was a desirable setting for festivities of all kinds. In King Farouk's day the building superintendent's apartment, the washhouse, and the servants' rooms on the back part of the roof had been set apart in such a way that it was impossible for prying eyes to look down into the palace garden. But since the Revolution everything was different. The large space, previously inaccessible, provided ample space for parties and weddings, and there were frequent drawn-out celebrations. Occasionally prominent personalities would attend, actors we knew from the cinema or singers familiar from the radio. It was there that I first saw a half-naked belly dancer.

In our free time we visited the museums or the old churches in Fustat. There, in Cairo's oldest quarter, stands the oldest synagogue in the country, the Ben Ezra Synagogue, the so-called Hanging Church, and not far away is the Mosque of Amr ibn al-As, the oldest mosque in Egypt. With pride we visited that structure built in around 640 after the Muslims' capture of Egypt. There had been no exquisite buildings like that in the Delta, and it was uplifting to know that our country had such shrines. At the time I don't recall that we made any distinction between Muslims, Copts, and Jews, but politics change a great deal. The language was becoming more aggressive. There was no longer any talk of Jews, but rather Zionists; no longer of Palestine, but of the enemy country.

School was a second shock. I was suddenly one of forty pupils in a classroom far too small: in Fariskur we had been only fifteen at most. Also, I missed Fatima, my beloved teacher. Now I was confronted with a large, robust woman with a hideously disfigured face, apparently the result of a burn. I was truly afraid of her. But Zahira was a wonderful teacher: She effortlessly managed to turn the forty children in her class into attentive and interested pupils. I owe to her the fact that I later played basketball and hand-ball, that I discovered a love of painting. She sent me to sports contests, she submitted work of mine that won me prizes. I often thought of her during my later studies and then during excavations whenever I needed to draw hiero-glyphs, tomb paintings, and reliefs. Zahira was a dear woman. I soon lost my dread of looking at her face, and she won my heart—for life. We remained friends even after I left school. Zahira named her only daughter Wafaa, and I was even with her in the last days before she died.

In Cairo Father was now working in the firm's administrative head-quarters. But barely two years after our move, in 1960, he was sent for the first time to Aswan and Kom Ombo. On January 9, 1960, Nasser and Soviet premier Nikita Khrushchev had together given the starting signal for the building of the High Dam at Aswan. Al-Sadd al-Ali or 'Father of All Dams,' as it was proudly called by the Egyptians, was to become the tallest concrete dam in the world at the time, a "bulwark against drought." Behind the dam the Nile was gradually backed up to form a lake five hundred kilometers long, extending far beyond the Egyptian–Sudanese border. The Nubians still living there were required to abandon their villages, to be resettled in new villages downstream near Kom Ombo. Father was one of the engineers who built the infrastructure for the new Nubia: canals that carried Nile water to the villages in the desert and irrigated the new fields.

At first he was away only for a few weeks, but then, beginning in 1962, without a break for four years. We would see him only four days a month, when he would come home from Kom Ombo for a visit. He would bring us dates, peanuts, and dried hibiscus; from the latter Mama would make a wonderfully refreshing drink, and Father would explain how important the date palms were for the Nubians. With the wood they built their houses, beds, and furniture; with the leaves they thatched their roofs; and the dates provided them with a living, for they are of such high quality that they are sought-after even outside Egypt. The Nubians' culture, their complex, close-knit society, is based on communal ownership of the date palms and cultivation of them. Millions of the trees would be submerged in Nasser's lake.

At that time I learned a great deal from Papa about the Nubians: about their culture that was thousands of years old, their exquisitely painted houses, their unique social relationships. In 1960 it seemed that all that was destined to be lost; the resettling of the Egyptian Nubians in Kom Ombo was described as a cultural catastrophe. Although UNESCO rescued the famous temples at Abu Simbel and Philae from being engulfed by the lake, and a number of western countries dismantled Nubian temple sites and reconstructed them in their museums, few people seemed to take any interest in the Nubians themselves, even though Egypt had tried to ease their greatest concerns with reparations and construction help. Needless to say, they were not happy about being the only ones to pay the price—and it was a terrible price—for Egypt's progress. Yet it soon became apparent that they too were indebted to the dam for employment, power, and water, even in dry years. Unfortunately, we were not allowed to visit Father in Kom Ombo. It was no place for children, he said, and he lived there very simply; it was hot, and there were snakes and scorpions. But he spoke with great enthusiasm about the Nubians. He claimed that they were born dancing and singing.

The Nubians' identity was not lost beneath the waves of the lake. They have preserved any number of traditions in their handicrafts—mainly basket weaving, ceramics, and leatherwork—and above all in their music. They hold fast to their close social ties, nurturing—as Egyptians—their Nubian culture.

In the 1990s, when I organized the first educational workshops for children at the Nubian Museum in Aswan, I was astonished at the craftsmanly genius of the girls and boys, their sense for color and form. The Nubians encouraged me: We won't lose our identity if we are determined to preserve it, to live it, knowing that it is something special.

During the entire Nasser period I was at a girls' school. We were very proud of being Egyptian and knew by heart the wonderful songs Oum Kalthoum sang about the country and the Nile, for example the famous song "Egypt Speaks for Itself." The curriculum included the use of firearms and nursing. The government required that in case of war, we female pupils could be of use in civil defense. I learned to shoot a simple rifle, but secretly I prayed: God grant that I never have to use it.

But then came the worst trial—not for us at school, but for my older brother Mohamed. After his graduation he was determined to attend the military academy. Father was not thrilled, but he respected Mohamed's wishes. After the beginning of the semester, Mohamed stayed away for months. It was the first time we had not seen him for so long, and we missed him terribly. Our big brother was a model for us in so many ways. He was always smartly dressed, listened to 1960s pop music—the Beatles and the Rolling Stones—read modern authors whom he would recommend to us, and would take us with him to the cinema, where we became familiar with all the glamorous film stars of the time. Thanks to him we felt far more grown-up and mature. When he finally came home from the military academy, we frantically hugged him and hung on his every word as he related his experiences as a soldier, which were as exciting as movies.

Less than two years after Mohamed entered the academy, Nasser decided that the military would support the socialist nationalists in Yemen in their rebellion against the king, Imam Muhammad al-Badr. The young cadets' training was abruptly ended; suddenly Mohamed was promoted to lieutenant and given a command in Yemen. My parents were shocked, and Father kept asking in bewilderment, "How can they send such young lads with no military experience into a country they don't even know!" Quite apart from the question of how sensible such a deployment was.

Today the world looks to Afghanistan. In the 1960s Yemen was Egypt's Afghanistan—a few years later one could have called it Egypt's Vietnam.

Nasser and Egypt were in for a disaster: changing tribal loyalties, assassinations, battles in impassable mountain regions with heavy losses, support of the adversaries by the Saudis, the British, and the Americans, who feared the encroachment of a pan-Arab socialism. In October 1962, Nasser sent five thousand soldiers into Yemen. Three years later there were fifty-five thousand. It was a brutal and dirty war, one that Egypt lost in 1967 with great loss of life.

Soon after Mohamed's deployment we received news that there were already many dead and wounded. Returning officers and soldiers made no secret of their discontent. To appease them, their pay was raised and they were presented with gifts, mainly cigarettes and alcohol. The first time my brother came home on leave, he was altogether changed, reticent and withdrawn. He smoked incessantly and drank too much. He spent his nights in nightclubs and went through a lot of money. When I questioned him, asked what was wrong with him, he took a long time before he finally said, "You can't imagine what we are experiencing. Terrible things." The king was hiring mercenaries who would attach themselves to the rebels and the Egyptian army. Outwardly, they behaved as though they were altogether loyal, and so ingratiated themselves into the Egyptians' trust. "But then, while we're asleep at night they beat and massacre my comrades. The imam has announced that he will pay cash for every decapitated Egyptian head. One morning when I went to my comrades' tents to wake them, I found their headless corpses. It was horrible. In our camp, we would find the hastily buried bodies of our own men in the loose sand beneath our feet."

It was almost a miracle that my brother survived that war, but afterward he was a different person. He came back from Yemen unwell, suffering from asthma and in frail health. It was a long time before he smiled again, and then only for brief periods.

On June 5, 1967, Egypt declared war on its archenemy Israel. My brother and his comrades were deployed to the Sinai. Young people like me were asked to donate blood and called up for civil defense. Mohamed was with the air-raid defenses. Even as a boy he had been a wizard at math, and now his abilities were exploited by the artillery. His unit was assigned to block the transport corridors on the Sinai, a deployment in difficult terrain. But the morale of the troops was good. This time he and his soldiers were fighting for

Egypt, not Yemeni rebels. In general there was a mood of victory. Egyptian radio incessantly broadcast patriotic songs, and the news reports were full of victories that weren't true. Little by little we learned the bitter truth: The war was already over before it had even begun. The Israelis had almost annihilated the Egyptian army in six days. Ten thousand young Egyptians lost their lives, and thousands became prisoners of war.

I saw my first war wounded in Cairo's hospitals. I was a member of the Egyptian Federation of Scouts and Guides—the Pathfinders—and our troop had decided to take presents to the wounded. I have never forgotten how in the military hospital we would stand in front of young officers and soldiers who had lost arms and legs only hours before. We had trouble holding back our tears, and it was only the brave smiles of the men that kept us from racing out of the room. But we remembered our oath as Pathfinders and kept going back, so we became used to the sight of the poor men.

With no news from Mohamed, those were terrible days for our parents. Little by little the magnitude of the catastrophe was becoming clear. Then came Nasser's speech on the radio. He confessed to the bitter defeat, assumed full responsibility, and declared that he was resigning as president. We were all stunned. It was a nightmare. Nasser, our Nasser, resigning! It couldn't be. At that moment I feared I would never see my brother again. We sat there sobbing, and Father, standing at the window, was just as distraught as we were. But Mother remained perfectly calm: "I know he's alive. Mohamed is not dead." I don't know how long it was, but at some point the bell rang. Father opened the door and there was Mohamed, pale and exhausted, marked by terror, by defeat, by several days in the desert without enough water and bread.

Again he never talked about what he had been through. He went to work and remained withdrawn. After a year, on one of his visits home, we all decided to drive to the sea and Alexandria. We rented a bungalow right on the beach and sat together until the moon rose above us. A fresh breeze was blowing off the sea. We were finally relaxed and feeling more positive. We at last ventured to ask him about his experiences, and he related what had happened to him in Sinai. I later wrote it down in my diary.

"My comrades and I were supposed to defend a strategically important Sinai corridor. We had not even settled into our emplacements when we were surprised by Israeli warplanes. They hit our positions, destroyed our air force on the ground, and knocked out the air-raid defenses. Because they also destroyed our convoys, there could be no new supplies and no organized retreat. We were completely cut off and being shot like fair game." Mohamed told us that he had lost Zakaria, his best friend and comrade from the war in Yemen. The Israelis had used prohibited incendiary bombs, presumably napalm, which the Americans were dropping in Vietnam at the same time. There were horrible injuries. "Then we saw Israeli tanks approaching along the corridor. We had absolutely no chance to stop them and were given the order to retreat. But how were we supposed to get away?"

My brother kept his head. He ran from one wrecked vehicle to another, and finally ordered two uninjured soldiers to install an undamaged engine in a battered but otherwise roadworthy truck. It must have been risky to try to install an engine in such circumstances, but they managed it. The wounded were gathered up from the base and loaded onto the truck. Along the canal, on the way from al-Qantara to Suez, he picked up as many survivors as the truck would hold. On the sides of the road were charred corpses and soldiers badly wounded by incendiary bombs. In Suez, which was completely destroyed, he realized the full extent of the defeat. Even the hospitals were destroyed, and Mohamed decided to drive to the closest hospital in the Delta. From there he drove on to Cairo.

Many years later a general spoke to me in the antiquities administration. "I owe my life to your brother," he said. "I was one of the young officers serving under your brother in Sinai." He confirmed to me the story of their flight in every detail.

But Nasser was not allowed to resign. It was said that "when the captain leaves it, the ship sinks." Suddenly all Cairo was out in the streets, the crowds shouting, "Gamal, Gamal, you can't go! Gamal, don't abandon us!" It was later written that even before his resignation speech, the party people closest to him had initiated the mass protests, if not actually organized them. Whether that is true or not, the Egyptians got their president back. But even Nasser couldn't alleviate the sadness and frustration of the coming weeks and months. The shock had shaken the country to the core.

Today the years between 1967 and 1970 are referred to as the time of the war of attrition. The dishonor of losing the war gnawed at people's souls. There were reports of massacres and senseless force, of the torture and murder of Egyptian prisoners of war by Israeli soldiers, of a bloodbath during the attack on Shedwan Island in the Red Sea—survivors had to be treated in psychiatric clinics. At that time we visited in the hospital a relative who had been on Shedwan. He no longer recognized his own mother and simply stared through her. In the eastern Delta the Israelis bombed the village of Bahr al-Baqar and struck the elementary school. I drove to the village. The people were all wearing black, mourning for their slaughtered children. They were inconsolable.

Gradually examples of Egyptian heroism became known, for example the battle for Ras al-Esh, in which the Egyptian army held its position despite heavy losses. Ras al-Esh became a symbol of heroism and a readiness for sacrifice. But the Israelis were sitting on the Sinai and showing no signs of ever leaving it, stoking a desire for revenge. The Egyptians wanted to drive the Israelis out of occupied Sinai—then suddenly the country was shaken by new dramatic news: "The Rais [Leader] is dead!"

Today it is hard to imagine what took place in Egypt's cities and villages after Nasser's death was announced. The notion of a nation in mourning doesn't do it justice. It was a form of mass hysteria. People simply wouldn't believe it. Everywhere they ran into the streets screaming, crying, and tearing their hair. A neighbor of ours wanted to throw herself from the sixth floor and was barely prevented from doing so—and she was not alone. Messages of sympathy came in from the entire Arab world. On the radio we kept hearing "Farewell, Gamal, beloved of millions!"

Nasser was by no means uncontroversial. As a statesman and commander he made many mistakes, and he had many critics and opponents set aside. He was no saint, but a charismatic figure, and the majority of Egyptians believed in him and adored him. I saw my father cry only twice—when my mother died and on the day Nasser died. And yet my father had been extremely critical of the president's policies.

Nasser's coffin was accompanied by a funeral procession of literally hundreds of thousands of Egyptians. It came close to being a tragedy, for everyone wanted to touch the dead man's coffin. We were in the midst of the throng with friends who had come from various parts of the country for the funeral. Finally the press of the crowd became more urgent and threatening. Women were fainting beside us, and we could no longer stand being shoved.

Mother called to us that we should leave; we could watch the procession on television at home. We wore mourning clothes for a week.

Nasser was ill. At fifty-one he had completely burned himself out in office, and he died from exhaustion. He ruled like an autocrat and sent his political opponents to prison. His pan-Arabism failed, his socialist economic reform suffocated in red tape. He lost two wars. But in spite of all, the Egyptians continue to honor him. Hosni Mubarak, by contrast, will always be remembered as a corrupt criminal. 'Nasserism' as a political program is a phenomon of the post-Nasser era. It is above all an expression of the yearning for an incorruptible, charismatic leader. During the revolutionary days in the spring of 2011, I saw young people carrying Nasser's picture through the streets, simply as a symbol of their hope for freedom and democracy. But did it have anything to do with a Nasserist program? We definitely need social justice and a distribution of the wealth of this country, but not a repeat of the socialist experiment. In retrospect, the Nasser era is now seen as Egypt's 'golden age.' That is pure romanticism, but I remember how we young people felt at the time. We all wanted to do something for our country. John Kennedy's famous "Ask not what your country can do for you—ask what you can do for your country" could have been urged upon us by Nasser, and we would all have responded. But for many, the policies of the subsequent decades stifled such enthusiasm and willingness to sacrifice. Yet not all of us have turned away in frustration. There have been and still are many people who have maintained their commitment. Some of them will be described in the following pages.

The parting from Nasser was also a parting from my childhood and teenage years. To be sure, from a distance of more than forty years I romanticize much of that time. I feel a sentimental nostalgia for it. And why shouldn't I? For the memory of my grandparents, my life in an extended family that seemed wonderful to me as a child; for a country and for figures who made it so easy for me to accept my country and my people and love them. I now hear many people complain that everything was better in the old days. No, of course it wasn't. But I object: To children there is no 'better' time. Only old people like us make comparisons with 'the old days.' To children the world is what it is. I know that by profession we museum people tend to preserve. But we preserve in order to answer the questions, Where have we come from? How did we become what we are?

There are some things that I miss, and I will never get over their loss: When we would visit the farmers in the huts they occupied for weeks out on the fields, they would sometimes make rice pudding for us with fresh cow's milk. That rice, the rice from my grandfather's fields, the Damietta rice with its unique flavor; I would love to taste it once again. But I look for it in our shops in vain. Just like the sugar from our sugar cane, the cotton from our fields. I miss the starry sky and the full moon, that vast cathedral towering above us. I now have to drive far out into the desert to leave the smog and dust of Cairo behind and rediscover that early, familiar silence. I miss the green expanse of the Delta. The villagers' fields have disappeared. Ugly concrete buildings are planlessly taking over the landscape, destroying the precious soils the Nile had brought from so far away. It strikes me that al-Sadd al-Ali, the 'Father of All Dams,' along with making us proud of our progress, has robbed us of our humility in the face of nature.

I miss the house of my scholarly grandfather, Alexandria's port director. He died in 1954. The house was filled with people. Many sobbing women in black, many men waiting outside for the coffin. They carried him to the mosque and then to the cemetery. Afterward the house was a different place. Without Grandfather it was empty, even though his spirit was still everywhere. In a glass cabinet Mama kept his glasses, pipe, pens, his crystal inkwell, the instruments he had used to study the stars, and also the fez he always wore when he left the house. After our move to Cairo in 1958, we always spent our summer vacations there. My brother Mohamed once took a photo of me with Grandfather's fez on my head, his glasses on my nose, and his pipe in my mouth, reading a thick book. During the 1967 war and the Israeli bombing attacks on Port Said and the area around Lake Manzala, Grandfather's house was also badly damaged. Since it was threatening to collapse, it was demolished in 1970. The house's park and garden, which Grandfather had given to the town, no longer exist. The town built unimposing office buildings on them. I can no longer find any green space in the town. In my childhood some 15,000 people lived there; today it has more than 250,000 inhabitants. I no longer like to drive to Fariskur.

So what happened to the familiar figures from my childhood? Grandfather's son Hassan al-Diasti, my mother's older brother who studied economics in France, ran the Banque Misr in Lebanon for twenty-five years as general manager. At the beginning of the civil war he suffered a stroke—he could not believe that the people of that beautiful country were capable of such savage battles. For twenty years, as long as the country's misery lasted, he was bed-ridden. He died at eighty-five.

Grandfather el-Sayed, the *omda*, the large landowner and member of parliament, died at eighty, a death that was altogether appropriate. He had spent the day out in the fields with the farmers. They had grilled fresh corn, which Grandfather loved. He died that same night.

My father, Taha El Saddik, wanted to return to Kafr al-Arab after he retired. He felt that he ought to return to his roots. The former engineer built a house in the village of his ancestors that would sap all his strength and ultimately cost him his life. The people in Kafr al-Arab had changed. The village office that my grandfather had headed for so long as *omda* was no longer the same. Father objected to the endless demands for money; private donations were expected here and there, bribes for petitions that were then held up, for work that was delayed. All his life he had held himself aloof from corruption and cronyism. With that last building project he lost his health, and died at seventy-six. He lies buried in Kafr al-Arab. My mother had died two years before him at seventy-four. We buried her in Fariskur. My older brother Mohamed took part in the Sinai campaign in 1973, which has gone down in the history books as the October War. He was wounded in his arm by a grenade fragment in Port Said, but refused to have it removed, as he considered it a decoration for the liberation of the Sinai. It was a proud and happy day for him when the Israelis withdrew. After the war he retired, and died at fifty-one.

Nur, my four-years-older sister, studied geography at Ain Shams University and became a teacher. Until her retirement she worked as the school's director. Safaa, my sister who was two years older, studied chemistry at al-Azhar University in Cairo. She followed in my father's footsteps and for a long time worked in Cairo's waterworks. Today she is a national secretary in the Ministry of Housing, Utilities, and Urban Development. Kamel, my brother who was two years younger, followed in my grandfather's footsteps and studied economics in Cairo. He was a director of the port of Alexandria.

When I now look back at my own path, I know that it began in my grandfather's library—and led me into the library of Cairo's Egyptian Museum.

3

ON THE GREAT PYRAMID

"To Giza, please!" I said proudly. "Cairo University!" And Aisha added, "Faculty of Arts!" Finally! By nine in the morning Aisha and I were already down in front of the building. We were so very excited and happy, two young women just turned eighteen. We were both wearing new dresses, new shoes, carrying new bags. Aisha looked very beautiful, and I—women don't forget such things—was wearing a turquoise dress. The taxi driver already knew where to take us. "So, today's your first day at the university, right?" In the rearview mirror we could see that he was missing a few teeth, but his smile was overwhelming.

Aisha el-Guhari had been my best friend since middle school. We were inseparable, and it was perfectly obvious to us that we would go on to university together. That day we drove up to the official entrance to the university like princesses with their toothless chauffeur. The campus lies in the middle of a park, and only members of the university have access to it. The buildings with their white columns and portals and the large, domed festival hall—President Barack Obama gave his Cairo speech there on June 4, 2009—seemed as awe-inspiring as the academic halls of Oxford or Cambridge. The university was founded as a private college in 1908, then nationalized in 1925. Its first rector was the famous philosopher and national politician Ahmed Lutfi el-Sayed, one of my great-uncle Abdel Rahman's closest friends. I had read Lutfi's autobiography, *The Story of My Life*, with enthusiasm. At that time Lutfi had been appointed to the Faculty of Arts by the blind Taha Hussein, a famous writer and former minister of education, known as the 'dean' of Arabic literature. By October 1968 both were only part of ancient university history. Yet when the famous carillon rang out from the clock tower, a sound every Egyptian knows from radio news broadcasts, I had the feeling I had arrived.

We newcomers were greeted by the dean in the great hall of the Faculty of Arts. He explained to us that all bachelor's degree students were obliged to pursue a general studies course the first year, after which we could focus on our major and a few selected minor subjects. I still remember how he laughed: "That is your fate. You'll have to learn a great deal." To me the broad range of courses was welcome, for I wanted to be a journalist. I dreamed of traveling and writing about the history, culture, and people of other countries—India, China, Mexico. My parents were by no means supportive. Father said that in Egypt journalism was a farce, the majority of journalists were political yes-men, and the few serious ones were either imprisoned or in exile. Mother also harried me; couldn't I see myself in the Faculty of Economics and Political Science? That was the most popular school at the time, for its graduates had a good chance at a career in the diplomatic service. With my grade average I would surely be accepted, but I didn't want that.

"And what about diplomats?" I objected. "Most of them are yes-men as well!"

But Father assured me that as a diplomat one could live abroad, in India, China, Mexico.

"And only be an exile! I don't want to be exiled," I replied. Father knew how stubborn I could be. I stayed with journalism and chose Egyptology as one of my minor courses. My parents didn't say anything more. They knew that since I was twelve I had devoured Grandfather's books on ancient Egypt.

I was also interested in politics, of course. How could I not be? The Egypt of my youth was highly politicized, and the year 1968 was a turbulent one, not only at universities in America and in Europe. There were university groups of all political persuasions: socialists, communists, liberals, and even then Islamists. Yet at that time none of the female students wore head scarves, not even those from Saudi Arabia. In fact, my Saudi friend Faiza wore shorter skirts than any of the rest of us. It seems unthinkable now, but at that time no one troubled us on the street. We listened to the Beatles, of course, but also to classical Arab music. In the West students were demonstrating in the streets against the war in Vietnam, for black and white equality, for greater civil rights. In Cairo, Alexandria, and Mansura they demonstrated for better study conditions. But they also went further, calling for greater democracy, an end to military dictatorship and censorship, and to the ubiquitous presence of secret police on campus. In February there was street fighting between students and police outside our building in Cairo. Thirty students were killed in Alexandria and Mansura. And for the first time you could hear chants of "Down with Nasser!" He promptly closed all the universities for four weeks.

At school I had written essays about Mustafa Kamil Pasha, the founder of the Egyptian National Party, and Ahmed Urabi, the leader of the 1882 revolt against the British. I wrote my first piece of journalism for the faculty's bulletin-board newspaper. Titled "Life in the City of the Dead," it was about al-Qarafa, Cairo's vast cemetery quarter, the beginnings of which go back to the era of the Fatimids and Mamluks. As far back as the Middle Ages, wealthy people built imposing family tombs and mortuary mosques at the base of the Muqattam Hills and the Citadel. But there are also thousands of small, unprepossessing tombs that stretch for kilometers along a dense network of alleyways. From the outside they can barely be distinguished from the single-story, flat-roofed houses of the suburbs. They were erected for the living as well as the dead, a custom—as I would learn later—that goes back to pharaonic antiquity. The cemeteries in Giza, Saqqara, and Thebes were also designed for the living. The priests entrusted with the cult of the dead lived there, and families would regularly visit their dead, perform rites, and celebrate festivals that often went on for days, with much feasting and partying.

Caretakers of tombs had always lived in Cairo's necropolis as well, but with the increasing flight from the countryside, and especially since the loss of the Sinai to Israel in 1967, more and more people were streaming into the city where there was no housing. The necropolis had become a makeshift settlement, so that by 1968 some ten thousand people were living in the tombs, the poorest of the poor.

In 1968 al-Qarafa was still a contemplative place. Sometimes Aisha would come along when I was interviewing people, sometimes my mother, who loved seeing the shrines and cenotaphs of the Prophet's family. Her favorite spot was the Mosque of Nafisa al-Tahira, a popular Egyptian saint. There were beautiful walks across the quiet Northern Cemetery, a veritable oasis in the midst of the metropolis. It has villa-like tomb structures and wider streets than the poorer southern section. There I got to know little Magda, an enchanting seven-year-old with curly blond hair. She knew all the families living there and introduced me to many of them, especially the women. I wanted to know how they could stand it. Weren't the children afraid of sleeping in a house with dead people lying in the cellar? Were they afraid of ghosts? The women told me that every day they had to walk long distances to fetch water from fountains and standpipes in the city. There was also no electricity. Their husbands worked as day laborers at construction sites or as paid tomb guards in the necropolis. They were mostly worried about their children's future. They yearned for healthy living quarters and good schools, and many of them were working as cleaning women to save up for them. The children did believe in ghosts, as did many adults. Ghosts moved through the streets like the living, Magda told me. "But they're harmless." Once a neighbor of hers was about to greet a man he met when he noticed that the man had four legs and four hands. "But don't be afraid," Magda assured me. "If you get too close to ghosts, they immediately disappear." For little Magda, al-Qarafa was a perfectly happy place. She always looked forward to visits from the owners of the tomb she was living in with her family. "They bring us dates and pastries," she said. "And sometimes they even give me money."

I was proud of the subject and my article. Most of my fellow students had never even heard about the people in al-Qarafa. Now it is estimated that three hundred thousand are living there, ignored by the authorities and tolerated by most of the owners of the tombs. Temporary shelters have become permanent dwellings. They have installed water lines and electricity, built streets; they operate shops and businesses—and have made their peace with the dead. What could have become of Magda?

Mother never came into the families' tomb shelters with me; her piety toward the dead held her back. But she would drag me to the structures at the edges of the necropolis. They were only derelict barracks in which people were living in the most squalid conditions—only a few kilometers from our wonderful apartment next to the Abdeen Palace. We visited one sick woman who lived in a cave-like cellar with no light, another who owned only the mattress on which she lay in a cellar filled with wastewater and an incredible stench. I asked Mother who these people were, but she didn't answer my question. Later, while writing my article, it occurred to me that all of them could have been women from the countryside from villages like Kafr al-Arab, that they had once been members of a family and a village community. I thought of Kafr al-Arab, the idyll of my childhood days, of the Nile, the fields, the friendly farmers. How many Egyptians, I wondered, have such memories of the cotton fields of their childhood, of the aroma of baking bread, of the sky above the Nile? But Egypt was changing so fast. How long would it be before the Egyptian village was only a memory, a myth. A cliché of sentimental films. The Egyptians' longing for their village persists—in the midst of the city. A painful discrepancy. I asked Mama again how she knew those women, and she answered only curtly, "They're living in misery, and we can see it. If we know that people are in need of help, we have to provide it, whether we know them personally or not." Many people we didn't know came to my mother's funeral, and we had no idea how they had known her.

Aisha and I lived with our parents, for at that time—as it still is today—it was improper for two unmarried young female students to share a rented room or apartment. We walked the same route and needed an hour to get to campus. Sometimes we would take the bus or a taxi, especially after attending some evening event, a reading, a play, or a concert. We would sometimes meet friends in the students' club or, on weekends, at the Rowing Club on the Nile. Since elementary school I had been a member of the Egyptian Federation of Scouts and Guides—the Pathfinders. And I continued my membership at the university, if only because of my fondness for group excursions. But scouting was not the same at the university as it had been at school. Now there were young women and men in the same groups. We would spend most of our free time together, taking long hikes, building rope bridges across canals, climbing cliffs above the Red Sea. I learned a lot about how to relate as an individual with a group, how to master difficult situations, and to have respect for the opposite sex.

During the semester break the Faculty of Archaeology also offered an excursion, this one to Luxor and Aswan. It was my first trip to Upper Egypt, and one that would change my life. We boarded the train heading for Luxor, and only a few hours later we found ourselves standing in a different world, a different time. Even though I knew the layout of Karnak, the huge field of ruins struck me as hopelessly confusing. I kept looking for the things I knew from my books: for the monumental statue of Ramses II, the obelisks of Hatshepsut, the Sacred Lake, the Red Chapel. But everything was disconcertingly different.

Professor Mohamed Abdel Qader led us past the former Nile quay, the statues of rams, and to the first of what were once ten pylons, or gateways. The area we were about to enter, Abdel Qader explained, was not only a single temple precinct. It comprised three large temple precincts and many smaller ones, on which construction was carried out for more than two thousand years—from the Middle Kingdom, around 2000 BC, down to Roman times. We were now standing before the virtual Vatican of pharaonic antiquity: the center of the most powerful priestly caste of antiquity, the great temple of the state god Amun-Re. There were but few places in the world where the power, splendor, and mystery of a religious cult had been carved so sublimely in stone—simply a wonder of the world.

We were familiar with the names of the pharaohs from the time of Karnak's flowering—the New Kingdom, the era of the Eighteenth and Nineteenth Dynasties: Hatshepsut, Thutmose III, Amenhotep III, Akhenaten, Tutankhamun, then Seti I and his son Ramses II, the greatest of the builder pharaohs. I had frequently stood before the mummy of the long-lived Ramses in the Egyptian Museum. We were now entering the common project of the three greats Amenhotep III, Seti I, and Ramses II. We passed through the pylon and were finally standing in a forest of massive, brightly decorated papyrus columns, the hypostyle. What a sense of space! In the great hall one's ego shrinks down to the size that God and the pharaoh accorded to select visitors—and they were surely the greatest of the great men of the kingdom. I looked up. The colors of the capitals were still wonderfully fresh even after three thousand years. The inscriptions on the walls were still legible, relating to visitors events important enough to outlive time. I was carried away by the size, the splendor, the aura of the place. My books had not prepared me for any of it. You have to experience it yourself.

Professor Abdel Qader then took us over to the west side of Luxor, to the mortuary temples and tombs in al-Assasif. At Hatshepsut's temple in Deir al-Bahari we met two of the country's most respected Egyptologists: Ahmed Fakhry, the pioneer of desert archaeology, and Abdel Moneim Abu Bakr. The two were seated in a tent poring over tiny limestone objects, and I still remember how curious I became when one of them assured the other that he had never in his entire career seen anything so beautiful. We had read books by both men of course. It was Fakhry who, in 1951, discovered another entrance to the Dahshur Pyramid on the west side in addition to its main entrance on the north. He also carried out pioneering excavations in the Bahariya Oasis. Abu Bakr's publications on the Giza necropolis are among the standard works of Egyptian archaeology. We were astonished that two such noted scholars had time for beginners like us. Possibly it was because Fakhry and Abu Bakr, along with Girgis Matta, Labib Habachi, and Ahmed Badawi, belonged to the first generation of Egyptologists graduated by the university's Faculty of Archaeology. They led us around the excavations at Deir al-Bahari, and from everything they told us about their work, and especially the way they told it, I had the sense that the two men spent their days in a different realm—at least not in our workaday world. What they told us was interesting, but they related it with such emotion. So there's another dimension to my book learning, I realized. The two shared a realm closed to others. And suddenly I knew that was what I wanted, too.

By the time I got back to Cairo, my mind was made up: I would major in archaeology and study philosophy and ancient languages as minors. I gave up journalism. At home I went through my grandfather's books, looking for the volume with gilt hieroglyphs on the binding that had fascinated me even as a child: E.A. Wallis Budge's *The Nile*, a popular, encyclopedic work on Egypt, its history, and the ancient Egyptian language. Mother was not particularly thrilled with this new development. "Archaeology is a science of tombs, for people who dig in cemeteries!" Moreover, "Work in the desert sand under the scorching sun is not for young women." My father waved her away. "Say what you will, she'll do what she wants." Mama gave in. Perhaps she consoled herself with the hope that after graduating I would marry like my sisters. Then there would be no excavations in the desert. Perhaps her daughter would work in a museum, dressed in a clean white smock. If only she had lived to see how dirty a white museum smock can get.

I began my study of Egyptology and archaeology in 1969. At first our class was made up of twenty-four students, but each semester there were fewer of us. Finally we were only twelve: eight women and four men. The more demanding our studies became, the more passionate I was, especially since we took more and more excursions to the necropolises of Saqqara and Dahshur, and again and again to Luxor and Aswan. Bemused, my father would ask whether I had succumbed to the 'curse of the pharaoh.' In truth, nothing interested me any longer but ancient Egyptian history. I spent a great deal of time in the library of the Egyptian Museum on Tahrir Square, surrounded by the voluminous folios of the first Egyptologists of the nineteenth and early twentieth centuries: the splendid *Description de l'Égypte*, Lepsius's marvelous *Monuments from Egypt and Ethiopia*, and the books by Auguste Mariette and Flinders Petrie. When my uncle Mohamed—at that time vice president of Cairo University—learned of my passion, he gave me books that stand in my library to this day: Sir Alan Gardiner's famous *Egyptian Grammar*, from 1927, and the standard work *Egypt of the Pharaohs*, published in 1962, shortly before Gardiner's death.

So I slogged through grammar, studied hieroglyphs and hieratic texts, learned ruling dynasties by heart. Aisha and I spurred each other on. The country needed Egyptologists on a par with colleagues from abroad. As an incentive, Nasser had guaranteed positions for all graduates of Egyptian universities. But our professors made one thing clear: "Excavating is a man's job!" Women could by all means accomplish distinguished work in philology, but practical fieldwork was best left to men. Aisha and I only rolled our eyes.

In 1971 I was named the leader of the female Pathfinders at Cairo University. In doing so I took on considerable responsibility. The universities were under constant surveillance by the security services; even supposedly nonpolitical activities were suspect. All student activities were monitored by secret-service informers. Our group was especially dedicated to blind students, most of whom were studying history, philosophy, and sociology. In our free time we would read their textbook assignments to them, which they would then translate into braille for others. I admired the endurance, strength of will, and diligence of those students—and years later I worked to see that workshops for blind children and young people were incorporated into the educational programs of our museums.

For the semester break in 1971, I proposed an extraordinary project: a hike from Cairo to Alexandria and on to Sallum on the Egyptian–Libyan border, a two-week journey through the Nile Delta and the desert, a rigorous trek through wind, sand, and sun. We would get to know our country better, the villages and cities, the desert and the coast. We could overnight in the hostels of Egyptian youth and health organizations. On such a hike we could demonstrate that women could be just as persevering as men. So that the idea wouldn't be squelched by our parents, I proposed that we take younger brothers along. I knew that my brother Kamel would be delighted to join us. And my friend Mona was able to persuade her younger brother to come too, so it was six young women and two boys who set out in early June, wearing the gray uniforms of the Egyptian Pathfinders, our green berets on our heads, and our old military backpacks and tents on our backs.

Needless to say, we aroused the curiosity of everyone we met. "What are you thinking of?" the fellaheen would call to us from the fields. And village people would ask, "Where are you coming from, and where are you headed?" But we were always welcomed hospitably. In each mayor's office we signed the *omda*'s registry. We spent some nights in village clinics, some at service stations. If we camped out, we were plagued by mosquitoes. One night the frogs in the canals were croaking so loudly that I couldn't sleep a wink. The city of Damanhur, in the northwest of the Delta, is known for the rudeness of its inhabitants, and it lived up to its reputation. The young boys there actually threw stones at us. We spent the night in the sports center—under police guard. At the end of the day we would stop freight trucks or motorists, sometimes we would lie exhausted on donkey carts. But in Alexandria we took a break for four days. The youth hostel had a fabulous view of the sea, was clean and well tended, and gave us a chance to put our gear in order. Since we all had relatives in the city, every evening we were well fed. During the day we would go sightseeing—the famous Pompey's Pillar that rises above the mysterious Serapeum, the catacombs of Kom el-Shuqafa, and the ostentatious hunting residence of the last khedive, Abbas Hilmi.

Restored and inspired, we set out on the longest and most arduous leg of our trek, the stretch between the coast and the desert, at that time a totally desolate, wonderfully beautiful landscape of yellow-gold desert dunes, white beaches, and the turquoise-blue sea. Today it is built up with vacation compounds, a seemingly endless array of the architectural monstrosities of wealthy Egyptians. In El Alamein we excitedly flung ourselves into the sea. The next day we were shocked and depressed: We had heard of the armored battle of El Alamein, of course, but what we saw was unimaginable. In the desert stood thousands of grave crosses and the wrecks of burnt-out tanks and bullet-ridden military vehicles, scrap that was being gradually buried by the desert sand. We camped in the desert and talked into the night about all the men, scarcely older than ourselves, who had died here.

Next morning we were awakened by a Bedouin. He had heard that we were staying there overnight and had come out early to warn us. He pointed to the barbed wire and told us not to venture across it. The whole area was mined. Since the war, people had been either killed or badly wounded there every year. Bedouin children would chase after runaway cattle only to die. We were horrified. For decades those insidious munitions had lain there in the desert, and neither the Germans nor the British had made any effort to remove the land mines they had left behind. They had waged their war on Egyptian territory and later thought nothing more about their murderous legacy. It hasn't troubled them—to this day—that thanks to their land mines, internationally condemned, children were still having to die. A huge part of Egypt was still a restricted area, accessible to no one, of no use to anyone. Later I would learn that subsequent generations of Germans had simply forgotten what they left behind.

We arrived at Marsa Matruh and were eager to make a side trip to the legendary Siwa Oasis, where Alexander the Great is said to have consulted the oracle of Amun. But the road was closed, we were told. We appealed to the governor, but he would not permit it. The road wasn't paved and shifting dunes blocked the way. We would get lost. We decided to visit the oracle some other time. It would be twenty years before I finally managed to see that mound of ruins. After two weeks we finally reached our goal: Sallum on the Libyan border. We were extremely proud of ourselves and had our travel documents stamped at the local police station. Then we took a bus back to Cairo. Ahmed Mursi, our professor of Egyptian folk literature and the Pathfinders director at the university, was so proud of what we had done that he informed the media: young women undertaking such a strenuous journey on foot! The next day I was interviewed at the university. Our patriotic act was praised on television and radio and in newspapers, and of course we basked in the attention.

Our university campus was still a green oasis at that time, and after the hike we were given permission to pitch our tents on the grass and show how we had fared. We would sit around a campfire with other students until late at night, discussing what occupied us most in those days—politics and literature. Everyone was familiar with the verses of two writers, Abdel Rahman al-Abnudi and Ahmed Fouad Negm. Al-Abnudi wrote exquisitely beautiful poems, Negm unbelievably polemical ones, and they were both extraordinarily courageous men critical of Sadat. Negm didn't even refrain from personal attacks on the president. The blind composer and singer Sheikh Imam made his works highly popular. Al-Abnudi, Negm, and Imam were all in prison, their songs banned, but they were passed around on cassettes, smuggled by students like drugs, though anyone who owned them could also be sent to prison. I began to be more interested in writing in the Egyptian vernacular. Thanks to my mother's bourgeois education, I had mainly known only classical Arabic literature. We would get together more and more often at the university just to listen to our fellow students who were also writers or artists. The Sudanese caricaturist Mohamed Hakim was part of our circle. The most gifted of the young writers was Zein el-Abdin Fuad. He was studying philosophy, was also a member of Cairo's Pathfinders, and we became friends. Later Zein came to be known as the 'poet of the resistance,' the 'singing bomb.' He was arrested more than once, and his works, banned in Egypt, were printed in Lebanon. Like most of our intellectuals and poets, he himself later went to England.

At that time Zein liked reading his works in our small, familiar circle, for example his poem "The Meeting of Lovers of Egypt in the Citadel Prison." At that time the prison on Cairo's Muqattam Hills was as famous for torture as Abu Ghraib is today. Zein and the poet Osama el-Ghazuli felt that I had a lovely, clear voice and distinct pronunciation, and asked if I might also read their poems in public. So I learned Zein's poem by heart and recited it in front of the assembled students and artists at a writers' convention on campus. I still know it by heart, and I often have to think of the last verses: "Whatever the wardens do to us only makes their punishment worse! Who dares to imprison Egypt even for an hour!" On January 25, 2011, these verses—from a poem dating back to 1972—could often be heard in Tahrir Square.

Protests against Anwar Sadat's regime culminated in late 1971 and early 1972. He had promised to allow greater democracy but created the opposite. In addition, there was disappointment and anger about the fact that Sadat was putting off the promised recapture of the Sinai. For years the young people in the military and at the universities had vowed to erase the dishonor of the 1967 defeat. I too was in favor of such a war. Like everyone else, I felt that the Sinai was Egyptian, its occupation by Israel intolerable, a reminder of the still open wound of the British colonial period. The demonstrations became increasingly vocal, with increasingly brutal deployment of police and arrests of students that were in turn answered with boycotting of classes. Students were humiliated and tortured in prison. Since their names were now on secret service lists, policemen would regularly show up at their families' homes. Even some of my girlfriends were arrested. Since most of them spoke several foreign languages, the public prosecutors accused them of collaborating with a "foreign entity," of being a kind of "fifth column." We had to ask ourselves who that perfidious "foreign entity" might be. Then freedom of assembly at the universities was drastically limited. If more than three students were seen standing together on campus, it could be seen as a political gathering and a threat to the country's security—hence reason for arrest. Sadat also issued the so-called defamation law—a vague, sweeping decree by which more or less everything that didn't suit the regime could be punished; at the very least it was a measure by which students could be expelled from the university without a hearing.

On January 15 and 16, 1972, there was a sit-in at Cairo's Polytechnic Institute, and on the 17th a large number of students assembled at Cairo University. Sadat had been requested to appear on campus and respond to the students' concerns. But the president chickened out. Then the state-censored press refused to publish a critical statement by the student unions. There was an assembly in the great hall of the main building. I was there, listening to speeches by student leaders about the current political situation in the country and at the universities. But I couldn't stay. I had arranged to meet Mother downtown. Only minutes after I left the campus, the police sealed off the university and arrested several hundred students. My guardian angel again.

On the morning of January 24, I was sitting with fellow students in the Faculty of Archaeology's lecture room, at that time an old villa next to the

Nile, not far from the main building of the university, though separated from it by the Botanical Garden. Suddenly Professor Gaballa Ali Gaballa was standing before us, staring at one after another in disbelief: "What are you doing here?" There would be no lecture that day. Outside, students from the Faculty of Arts were assembling to march en masse to Tahrir Square. "You want to stay here?" In the villa we hadn't heard what was taking place on the other side of the Botanical Garden. To be sure, someone had written on the blackboard "Where are you, students of Egyptian history?" and we had wondered what that meant. Gaballa attacked our honor as students, "So, don't you want to march too?" Aisha, Mona, and I ran straight across the Botanical Garden and finally came upon the crowd of students. Our friend, the poet Zein el-Abdin Fouad, was shouting through a megaphone, "Yesterday many of our fellow students were arrested, among them the student union chairmen Alaa Hamrush and Arwa Saleh. Let's all head for Tahrir Square!"

Alaa Hamrush was president of the university's student council. His father Ahmed was a famous journalist and writer. Alaa was studying philosophy and, like Zein and many others at the time, was a committed communist. Outside the university gates we were joined by students of the Law, Economics, and Engineering faculties. We chanted "Freedom for our arrested colleagues!" Aisha, Mona, and I marched with one group along the Nile through Garden City, another group headed down Qasr el-Aini Street in the direction of Tahrir Square. There students from Ain Shams and al-Azhar universities were already waiting. The square was filled with young people chanting louder and louder, and with increasing self-confidence, "Freedom and justice! Freedom for our jailed brothers!"

Suddenly someone grabbed my arm, a member of our Pathfinders group. "You should get out of here, and fast!" She looked at us imploringly, then whispered to me that her brother worked for the secret service. He had told her earlier that he knew that a great number of students would be arrested that day, and urgently advised her to stay at home. But our friend had nevertheless raced to Tahrir Square to warn us. "The police will be here any minute! Let's go!"

I thought of my mother, my family, but also of Aisha and Mona. For months Father had been working on a water project in Libya, Kamel was studying at the university in Benghazi, Mohamed was stationed at the Suez Canal, and my two sisters were occupied with their babies. What will it do to them if I allow myself to be arrested? We deliberated briefly, and all agreed to leave the square. As it happened, security forces brutally broke up the demonstration and two thousand students were arrested. Among them were many we knew, and close friends we would not see for months.

It was clear to us Scouts that we needed to somehow help our fellow students in prison. Zein supplied us with the names and addresses of arrested students and their families. Again we were warned by our Pathfinder friend: If State Security (Amin al-Dawla) were to get wind of our activities we too could land in jail. But there are subtle, unsuspicious ways to show solidarity. We collected money, copied material from ongoing classes, and got everything to the families, who passed it along to their jailed children. When they were finally freed, they thanked us. The study material had helped to distract them from the prison routine. Only my girlfriend, lovely Arwa, didn't say anything. She was repeatedly arrested, but nonetheless, immediately after she was released, continued to write articles against the Sadat system for the bulletin-board newspapers. We knew that she was beaten in jail. But Arwa didn't say a word. On the contrary! She had her hair cut short and joked that she would soon be sitting in a cell again. Fifteen years later she took her own life.

Many friends and acquaintances who were with us in Tahrir Square and were arrested died between the ages of thirty-five and forty-five. The student leader Alaa died at fifty. His long imprisonment under Sadat had ruined his health. They died because, as Zein had written, they loved Egypt. Their only crimes were believing in a better future and committing themselves to civil liberties and the rule of law. Mohamed Hakim continues to work as a caricaturist for opposition newspapers to this day. Zein I have not seen since those student years. In the year of the Revolution, 2011, he could often be seen on television. And once again his books are frequently discussed. Aisha—like many others from our Egyptology circle—became a tour director after she graduated. We saw each other later when she would come with her tour groups to the Egyptian Museum.

Our circle consisted of maybe twenty-five students. We talked a lot about politics, about Egypt, about Sadat, about the future. How I became the person I am today goes back to those January days in 1972. At that time, and also under Mubarak, I never dreamed that we would change the system with our demonstrations. I had seen how brutally the regime proceeded against its opponents, and I myself had been more than once protected by my guardian angel. I took to heart my father's words, "You need to know how far you can go, but you have to envision the consequences of your actions and be able to face them." At that time I set out on the course that my mother had lived before me, which I still follow today: Even in seemingly little ways you can change a great deal. You can become engaged, maintain your integrity, and show people that you haven't become disheartened, have not abandoned your belief in change. It was always clear to me that I would never endanger my family with my behavior or involve it in any way. I had seen how dear and courageous people were broken by torture and rape. They were heroic, and we would cherish their memory with great respect. They are sorely missed when it's a matter of improving the education of our children, abolishing the country's pervasive poverty. We could have used them as teachers, journalists, artists, politicians, parents, and friends.

I met the pharaoh, the 'Rais' Anwar al-Sadat, on two occasions. In 1975, during the state visit of Shah Reza Pahlavi and his wife Farah, and again on March 11, 1979, during the state visit of President Jimmy Carter and his wife Rosalynn. In 1975 I was still too young to be asked to guide such exalted guests, but as assistant inspector of the pyramid precinct I was there when Sadat showed his friend, the Shah of Iran, the Great Pyramid. I remember the Shah most clearly. A very elegant, reserved, and surprisingly small man. The photographers and film people paid more attention to his wife Farah. They both inspected the wonder of the world, listened attentively, and nodded politely without asking further questions. Jimmy Carter was altogether different.

In the spring of 1979 Iran's Islamic Revolution was in high gear. Ayatollah Khomeini was back in Tehran, and the deathly ill Shah, the longtime friend and ally of Egypt and America, was in search of asylum. The political situation in Egypt was palpably strained. I had been the director of the Khufu Boat Museum for only a few weeks and was supposed to welcome the state visitors. Three days before their visit, the pyramid plateau had already been sealed off by security people within a radius of three kilometers. One of the officers informed us that all our coworkers would have to stay at home for the next three days, that the area would be completely evacuated. "We will shoot anything that moves." That would have been extremely hard on our guards, for many of them lived with their families in the precinct at the edge of the necropolis. I explained to the officer that I would vouch for our people, that they were no security risk, and would stay in their homes, that one simply couldn't throw them out into the street. The security people were finally satisfied to simply have a register of their names.

That March it was already quite hot on the plateau. The security personnel standing all day under the scorching sun had no chance to change their sweat-soaked uniforms. They also didn't have enough food and water and after an eight- or ten-hour watch, some of them keeled over. Their comrades would then drag them into the shade of a stone block. We were so sorry for some of them that we gave them food and water in the Boat Museum. On the morning of the state visit, the whole area was crawling with generals. One of them barged into our museum with a cigarette in his mouth. When I asked him to smoke outside the door, he roared at me. Who did I think I was to challenge him? He was responsible for the president's safety. "And I am responsible for the safety of this boat," I countered. Would he like to be responsible for incinerating forty-five hundred years of Egyptian history? One spark would be enough to ignite the ancient wood. He nearly exploded with rage, used his walkie-talkie to find out who I was, and finally left.

Given the political situation and the heightened security measures, I expected two tight-lipped, solemn statesmen, but quite the opposite proved to be the case. As host, Anwar Sadat appeared at the head of the entourage of security people and representatives of the press, completely relaxed and clearly in a good mood. "Ah, you're the director?" he called to me in his sonorous, deep voice in the foyer. "You're still so young! What will you have to tell us, my daughter!" Sadat smiled and lay a hand on my shoulder. He presented himself as paternal and benevolent, altogether the winning, charming personality. By contrast, Jimmy Carter and his wife Rosalynn were reserved but pleasant. Sadat's wife Jehan was there as well. But she seemed unapproachable, at least for us mere mortals. Decades after the death of her husband, she often came into the Egyptian Museum and seemed truly interested in our work with blind children and young people.

I led the tight-knit group up to the boat and could see that Carter had been truly moved by his encounter with the Sphinx and the pyramids. "Forty-five hundred years!" he quietly said to his wife. "And we talk of America's two hundred years." Carter attentively studied the wood-and-rope construction of the ship, asked questions, and seemed to be unconcerned that only ten minutes had been scheduled for this part of his visit and that all the people around him kept looking at their wristwatches. When I took a step back, I happened to step on someone's foot. I turned around to apologize, and looked into the smiling face of Hosni Mubarak, Sadat's vice president. At that time the Egyptians simply called him *La vache qui rit* (the laughing cow) after the French cheese. He never said anything, and on television he could always be seen wearing a tight-lipped grin. A few meters away from him stood Jimmy Carter, with his gentle, kind eyes.

Sadat was in a jocular mood, and on that morning he was nothing like the man who shouted down his political opponents on television in cold rage. I was not afraid of him. I told myself, "They're all only people. And it's they who are wanting something from you, not you from them." They had to scoot along behind me in their felt museum slippers—Sadat, Mubarak, Carter. Finally, Sadat once again extended his hand with a friendly smile. Carter said, "I have to come back again. And bring more time with me." In fact he did come back, after his term as president, and I was able to guide him and his wife once again. But that was long after the hostage drama in the Iranian desert, long after Camp David, and after October 6, 1980. Naturally my friends and colleagues asked me, So what is Sadat like? I told them that he was paternal, friendly, intelligent, that he was in fact a charismatic figure who doubtless managed to make people like him in direct, personal contact. But to his people he remained aloof. In 1977, when he was suddenly standing before the Knesset, I gazed at the television screen in disbelief, just as skeptical as the majority of Egyptians. Also, I still think that the agreement Carter and Sadat negotiated at Camp David was not good for Egypt. The Sinai became a restricted area, with all the consequences we are having to deal with today: a region in which drug and weapons dealers, al-Qaeda, and members of the so-called Ansar Beit al-Maqdis—an Egyptian faction of the 'Islamic State' (IS)—pursue their murderous activities.

In the summer of 1972 I ended my four years of study at Cairo University with a bachelor's degree. It was clear to me that I would then go on to earn a master's. For a year I took preparatory courses, at the end of which there was an examination on the history of ancient Egypt, also requiring translations from hieratic, Coptic, and hieroglyphic texts. In 1973, finally, I enrolled in a master's program. Graduates with a bachelor's degree were automatically assigned a post in the antiquities service, but by law I could not accept one for a year. Inasmuch as young men were required to perform a year's military service, for fairness' sake women were required to postpone their careers for a year as well. Even so, I didn't have to look for a job: One would come to me; I only had to wait. At that time my father was working in Libya, assigned by the Egyptian government to set up a laboratory for the desalination of seawater in Ajdabiya. Father asked whether I would be interested in coming to Libya, like my younger brother Kamel. I decided that I might write my master's thesis on Egyptian–Libyan relations during the pharaonic period and finally left for Libya in mid 1973. It was my first trip abroad. Although Libya was so close and we shared a language and a religion, the country and the people were still very different, with different customs and traditions. I wore modern European clothing, went out into the street without a male escort, and had a job. Possibly I would be constantly harassed by men.

Father asked around in his circle of friends whether anyone had contacts in the Libyan antiquities administration. And as it happened someone put me in touch with the director of the Department of Antiquities in Benghazi and arranged an appointment with him. I told the director that I would like to use my year off to do research for my master's thesis, but he regretted that he was unable to help. His department was concentrating on providing administrative and technical assistance to the foreign excavation missions in Libya. Unfortunately, it was not fielding any scholarly projects of its own. However, he would be happy to introduce me to the director of the British excavation mission at that time digging in Benghazi. Perhaps I could volunteer there and pick up some useful information. I was ecstatic. I so wanted to work at an excavation sometime.

The next day, as arranged, I met the director of the British mission. He was very pleased that I was interested in its work and wanted to learn modern scientific excavation methods, and he introduced me to his colleague Carolyn Dallas, a Bermudian woman, sun-browned and with long black hair. We immediately took to each other, and she led me to the dig. Young archaeologists were crouched in small pits; others were seated in a plan quadrant marked out with twine, using little brushes and trowels to expose tiny pieces of ceramics, which they then carefully placed in banana crates. In the evening, in the excavation hut, they would then draw them, classify them, and attempt to fit them together with adhesive. Others were taking photographs, making measurements, and drawing the precise locations of the finds on transparent foil. Carolyn explained to me why the location and history of this Libyan dig was of such interest for Roman provincial archaeology.

I was elated. I was being given a chance that I could only have dreamed of in Egypt. During my time in Libya I learned things you cannot learn at university: excavation technology, practical scientific know-how. I was there every day, and Carolyn let me take part in every step of her work, tirelessly explaining how and why things are done. At the beginning, I admit that I thought that, compared to what we retrieve from the ground in Egypt, these were not particularly spectacular finds. But I was soon converted. Even the most unlikely find can provide exciting information that on-site excavators may not necessarily recognize. It may be that the importance of the finds is revealed only later, and only thanks to extremely conscientious and precise notes of the on-site archaeologists. The painstaking, scholarly excavation report then serves as an indispensable source for new insights. The humility and patience of the professional excavators impressed me enormously.

In that very year, 1973, Muammar Gaddafi commanded that everything reminiscent of former colonial rule by Italy be destroyed. Italians living in Libya were requested to exhume their dead and convey them back to Italy. His order even called for the destruction of archaeological sites from the Roman era, as they were symbols of early colonization and enslavement. The British archaeologists were just as shocked as I was. I knew that many young Libyans in the General People's Committee would not hesitate to implement the demands of their supreme brother Gaddafi. I spoke with Father about this act of barbarism, and he called his friend Mohamed Faid, a Libyan journalist who worked for a newspaper in Benghazi. When he visited us, I begged him to write something. The Libyan people had to recognize that the ancient sites were a part of their own history, built for Romans, to be sure, but still erected by their Libyan forefathers. Faid in fact published an article. The next day the publisher of his newspaper received an enraged letter from Muammar Gaddafi. Who the hell was this Wafaa El Saddik that she should have the effrontery to mix in Libyan affairs? Faid laughed: "The message was received, and

Gaddafi obviously understood it. That in itself is worth something." Faid was married to a Swiss citizen, so he didn't let himself be cowed by Gaddafi.

It was then that I received a letter from the employment office. An inspector's post had opened up and I had to return to Cairo. Faid again mentioned me in an article. The Egyptian archaeologist Wafaa El Saddik was returning to Cairo. He told my father the next day that his publisher had received another furious letter in which Gaddafi asked, who is this person?

I had to think of that episode when I saw the revolutionary leader on the television screen screaming and raging and asking a crowd of his faithful: Who are these rebels? It was the same language. In any case, the threatened destruction of antiquities was never carried out. Had the revolutionary leader simply forgotten his own instructions, or had he had a change of heart? Since that time I am always delighted when I receive letters from Libya. They carry very beautiful stamps—with motifs from ancient Cyrene, Apollonia Susa, Sabratha, or Leptis Magna.

I am friends with Carolyn Dallas to this day. She has visited me in Egypt several times and I have visited her in England. We have traveled together to Aswan, Alexandria, and the Red Sea, also to London, Oxford, Cambridge, Norfolk, and York. Carolyn was injured by a worker's axe during a dig in Afghanistan in the late 1970s. The accident caused her to lose her left eye— and the work she loved so much.

In Cairo the document appointing me to a new position was awaiting me at the antiquities administration. My anticipation had been great and my disappointment was complete. I was only going to be working in an administrative building near the Egyptian Museum. I had thought I might be assigned to an excavation, or at least to the Egyptian Museum. Shortly after my return from Libya, my great-uncle visited one evening. He listened to my enthusiastic report about the excavations in Libya and could see how disappointed I was with the job in the antiquities service. The next day he sent me a letter of recommendation to his close friend Youssef el-Sebai, head of the Ministry of Culture, which had oversight of the antiquities administration, and had already arranged an appointment for me. On the telephone my great-uncle explained that I should not hesitate to tell the minister what I wanted. "Don't be coy, Wafaa, connections are there to be used. And don't kid yourself, jobs like those in Giza or Saqqara are only awarded through connections."

In fact I met the minister. He was extremely nice and courteous. But I didn't ask him for a better position. I could see that he was annoyed. He was doubtless wondering, what does this young woman want from me? But the moment I extended my hand, it was clear to me that I wouldn't ask anything of this friendly man. There must be some other way. I went home and said to myself, They've given you a position; make something of it. But I confess that I had to wonder whether my pride had ruined my chances.

What I had to face each day from then on made me furious. For excruciatingly long hours I would sit with two dozen women in a much too crowded office. We all had jobs, to be sure, but no work. We had absolutely nothing to do. Some would brew tea or spend hours shopping, others would chop vegetables at their desks in preparation for making dinner at home. I wasn't interested in either; I started going to the library of the Egyptian Museum to continue my university studies. So it went for a few weeks until one morning there was an unannounced inspection. It was led by the 'General,' a retired officer who was the head of the Labor Control Committee, and a man before whom everyone in the agency trembled. The committee discovered my absence. When I got back from the library, books and documents under my arm, a colleague warned me, "Better not go in. They're waiting for you." When I entered the office, the waiting gentlemen unleashed a storm of abuse on me. What was I thinking of? Why wasn't I at work? But I refused to be humbled. I felt I was in the right. "I've been in the library. Working. I am studying. I'm not here to chop vegetables." I hadn't studied Egyptology for that. The General roared at me, "I see! The lady is somebody special!" And just what did the lady picture herself doing? "I want to dig," I shouted. "I want to do scholarly work!" Suddenly the General calmed down. With an undertone of smugness he announced, "Well then, young lady, so go! Downstairs there's a car waiting that will take you straight to Giza. Get down there! Go!" He didn't have to tell me twice.

The Giza excavation inspector's Jeep was indeed standing in front of the building. It was old, a discarded military vehicle. I drew myself up before the driver and explained, "I'm the new inspector. Drive me to the pyramid plateau. I want to get started today." The driver drew back, then laughed out loud, showing me his yellow teeth. "So now a young woman is working with us, that's something new," he brayed with laughter. "I simply don't believe it!" I paid no attention to his amusement, climbed in, and told him my name. He immediately collected himself, said that his name was Umran, and we set out. His clothes betrayed his miserable origins, but his eyes and his voice made it clear that he was a kind soul. During the trip he told me what I already knew: "The work in the desert is very hard. It's not for women. The sun is simply too strong. And sun-browned women aren't attractive!" I could hear my grandmother Sakina, who was forever scolding my mother, "Get the children into the house. They've been playing too long in the sun. Do you want them to get ugly?" The Egyptians' ideal of beauty, and presumably that of men in the entire Arab region, is a light-skinned woman. I had to tell myself that in this respect men haven't changed much since antiquity, for in ancient Egypt, as well, the women were pictured as light-skinned, the men with dark complexions. Umran asked me over and over, "Do you really think you can stand it out there?" I answered stubbornly, "Yes. Why not? For years I was the leader of the Pathfinders at the university. I know very well how to deal with stress."

By the time we finally arrived at the inspectors' building, I was soaked with sweat and covered with dust. The chief inspector studied me nonplussed: "So who are you?" "I'm the new person," I told him. Nassef Hassan stared at me uncomprehending. If I thought he would send his Jeep for me every day to take me out to Giza, I was greatly mistaken. Instead, I had to take the long trip from downtown Cairo to Giza myself. The buses were overcrowded, the schedules irregular. There was no telephone I could use to explain to my worried parents that I would be getting home later than usual. As a result of my work, I turned dark brown. My mother would surely have preferred it if I had worked in a library.

The inspectors' building is a small, mud-brick structure with a double roof against the summer's intense heat. It was built at the beginning of the twentieth century behind an old excavation dump northwest of the Khufu Pyramid. We were perched in the middle of the pyramid plateau, yet the building did not obstruct the wonderful panorama. And we also enjoyed a spectacular view of Cairo and Giza. On a clear day we could see the Salah al-Din Citadel, the Muqattam Hills, and the Tura limestone quarries, and of course the broad fields that still lay on the plain next to the bank of the Nile at that time. Nearby was the famous Mena House Hotel, with its expansive golf course. In addition, there was a very lovely guesthouse belonging to the antiquities service, to which I liked to invite my family on holidays. But suddenly, from one day to the next, Sadat appropriated it for his own private use.

Our building housed the office of the chief inspector of the Giza antiquities administration, the office of his two assistant inspectors, two smaller offices for the architectural draftsmen, and the secretaries' office. We were responsible for the archaeological sites over a huge area. It included the Giza pyramid plateau, also the sites in Saqqara, Helwan, and the Tura limestone quarries, as well as those in Heliopolis and Imbaba. Then there were the sites in al-Beheira governorate and the monasteries in Wadi Natrun. It was our job to ensure the integrity of the monuments and depots, to determine whether grave robbers or young hooligans were at work anywhere, and to prevent farmers from illegally expanding their fields onto excavation sites. We also had to monitor foreign excavations, to make sure that the archaeologists were staying within the limits specified in their licenses and not venturing into other areas. And of course we also tended to state visitors. There were many days on which, during international conferences, we would conduct as many as ten guided tours for prime ministers, ministers, or diplomats.

Nassef Hassan, the chief inspector of the Giza precinct, was a typical Egyptian official, obedient to his superiors. He performed his prescribed routines but would not have dreamed of initiating anything on his own. He spent most of the time seated in his office dealing with correspondence. In winter he would sometimes sit outside the building in the sun, in summer in the small shady garden. But he had one young ambitious inspector who knew everyone on the plateau and who was known to all: Zahi Hawass. We got along well; he was full of humor, always ready with a joke, and I have many pleasant memories of our time together on the plateau. His later wife is a good friend of mine. She and Zahi were from a village near Fariskur, and Zahi attended the same school there as my brother Mohamed.

Our chief inspector was primarily concerned with the state guests and other prominent figures who regularly needed to be shown the sights on the plateau. Otherwise, he unquestioningly followed his instructions. One morning an unusual letter lay on his desk—a personal request from President Sadat. When sitting on the terrace of the recently appropriated guesthouse, Sadat was disturbed by the fact that three-fourths of the steps of the Khafre

Pyramid were covered with desert sand. In addition, it offended him that the facing stones at the top were not the same color as the pyramid's lower steps. So Sadat was suggesting that the pyramid be thoroughly freed from "debris" and the upper part "cleaned." In any case, he wanted it a uniform color. The Khafre Pyramid was to look like the other two.

My superior didn't dare oppose this hair-raising command or discuss it with the secretary general of the antiquities administration in Cairo. He called me into his office and explained that I was to oversee the cleaning project. I couldn't believe my ears. I explained to him that it had long since been proven why the stones were different colors: They reflected two separate construction phases. For the bottom, oldest part, the stone came from the pyramid plateau, while the remaining facing stones were from the Tura limestone quarries. I told him that 'cleaning' the pyramid, whatever the method used, would be an incalculable risk to the stone itself, and could by no means produce Sadat's desired effect. But the man was totally intimidated. There was no talking to him.

The next morning I showed up with twenty laborers on the west side of the Khafre Pyramid, directly across from Sadat's guesthouse on the pyramid plateau. The workers, armed with brooms and shovels, climbed up the high steps, and suddenly it became clear to me how dangerous our undertaking really was. Having arrived at the top steps, the workers began plying their shovels and the first chunks of stone began to fall, followed by smaller avalanches of detritus. I told the workers to stop immediately and said to the foreman, "That's tons of material. We'll damage the pyramid. Moreover, it's far too dangerous. What if somebody loses his balance?"

The foreman, Sheikh Mohamed, nodded in relief. "You know, Madam Wafaa, that the men are not even insured."

I couldn't believe what he was saying. "What do you mean the workers aren't insured?"

The foreman only shrugged his shoulders. Fuming with rage, I returned to my superior's office and shouted, "How can you permit laborers to work without accident and health insurance?"

Nassef Hassen looked at me dismissively. "Why haven't you finished the job? How can you dare oppose a directive from the president?"

I responded equally firmly, "How can you dare to order such nonsense?" I once again explained to him that the second pyramid was built with different types of limestone. That was confirmed by the fragments of stone that had just fallen. I would in any case refuse to continue even if I had to deal with sanctions. But I would write a report spelling out my position, and would relieve him in writing of any responsibility for my behavior. But that didn't satisfy him either.

He threatened, "If I get only anger from you, I'll dismiss you immediately."

The rest of the day and night I sat at my desk compiling a report complete with the relevant construction theories and scientific proofs. In addition, I declared that whoever gave the order for the cleaning work would have to take responsibility for the integrity of the pyramid and the safety of the workers. The next morning I submitted my report to the chief inspector and tried to put his mind at ease. Would he kindly forward it to the secretary general. I was certain that both the secretary general and the president would agree with my conclusions. In any case, the first obligation of the antiquities service and the government was the protection of monuments and the lives of workers. A few days later the project was called off. My protest had no negative consequences for either Nassef Hassan or for me. A pyramid-size weight fell from my shoulders. It could have meant an early end to my career. At the same time, I was proud that what I had learned from my parents had once again been substantiated: "The straight and narrow is the only way."

After several incidents of this kind, in which I consistently raised objections, it got around that I was the young woman who was standing up to her superiors. Strangely enough, it didn't harm me. On the contrary, in 1976 I became the first Egyptian woman to be given responsibility for an archaeological dig. And I also refused to ever ask a minister for a favor. I worked with persistence and candor to gain the respect of my excavation workers. I later met the 'General' from the antiquities service once again. "I remember you," he said with a smile. "You were the stubborn one."

The time I was able to spend on the pyramid plateau now seems like a dream. From the very first day I was fascinated, even possessed by the place. I would tell my parents that I was late getting home because of poor bus connections. And often enough that was true. But many evenings I would wait like an addict to watch the sunset over the Great Pyramid. When there was a full moon I would stay with the guards. Sometimes I would get up in the middle of the night so as to be able to watch the sunrise on the Great Pyramid. At that time there were a few young men interested in me. They must have thought me somewhat snobbish, but the idea of marriage never crossed my mind. I know that the magic of the place has been evoked so often as to become a cliché. No one wants to hear about it any longer. But there is a magic there, and at the time it had me powerfully under its spell—pursuing me even into my dreams and nightmares. In my sleep I would dream of the interior of the Great Pyramid. A voice commanded me to study more closely the five mysterious relieving chambers above the King's Chamber. Or the unfinished room and the vestibule carved out of the bedrock beneath the pyramid. In one recurring dream a man was falling from the Great Pyramid. I could clearly hear his screams. How appalled I was one morning after one such nightmare to learn when I arrived for work that at sunrise a man had in fact fallen to his death. I looked at my colleagues and wondered whether I was still dreaming. I frequently climbed the Great Pyramid myself. I knew the fever that grips you as you pull yourself upward, step by step, meter by meter, so as to experience an indescribable feeling of breathless joy at the top. But I also knew the attack of vertigo when you look at the way back down, the terror when you realize that the descent will be far more dangerous, the fear of losing your balance. I was relieved when the administration banned any further climbing on the pyramids.

4

DINNER WITH CLEOPATRA

A few weeks after the cleaning incident at the Khafre Pyramid, I was introduced to the Austrian archaeologist Karl Kromer in Chief Inspector Nassef Hassan's office. I was assigned to oversee Kromer's spring campaign on the Gebel Qibli, the south hill of the Giza plateau. Roughly three kilometers south of the Great Pyramid, his mission from the University of Innsbruck was searching for traces of early, predynastic settlement.

We drove out to the site in Kromer's Jeep. It had rained the previous evening, and the air was clear and fresh. The sun rose above the eastern horizon, gentle and benign, bathing the west side of the Nile in wonderful light. I love days like that. Earlier I had looked down from the balcony of our apartment into the garden of the Abdeen Palace, and the green of the trees appeared newly washed. Then I saw the Giza pyramids, and knew that it was going to be a delightful January day. From Giza that morning it was possible to make out the pyramids of Abusir and Saqqara, and even the two pyramids of Snefru at Dahshur, a rare occasion. At that time the plateau was not yet surrounded by a fence; the area was open on all sides. And after rain the sand was much firmer underfoot, and walking less difficult.

There were already two tents set up at the south hill excavation site—
one for the Egyptian laborers, one for the Austrian scholars. Kromer gave
me a brief explanation of the excavation's goal, the manner in which it was
proceeding, and the number of coworkers and their respective responsibili-
ties. Some of them were students my age who were here receiving practical
training. "We start work quite early," Kromer said. "At seven o'clock. But
that doesn't concern you. It will be quite enough if you look in on us every
few days."

Kromer was being friendly, but I felt a surge of anger. "It is my job to
accompany the progress of the work here on-site, to keep a record of your
finds every step of the way," I explained. "Moreover, it has been agreed that in
doing so I will also get practical experience and instruction. I have no intention of only popping in as an occasional observer." I felt annoyed, and asked
myself why foreign archaeologists so readily assume that their Egyptian colleagues are less curious and ambitious than they themselves. In a huffy tone
I explained to the startled professor that I would be there promptly at seven
the next morning to get to work with the other archaeologists, that I did not
intend to miss an hour of project, just as my assignment as inspector required.

Kromer was nonplussed. That was something new, he assured me. "I'm
only sorry that with these miserable road conditions you'll have to come out
here to the south hill." It would indeed be a long trek every day, alone and
on foot. "You should ride a horse," he suggested, and reached for his wallet.
He wanted to give me money for the horse rental. But that annoyed me even
more. I was almost ready to surrender the job to a colleague, but once again I
felt that my honor as an Egyptologist had been impugned.

"I receive a salary from the government. It is difficult for me not to see this
as an attempt at bribery." But no, a mere misunderstanding, Kromer replied,
and emphatically apologized. I needed to understand that in past years they
had become accustomed to providing inspectors with financial assistance for
transportation. By no means had he meant to offend me, and certainly not to
bribe me. I accepted his apology, but our parting was awkward.

Why did foreign scholars look down on us so? Why did they give us the
feeling that they alone were Egyptologists to be taken seriously? Depressed,
I trudged the long way back to the inspectors' building. In my dealings with
foreign colleagues I had often felt that we Egyptians counted for little in our

very own discipline; people thought of us as dilettantes. I looked across at the towering tips of the pyramids, at which, long ago, Napoleon and his scholarly mission led by Dominique Vivant Denon had gazed in awe. It is true, we are greatly indebted to European scholars. To the Frenchman Jean-François Champollion and the German Karl Richard Lepsius, who laid the foundations of our profession in the nineteenth century. Europeans recognized the importance of Egypt's advanced culture early on, studied our monuments, revealed them to the world, and salvaged a great deal—also for their museums.

I thought of the many tourists who gaze up at the light-colored limestone panels on the red façade of the Egyptian Museum in Cairo and see all those European names: Lepsius, Brugsch, Dümichen, Rosellini. . . . With the exception of Ahmed Kamal Pasha, at the time of the opening of the Egyptian Museum in 1902 there were still no Egyptian Egyptologists whose names might have been immortalized on the museum façade. Few visitors make their way to the court of honor at the grave of Auguste Mariette next to the left wing of the museum, and few know the names of the men whose busts are ranged around Mariette: Ahmed Kamal; Selim Hassan; Mohamed Zakaria Goniem, the discoverer of the Sekhemkhet Pyramid at Saqqara; Labib Habachi, noted for his study of Egyptian obelisks. But what about all the others worthy of inclusion in this small Egyptian gallery of notables? Ahmed Fakhry, who studied Egyptian oases. Abdel Aziz Saleh, discoverer of the workers' cemetery near the Menkaure Pyramid. Or Abdel Moneim Abu Bakr, who carried out important excavations in Giza. And there have been plenty of other worthy Egyptian Egyptologists.

I would follow narrow, more or less established tracks through the soft dunes of the plateau, past the waste dumps of former excavations. The plateau is strewn with 'mole hills,' behind which archaeologists from all over the world have uncovered tomb sites. Foreign scholars had done incalculable service for Egypt, and continue to do so to this day. We have them to thank for the decipherment of hieroglyphics, the first dictionaries and grammars, the methodology of our scholarly discipline, sophisticated excavation techniques, and conservation and restoration methods. But for all too long they had attempted to keep all that for themselves, as knowledge that we wouldn't understand. To be sure, Frenchmen like Champollion and Mariette had also pressed for the first antiquities law passed in 1835, the establishment of the

Service des Antiquités de l'Égypte on February 29 of that year, and for the museum in Bulaq in 1858. Yet the Europeans also saw to it that they did not have to share the fame of discovery with Egyptians. The French considered the directorship of the antiquities service as their exclusive right, in exchange for leaving the business of government to the British. After the bankruptcy of the khedival government in 1876, the Egyptians were above all their debtors. With the antiquities laws passed under the khedives and the protectorate (1914–22), the Europeans reimbursed themselves for their cultural commitment. Anyone who now visits the Louvre, the British Museum, or Berlin's Museum Island has to admit that in this respect Egypt owes them nothing.

What truly saddened me on my way home was the modern divide between us and European scholars. Unfortunately, it has a long tradition. Frenchmen like Gaston Maspero, from 1881 to 1888 and again from 1899 to 1914 the Director General of the Service des Antiquités de l'Égypte, resisted the demand of "Egyptology for Egyptians" voiced by such Egyptian scholars as Ahmed Kamal. Maspero prevented them from being trained, fearing for his own authority and that of other Frenchmen. The British-controlled school system excluded ancient Egypt from its curriculum. German, British, and French Egyptologists were by no means congenial. They all spoke dismissively of the others' approaches. But they agreed in their belief that Egyptians were fundamentally unsuited for archaeology. This meant that it was only after its independence in 1922 that Egypt could begin to train a first generation of Egyptologists of its own—one hundred years after Champollion had deciphered hieroglyphics.

The British Consul-General Lord Cromer—a man who in Egypt continues to stand for the arrogance and brutality of the British Empire to this day—flatly declared that Egyptians were not "civilized enough" to deal with their antiquities. To be sure, in many Egyptian villages the remains of mudbrick walls of ancient settlements were being used to fertilize the fields, temples were treated as stone quarries, and tomb treasures turned into money. But the wealthy European collectors, dealers, and museums who shook their heads over the ignorance of the poor and backward Egyptians deliberately exploited that ignorance. In many places they were the unscrupulous sponsors of tomb plundering and the illegal trade in antiquities, of the bribery of authorities, and of the bending of any rules that had not been framed in their favor. It was simply not in the foreigners' interest that Egyptians recognize and protect their cultural heritage as early as possible—that would have meant that the so-called civilized foreign countries had to dig deeper into their pockets for that cultural heritage. It is true that there were Egyptians at that time whose excavations were primarily commercial in nature. But European scholars also had to keep their sponsors happy with finds as prestigious as possible. There was an obvious commercial interest that museums in Paris, London, New York, Turin, and Berlin continue to profit from to this day in marketing 'their' treasures.

The next morning I set out very early. I naturally wanted to be at Kromer's dig on time, not to show up late the very first day and thereby confirm his preconceptions. The bus took an hour to get from Abdeen Square to the pyramid plateau. It was then a three-kilometer trek on foot through the sand. It was winter and still dark at that hour. Near the village of Nazlet el-Simman, which lies below the pyramid plateau, I had to cross through the cemetery. I was utterly alone, and suddenly a black figure sprang toward me. I froze, and thought of my grandfather's *ghaffir*s in Kafr al-Arab and their stories about the goblins and evil spirits that lurk in cemeteries. A man stood before me, swathed in a filthy old sack with holes for his head and arms. I looked about, hoping to find help somewhere, but there was no one to call to. My heart was pounding. But the man kept standing there as though rooted to the spot, and finally almost tearfully begged me for a piaster: "I haven't eaten for days." I was trembling so much that I could barely open my bag and finally hand him ten piasters. Then I told him that from then on I would be coming through the cemetery every day at this time, and would bring with me something for him to eat. He took the ten piasters and accompanied me across the cemetery, gratefully praying the entire time, until he vanished as suddenly as he had appeared. I too thanked my guardian angel.

At the entrance to the dig I met one of our guards who was responsible for the south hill. He was somewhat surprised. An inspector at this hour, a young woman, and on foot? "Such a thing has never happened before." I told him about the man in the cemetery, and he laughed, "Ah, that's only a homeless man, a harmless old geezer who never hurts anybody." But the *ghaffir* advised me never to cross the cemetery alone again. Allah had protected me this once. From then on the *ghaffir* would wait for me every morning down at the street. "There are stray dogs here, even wolves that live in the hills. When they get hungry they come down as far as the cemetery." Again I had to think of the scary stories from Kafr al-Arab. As it happened, Saad al-Abbadi did wait for me next to the cemetery every morning, wrapped in his gallabiya and a thick black cloak, armed with his big stick and a pistol. Still today I often think of the dark-skinned Saad from the tribe of the al-Ababda from the southeastern desert. He lived with his wife and four children in a small mud hut at the foot of the south hill. Saad saved my life, but I wasn't able to save his. But that can wait.

Professor Kromer greeted me with a friendly smile and invited me into the tent for tea. We talked about the status and progress of the dig. The finds of potsherds and stone tools had confirmed his theory that this area had been occupied before the age of the pyramids, or in predynastic times. I was given a glimpse of the excavation reports and spent hours studying plans and drawings of ceramics—but I was not invited to engage in any practical work myself. It was obvious that Professor Kromer found my presence disruptive. Once again I fought down a rising resentment about the way foreign missions automatically thought of excavations as exclusively 'theirs.' I thought of the hundreds of foreign missions living in their excavation houses as quasi-extraterritorial fiefdoms. That too was a legacy of the so-called imperial archaeology of the nineteenth century, the competition between European countries for historic buried treasure in the Near and Far East.

*

First there were the treasure hunters, self-made excavators and collectors like Giovanni Belzoni, Henry Salt, and Heinrich Schliemann, who searched for art treasures at their own expense. But then archaeology became a national affair. Employing almost military strategy, archaeological expeditions from the European countries planted their banners on ancient deserted settlements. With their shovels they competed for the legacies of Greece, Babylon, and Egypt. An 'excavation license' was comparable to a prospector's claim in the California goldfields. The lucky ones came to own a tell, a hill formed from the remains of an ancient town, from which they extracted an ample booty of art that enhanced both the fame of the excavator and the prestige of the discovering country. The Louvre, the British Museum, the Turin Museum, and the Berlin museums were in avid competition for the most spectacular showpieces. None of them wanted to lag behind the others. For a long time they treated their finds as their own property. When the British scholar William Flinders Petrie was about to return home with his providential booty after his first Egyptian sojourn in 1880, his French colleague Gaston Maspero, though at that time director of the Egyptian antiquities adminstration, simply advised him not to declare his finds at customs, but to quietly smuggle them out of the country. In general, the Europeans who shared the responsible positions in the antiquities service tended to be extremely liberal among themselves, or, as Maspero put it, to maintain an "openness of spirit," especially in the division of finds or in the "broadminded interpretation" of Egyptian laws and regulations. European customs inspectors waved through antiquities exported to Europe—often enough, Egyptian interests played only a secondary role. That would change only with Howard Carter.

The year 1922 was a memorable one. Egypt achieved its independence, and Howard Carter discovered the tomb of Tutankhamun. A new era was beginning for us Egyptians in terms of politics, only Howard Carter was obviously unaware of it. He continued to treat the Egyptian antiquities service, the Egyptian government, and the Egyptian public in the same colonial manner. His first telegram after his discovery was not to Pierre Lacau, the head of the antiquities service, but to his sponsor, Lord Carnarvon. It wasn't Lacau, but Carnarvon, who set the date for the official opening of the tomb; and it wasn't Lacau who selected the guests for the official opening, but Carter. The Englishman did not delay the opening for Lacau—in fact there was not a single representative of the antiquities service in attendance, since Carter was unwilling to change the date to accommodate them. His exclusive contract with the *Times* newspaper shut out the press of his host country. February 12, 1924, the day on which the lid of the sarcophagus was to be raised, was the last straw. Even before the arrival of the official governmental delegation, the wives of the excavation's coworkers were allowed into the tomb—despite warning protests from Cairo. Carter was a self-centered, obstinant character; his British arrogance could only provoke the Egyptians' pride. Imagine what would have happened had a foreign archaeologist discovered an untouched royal grave in England in 1922, admitted only his own reporters, made up his own guest list, and offered his sponsor half of all the gold treasures before sharing any with the British monuments protection authorities.

But in Egypt another wind was blowing in 1922. The forces striving for national independence under Saad Zaghloul were becoming stronger and stronger, their organized protests more and more violent. The British found themselves forced to upgrade the protectorate they had proclaimed in 1914 at the beginning of the First World War into an independent constitutional monarchy. During the protectorate, the son of the former Ottoman viceroy had been promoted to sultan by the grace of the British, and now they installed him in the kingship. But King Fuad I found himself torn in different directions: he had to shut the Wafd nationalists under Zaghloul out of the government to please the British, and he had to keep the British in check so the nationalists wouldn't put him under even greater pressure. It was in this situation that Howard Carter, with his imperious behavior, presented the nationalists with the ideal target. Their mouthpiece, the newspaper *al-Ahram*, blasted him: "They're not your treasures!" Now that Egypt was a nation for the first time, Tutankhamun was declared national cultural property. Demands that Egyptians themselves should finally take charge of their antiquities adminstration became more and more insistent.

Director Pierre Lacau had to fear for his own and by extension France's leading position in the antiquities administration. He had Tutankhamun's tomb sealed, forbade Carter access to the Valley of the Kings, and introduced more stringent antiquities legislation. In January 1924 Zaghloul finally became prime minister. In 1925 Cairo University became the first national university, and Egyptology was introduced as one of its disciplines. The Tutankhamun tomb treasure became national property, and Lord Carnarvon was reimbursed. Moreover, it was at just this time that the Nefertiti bust was publicly displayed for the first time in Berlin—more than ten years after its discovery. When a photograph of it appeared in Egyptian newspapers, Lacau had no choice but to demand the return of the bust from Germany as a national treasure. He knew that pressure on him would become still greater were the Egyptian public to find out that the French were responsible for its leaving Egypt in 1913.

*

With all this in mind, I sat near Kromer's dig on the south hill watching his students at work. For a week. Then I couldn't take it anymore. I explained to Kromer that the situation was unbearable. "I have to work! I want to learn something!" I told him that I had already done practical work with British colleagues in Benghazi and had gained some experience.

Kromer was surprised. He was sorry if he had once again upset me by his behavior. "But never before has an inspector asked to take part!"

From then on our relationship was transformed. I became a part of the team, and Kromer, the members of the mission, and I came to enjoy an easy companionship. In the weeks we worked together removing sand and rubble with our shovels, trowels, and brushes, other thoughts went through my head: The disrespect by foreign colleagues was hardly surprising. Our inspectors were supposed to protect the archaeological sites, to see that there was no plundering or illegal construction in the precinct, and that farmers didn't extend their fields onto archaeological territory. I looked down on the valley of the Nile and saw that the monument protection authorities had not prevented illegal settlements from proliferating right up to the plateau. The laws could not prevent the fact that intensive agriculture was raising the groundwater level and drowning tombs in the Delta; they hadn't prevented influential families from constructing their villas.

I saw how diligently the students worked. In the afternoon we would discuss the day's results, draw and catalog ceramic finds. Their concentration and enthusiasm were infectious, and I learned more every day: about pre- and early history, about which little was taught at our universities. Moreover, I learned a little German. Only bits of course. I liked the sound and rhythm of the language, and determined to learn German, especially since it had always annoyed me that I was unable to read important scholarly essays and books. I enrolled in evening courses at the Goethe Institute, which was fortunately not far from our apartment.

When I compared my knowledge with that of the other students, I had to ask myself what they must really think of Egyptian inspectors who spent their days drinking tea and reading newspapers, showing little interest or ambition in their own field. I would hear the students exchanging opinions about the scholarly literature, and think of our own studies: how we learned by heart the writings of notable European Egyptologists like sacred texts, without being encouraged to form any interpretations of our own. We were content with excursions, without gaining any practical excavation experience of our own. To this day excavation techniques are not a part of our curriculum. When I took over the direction of the Egyptian Museum decades later, I discovered that a large number of its curators and restorers had never been at any archaeological site aside from the Giza pyramids. I put together a continuing education program, with lectures on important archaeological sites, which we would then visit one by one. It is ridiculous that a curator responsible for a museum's archaeological collection should have no clear idea of where the objects he or she looks after came from. I sadly had to ask myself whether it wasn't our own fault that foreign colleagues didn't take us seriously.

In fact, our universities were completely overburdened. In 1972 there were twelve of us earning bachelor's degrees. Today our universities graduate several hundred Egyptologists each year. Egyptology has suddenly become a fashionable major, and instructors can no longer deal with the masses of students. Research and teaching suffer accordingly. It is scarcely possible for us to offer training of a quality comparable to that of European universities. That naturally contributes to the inferiority complexes of many of our Egyptologists. So why are so many young people nevertheless studying Egyptology? In Europe I read that it is probably a response to a secret yearning on the part of young Egyptians for ancient splendor and glory, a kind of patriotric 'repatriation' of their own cultural heritage—Egyptology as reassurance of a onetime high culture at a time of national and political decline. It may be that that also plays a role. For many young people it must be all the more frustrating that their country is unable to give them any work.

Months later I had the same experience with the mission from Harvard University and Boston's Museum of Fine Arts that I had had with Professor Kromer. The Americans were documenting the graves in the necropolis to the west of the Khufu Pyramid, a project begun in the first half of the twentieth century by the famous American archaeologist George Reisner. 'Papa George' was legendary. In 1925 he discovered a shaft on the east side of the Great Pyramid that led at a depth of thirty meters to a wall sealed with limestone blocks. Behind them lay the tomb chamber of the 'Great Royal

Consort' Hetepheres, who lived between roughly 2551 and 2528 BC. She was the mother of the pharaoh Khufu and wife of Snefru, the first of the ancient Egyptian kings of the Fourth Dynasty. The expectations in 1925 were naturally enormous—three years before, Howard Carter had found the undisturbed tomb of Tutankhamun. But here was an obviously undisturbed tomb from the Fourth Dynasty, or roughly twelve hundred years older than the royal tombs in the Valley of the Kings. And in fact Reisner did discover that everything in the small chamber was undisturbed: the alabaster sarcophagus, the canopic jars, chests filled with fine linens, salve jars and cosmetic utensils in gold and copper, armbands of silver, a gold-studded bed, and other pieces of furniture adorned with marquetry. It was only the contents of the sarcophagus itself that were a disappointment—the coffin was empty. Clearly Reisner had come upon Hetepheres's second tomb. The first, we now assume, had probably been plundered, and the queen's mummy either destroyed or stolen. Here a new tomb chamber had been created for her at the foot of the Great Pyramid—but without her mortal remains. Her tomb treasure can now be seen in the Egyptian Museum in Cairo.

Reisner made a great contribution to the study of the Old Kingdom and its necropolises, and in the mid 1970s William Kelly Simpson was carrying on with Reisner's work on the plateau. After the predynastic dig on the south hill, I was looking forward to studying the following period. Or so I thought. But Simpson too made no effort to include me in the mission's work. "Make yourself comfortable here in the office. If I need anything or have any problems, I'll come to you. Have a nice day!"

I was about to turn around, when I burst out that I would insist on being present at the dig so as to be able to write detailed reports. I was not angry at Simpson, or about the fact that in my second assignment as inspector I was being dismissed in the same way. I was angry at my own people. It was intolerable how we presented ourselves to foreign colleagues. Then Professor Simpson and his colleagues also took me on without hesitation, and we are still friends to this day.

I had accompanied two American excavation campaigns and learned a great deal about the scientific recording and documentation of tombs. During my excavation work in Benghazi, it had already become clear to me that I wanted to write my master's thesis about an archaeological site that had not as yet been scientifically studied, and I began looking around the area with a purpose. Which of the many tombs could be an interesting research project? During the Austrians' excavations on the southern edge of Gebel Qibli, a tomb had caught my eye whose architecture clearly differed from that of the Old Kingdom tombs. During a lunch break I ran over to the other side of the south hill to look at the tomb up close, and was astonished. The exposed outer walls were made of a fine Tura limestone, on which were wonderful reliefs. They were quite similar to those of the Old Kingdom, yet somehow different. The tomb chapel was in the form of a cross. I could not get inside, for the entrance was partly walled up and secured with a heavy iron door.

In the library of the Egyptian Museum I looked to see whether any information on the tomb had already been published, and finally found it. The British archaeologist Sir Flinders Petrie had cursorily described the five rooms in 1906 and prepared a series of relief drawings. The Tomb of Thery—the more I dug around in the archive, the more clear the outlines of a tragedy became, one that was altogether typical of the fate of many ancient monuments: Petrie had had a large part of the sand beneath the slope of the hill removed and the tomb chapel cleared of it. He was fascinated by the quality of the reliefs, especially those of the eastern chamber. His drawings, published in 1907, pictured Thery seated before the offering table and his two sons, Psamtik and Gem-ef-set-kap, presenting offerings. Above them sat Anubis, the god of the necropolis. In front of Anubis one could see the symbol of the tomb, the ankh (the sign for life) and the Horus or udjat eye, beneath which, in turn, were the signs for 'beautiful' and 'gold.' I read that Petrie and also Gaston Maspero, then chief of the Service des Antiquités, had intended to remove a few portions of the wall. Petrie wanted the reliefs for a British museum, Maspero for the museum in Cairo. But apparently both of them lacked the time, money, and necessary sponsors, so the walls were left intact. Petrie had the tomb refilled with sand. But that precaution came too late. His discovery had long since been talked about, and tomb robbers had their eyes on it. Apparently at the request of foreign antiquities dealers, they cleared the sand from the out-of-the-way tomb and chiseled from the wall the very blocks that Petrie and Maspero had coveted. They also ravaged other reliefs, carving out entire scenes. What was scandalous was the inaction on the part of the antiquities authorities. In 1911 Inspector Georges Daressy permitted the stolen blocks to be shipped to London—"unknowingly," it was said, though the thirty crates were declared as "ancient blocks," "stones," and "fragments." Maspero was so enraged that within weeks he initiated a new antiquities law that went into effect on June 14, 1912. One more piece of antiquities legislation pointing in the right direction, but one that accomplished little—for only a year later the Nefertiti bust left the country in the same manner.

I told Professor Simpson about the tomb, and he immediately agreed to look at it with me. We were enchanted by the reliefs on the outer walls: Osiris seated on his throne, accompanied by his sister–wife Isis and their sister Nephthys—actually scenes found in temples, not tombs, at least not usually in those of the Giza necropolis. We concluded that many of the standard Old Kingdom scenes were found in this tomb, but also some from the pictorial inventory of later centuries.

"The tomb has to be documented before it deteriorates still further," I told him. "Petrie's notes leave a lot of uncertainty."

Simpson felt that the tomb definitely had to be measured, documented, and published—a very nice scholarly project. "I'll tell you what. I'll arrange for an invitation to you from the Museum of Fine Arts in Boston. There you can study our documentation of the Giza necropolis and also make use of the archive at Harvard University. I'll see that you can have a room in the museum's guesthouse. But you'll have to arrange for the plane ticket to Boston yourself."

On the way home I could hardly believe my good fortune. Simpson was not only entrusting me with such a project, he was paving the way for me. But where was I to get the money for a plane ticket to Boston? I was earning LE25 a month. The flight would possibly cost $1,000. I couldn't pass up the opportunity for lack of money. I would broach the issue with the vice president of the antiquities service.

Fuad el-Oraby had a reputation for throwing tantrums and was considered impossibly difficult: a former officer who bossed his intimidated subordinates around like common soldiers. I had not as yet met him, but I remembered my experience with the 'General' three years before and summoned up all my courage. I would simply explain to him how I envisioned the trip. A few weeks before, I had been awarded a small stipend from the British Council for a fourteen-day language-study stay in England. And now there was the invitation to America as well. So all I needed was a ticket from London to Boston.

I was given an appointment in Bab al-Luq. The secretary announced me and led me into a very simple office. Fuad el-Oraby was seated behind an uncluttered writing table, reading in a file. He promptly looked up and said, "I'm proud of you. I see that you've received an award from the British Council. A stipend for England! I congratulate you." An encouraging greeting. So I told him about the invitation to Boston—that I wanted to work on my master's thesis but needed a ticket to America. Fuad el-Oraby listened attentively, reflected for a moment, then suddenly brightened. "I have a solution! I will add your name to the list of official delegates to the opening of the Tutankhamun exhibition in New Orleans. What do you think of that? That way we kill two birds with one stone. You have your ticket to America, and I get to send somebody in place of these people who know nothing about Tutankhamun!"

On September 10, 1977, I boarded a jumbo jet for America. During the sixteen-hour flight I had a lot of time to think. Contrary to expectations, this 'general' had also given me a chance, and his suggestion exceeded my wildest hopes. I was the youngest member of an official Egyptian delegation. Behind me sat the minister of culture Abdel Moneim El Sawy; his wife; and the director general of the antiquities administration, Professor Mohamed Abdel Qader. Ahead of me was a ten-day tour to five major cities in the United States: New York, Chicago, the opening of the Tutankhamun exhibition in New Orleans, then California with San Francisco and Los Angeles. A dream journey. To be sure, I hadn't anticipated the amount of envy this trip would provoke among my older colleagues in the antiquities service. Such a young woman, not yet twenty-seven years old, and with no travel experience! They can't send such a person! But I also heard kind words. "My dear, you'll make precisely the right impression abroad of the young generation of Egyptian women," the friendly minister assured me. "You're the perfect ambassador for this exhibition," his wife seconded.

Over the Atlantic we ran into violent turbulence. Behind me I could hear the soft murmur of Qur'an suras. I could only think of Mama, who on a flight home from Benghazi landed in Cairo in a plane on fire, and despite the flames climbed out unfazed. She was absolutely certain nothing would happen to her. For hours I gazed down at a sea of scudding clouds and waves.

Then finally the pilot announced that the Manhattan skyline would soon be visible on the horizon: New York—city of dreams. Below us cruise ships and skyscrapers were glistening in the sun. During the descent I shut my eyes, calling to mind scenes from American movies. At the airport I still found myself in such a dream: A large committee met us, luxury limousines drove us into Manhattan, motorcycle police escorted us in front and behind. By the time the car door was opened in front of the famous Plaza Hotel, my neck already ached from constantly staring upward. We were told that we should freshen up, and then the visiting schedule could begin. I was suddenly exhausted. In Cairo it was two o'clock in the morning. But I suppressed the desire for sleep, took a hot bath, changed my clothes, and went back down to the lobby, ignoring my need for rest. We were immediately whisked on to the Metropolitan Museum on Fifth Avenue. I was stunned as I stood in the Egyptian Department: The Metropolitan owns more statues of Queen Hatshepsut than the Egyptian Museum in Cairo. From the late nineteenth century to the beginning of the twentieth, the museum owned the license for excavations at Hatshepsut's Temple in Deir al-Bahari. But how could it be that it was able to take home such quantities of unique objects? The museum people mostly wanted to show us the Temple of Dendur. It had been faithfully reconstructed in the Sackler Wing—a gift to the United States from Egypt in gratitude for its help in the archaeological campaign to rescue Nubian monuments threatened by the reservoir of the Aswan dam. I liked the way they had rebuilt the temple under a large glass roof.

On our way to the Brooklyn Museum I could see out of the limousine window only poverty and misery: black people lounging on stoops, drunks, jobless people, mountains of trash on the sidewalks. Was this America, one of the wealthiest countries in the world? The driver asked that we lock the windows and doors. We were not to go out onto the street alone at night, not to open our hotel room doors. I had been living in a city of millions, but at that time Cairo was truly a peaceful and safe metropolis. I suddenly felt oppressed by the canyons of steel and concrete, and it was only when I saw the view from the Empire State Building, and then from the Statue of Liberty, that my sense of elation returned.

I could scarcely believe it. Only shortly before I had been kneeling in the dust of the pyramid plateau, and now here I was standing in the General

Assembly of the United Nations at the invitation of Egypt's ambassador to the United Nations, Ahmed Esmat Abdel Meguid, who would years later be Egypt's foreign minister and president of the League of Arab States. There was to be a formal dinner with a great number of politicians and diplomats in attendance. I was somewhat intimidated, but the minister and his wife took me by the hand like a daughter. The ambassador's wife also graciously introduced me to their guests. I was asked to tell them about my work on the pyramid plateau. They were astonished that such a young woman had worked in the desert, and then they wanted to know whether I rode past the pyramids on a camel the way one saw people doing on television. In the course of the trip I met many Americans who actually believed that the camel was the standard means of transportation in Egypt and that attacks by Nile crocodiles were a frequent cause of death. I had to wonder about the image of my country conveyed by the media. We lived in the land of the pharaohs, to be sure—but time hadn't stood still for us either.

We left New York the next day, and in Chicago we were treated to the same scenario: a reception committee at the airport, luxury limousines, a luxurious hotel with a view of the lake, the warning not to open our doors and not to go for a walk at night. In Chicago's Field Museum I saw my first dinosaur skeleton, 'Sue,' the famous *Tyrannosaurus rex*. In the Egyptian Department we admired the many artifacts excavated in Egypt since 1924. Two days and a night later we were in New Orleans—a city surpassing everything we had seen before. We were greeted as though we had landed as aliens. On the drive into town, accompanied by an escort of police cars and motorcycles, I was struck by the way the streets were decorated with palms and ancient Egyptian motifs. For the opening of the Tutankhamun exhibit, the entire city had been adorned in pharaonic style, boutique windows featured ancient Egyptian costumes, and the hotel lobby had been turned into an Egyptian temple. Then came a shock: For the opening ceremony we were asked to wear tuxedos and evening dresses. I didn't have an evening dress. But the minister and his wife and the other members of the delegation were also unprepared. No problem, we were told, and a short time later we were provided with formal wear from a rental service. The minister's wife and I laughed out loud. But the wife of the Egyptian ambassador in Washington explained that that was perfectly normal in America. Plenty of people, even the well-to-do, rented tuxedos for an evening.

It was an evening filled with surprises. We went on foot to the hall a few steps away, noting that the palm-lined street had been dyed blue to represent the Nile. Hardly had we entered the hall when I felt I was at a masked ball: All the American women were dressed the same. They all wore variants of the costume that Elizabeth Taylor had worn in *Cleopatra*, and even their hairdos were imitations of Liz's. The courses at dinner were served with Egyptian twists, colorful sweets arranged as Tutankhamun masks. Among the horde of guests I recognized well-known Hollywood stars, and you cannot imagine what I felt when I was seated as a table partner next to the wonderful actor James Mason. An entire, much too short evening next to the incredible James Mason! His questions were unsurprising: "How can such a young woman work in the desert? Aren't you afraid of snakes and scorpions?" No, I assured him, wild animals are more afraid of us than we of them. And wasn't the desert one of the most enchanting landscapes on earth? We talked about Tutankhamun, speculating about the pharaoh's early death, but also about modern Egypt, about Cairo and the university. While we were eating, I felt the attentive glances of a woman from the neighboring table. She was the only one who wasn't dressed like Elizabeth Taylor. It *was* Elizabeth Taylor. We nodded to each other, and I felt that she had the most beautiful smile in the world. After dinner she came over to us. James Mason introduced us, and for a long time I thought I had strayed into a film. With a winking glance at the ladies around us, Elizabeth Taylor said, "Oh well, we now know perfectly well what ancient Egyptian women looked like. But here's an Egyptian who outclasses them all. You are very beautiful!" James Mason looked at me and smiled. Elizabeth Taylor looked at me and smiled. And all I could say was something dumb like, "Thank you. But so are you!"

Tutankhamun was the most spectacular exhibition Egypt ever sent abroad. It displayed a large selection of the most important objects from the tomb treasure and, of course, the famous eleven-kilogram mask made of gold and semiprecious stones. None of these would ever leave Egypt again. Americans and some 40 million people around the globe were stunned by the show. The proceeds helped to compensate for Egypt's war losses and improve its tourist infrastructure. It was the most successful publicity show the country had ever undertaken.

After the dinner and the opening ceremony, museum colleagues invited us to a Bourbon Street jazz bar. The following day I saw the Mississippi, flowing a dark gray beneath clouds. It began to rain, and never again have I seen so much water lash down in such a short time. The blue-dyed street turned into an actual river. I had to think of Cairo: Whenever it rained there, even a few drops, people stayed home from work, as the streets descended into absolute chaos.

So we were happy to be able to set out for sunny California. Our days in San Francisco were overscheduled and flew by. I remember Chinatown, the Golden Gate Bridge, and the oldest gigantic trees in the world. Afterward came Los Angeles with its Universal Studios, the film tricks with which Charlton Heston had crossed the Red Sea in *The Ten Commandments*, and the gigantic gaping jaws of the "great white" in *Jaws*. At Disneyland I began to be bored, but our time had run out in any case. The delegation had to return to Cairo, and I was expected in Boston. Minister El Sawy's wife parted from me charmingly and wished me much success in my work in Boston. The minister and the president of the antiquities service thanked me for my commitment.

A day later I was standing in the arrival hall of the Boston airport. My reception committee consisted of Peter Der Manuelian, now the Philip J. King Professor of Egyptology at Harvard University, and Professor Simpson, who drove me to the museum's guesthouse. We had a small snack with the other residents. I had returned to an altogether normal life. At night, thanks to the jet lag, I lay awake. I would have liked to be able to take a walk, but in Boston too that was not advised. So I spent my days at Harvard University, sifting through the data relating to excavations on the Giza plateau. Everyone was extremely friendly and helpful. We often went to the shore. I would breathe the fresh sea air, eat fish and lobster outdoors, and enjoy it all enormously. Again I could see how diligent my American colleagues were. They would work tirelessly and with dedication from morning to night, and I could see how precious this study was to me. I learned how tomb reliefs were documented and was inspired by modern ways of displaying them.

But in the United States I had another experience that would stay with me: I visited an exhibition titled *Dialogue in the Dark*. The visitor entered into a completely dark space. For two hours, armed only with a cane, you moved with a group of people led by the voice of the guide. At first I was panicked. I was supposed to cross a highly trafficked street, honking cars were racing past me, and I didn't dare step off the sidewalk. I was supposed to search for a seat in a restaurant, shop in a supermarket, and count my change. I was totally disoriented, with only the voice of the guide for help. She had noted all our names, and spoke familiarly to each of us. "Wafaa, here we are! Only a few steps to your right." I groped my way through the darkness and began to realize what it means to live one's life in utter, inescapable darkness. Once we were seated in the dark restaurant, I asked our guide how she managed to find her way around. She answered, "I'm blind." I can't describe how that struck me. But I finally felt my anxiety subsiding, and I noticed that I began to smile. I have no explanation for this phenomenon, but I have since encountered this smile again—it made me very happy later during my work with blind children in the Egyptian Museum.

In London upon my return I was on my last legs. I landed at Heathrow early in the morning. My first meeting with the director of the British Council and the directors of the educational program for recipients of the Near Eastern stipend was scheduled for nine o'clock. Because of jet lag my eyes were drooping. I had a hard time listening and barely understood what they were saying. We were then taken to the British Museum. Henry (Harry) James, the keeper of the Egyptian Department, could see I was totally exhausted. I explained to him that the visit to his museum was perhaps the most important part of my trip. "Could we possibly put off the museum tour for a day? I need to rest." Mr. James smiled with understanding, and we postponed the date. The British Council also recognized that as an Egyptologist I wanted to spend more time in the museum. I had thought I knew the British Museum collection from catalogs and books, but I was overwhelmed by the sheer abundance of its rare and important objects. At the same time, I was impressed by the swarms of visitors. In New York, Chicago, and Boston I had already seen that most museum visitors immediately head for the Egyptian departments and stand fascinated in front of the displays. Of course I was accustomed to the sight of crowds of tourists in front of the pyramids or the Sphinx. But here it once again became clear to me what fascination ancient Egyptian culture holds for people all over the world. I was a little proud of that, but also sad about what enormous losses our museums had suffered.

In the evening I would walk along the Thames, past the Tower of London and the venerable Houses of Parliament and Big Ben. After my time in the New World, I was enjoying the aura of the old one. I visited Westminster Abbey and admired the government buildings of Whitehall. At the changing of the guard in front of Buckingham Palace I thought, This is the center of the British Empire. It was from here that the colonies of India, Australia, New Zealand, South Africa, Canada, Hong Kong, lands in the Caribbean, and Egypt were ruled. It was from here that were issued the orders to put down the Urabi Revolt and to invade during the Suez crisis. I looked at the mix of nations and cultures around me—and I didn't feel foreign. Strange, I thought, for decades we Egyptians tried everything to cast off the British yoke, and now I have the feeling that I too am part of the British Commonwealth.

My friend Carolyn picked me up, and we drove to Oxford to see the Ashmolean Museum, to Cambridge and the Fitzwilliam Museum. There too I admired the museums and the wealth of their collections. Seeing the abundance of Egyptian objects, I had to think that we Egyptians were no longer part of the Commonwealth and its privileges, while the British still enjoy the most precious works of the ancient East. Beyond all political and intellectual differences, that should unite us—a 'commonwealth of culture.' Artifacts form the cultural bridge between us. Couldn't they help overcome the barriers between rich and poor? Carolyn and I got along wonderfully. We laughed a lot. Since her time in Benghazi and despite her accident in Afghanistan, she hadn't lost her sense of humor. We spent delightful days together. But I was already feeling homesick. I missed my family, the sun over the pyramid plateau, the laughter of my countrymen.

I left London with a suitcase that weighed a ton, packed with books, catalogs, publications, and my workbooks. I landed in Cairo happy, full of enthusiasm and eager to get to work. It was time to put theory into practice. I was burning to get back to Thery's tomb, even though I would be able to visit it only at odd hours on account of my obligations as inspector. Back in Giza my colleagues reacted to my plans with reservations. When Chief Inspector Nassef Hassan heard what I had in mind, he enumerated all the possible objections to it. It was too far away, the terrain was difficult, even dangerous. In any case, he could not put a car at my disposal. But he did agree that I might work in the tomb. So I would set out in the early morning on foot and trek the three

kilometers through the desert sand, my notebooks, my camera, and my drawing utensils under my arm. My colleagues gave me no support, either moral
or practical. Often enough I would find the inspectors' building locked in the
afternoon. Hassan and the others had already headed home in the Jeep and the
minibus. I would trudge down to the bus stop from the plateau, my hair and
clothes full of dust that I would have to shake off outside the door at home.
My mother would be dismayed to see me in such condition. "My child, what
are you doing to yourself? Do you really have to do this?" "Yes, I have to,"
I would tell her.

But I was not entirely alone. Saad al-Abbadi, the *ghaffir* from the south
hill, supported me. Whenever he saw me heading for the tomb behind the hill,
he would accompany me, and ultimately even bring along a few excavation
workers. Saad helped me to open the heavy iron door that must have been
installed in Maspero's time. All of us set about clearing away the sand that
kept sifting into the tomb's interior.

The south slopes of the plateau are treacherous terrain. The limestone crum-
bles, the sand is fine and shifting. In addition, it is riddled with tomb chambers
whose shafts, as much as twenty meters deep, are neither secured nor marked.
They have no surface structures and the shafts are in no way encased. Sand
trickles into the openings, partially covering them, so that anyone unfamiliar
with the area risks falling into one, where it is not uncommon to find nests of
snakes and scorpions. Naturally I didn't tell Mother any of this. I had no fear of
the shafts. The guards and laborers knew exactly where they were, and I quickly
memorized their locations. Eager for adventure and with a lust for discovery, I
would have liked to climb down into some of them and investigate, but the men
urgently advised against it, for which I am still grateful to them today.

I began by documenting the exterior walls. The pictures show the owner
of the tomb and his wife praying to the deities Osiris, Isis, and Nephthys. The
style of the relief drawings is very like that of the Old Kingdom, but the motif
itself wasn't used in tombs in that early period. From the hieroglyphic texts
on the exterior walls I knew that Thery was a police overseer, an office he
had inherited from his father, Gem-ef-set-kap. His mother's name was Tadi-
Hor, and she bore the title 'Lady of the House.' One of Thery's two sons was
Psamtik—and this name is an indication that he had been given it in honor of
Thery's lord, the pharaoh Psamtik, a ruler from the late seventh century BC.

On the Giza plateau, with its pyramids and necropolises, there are mainly monuments from the era of the Old Kingdom (ca. 2650–2100 BC), but there are also a small number from the time of the New Kingdom (ca. 1550–1100 BC), especially the temple structures in front of the Sphinx. Archaeologists concentrate mainly on the monuments of the Fourth Dynasty (ca. 2613–2294 BC). That there are also traces in the necropolises of the Late Period, that is, the era of the Twenty-sixth Dynasty (ca. 664–525 BC), was still not fully recognized in the 1970s. Thery's tomb was constructed around 640 BC. That was the time of the so-called Saïtes, rulers whose residence was in the city of Saïs in the Delta. The Twenty-sixth Dynasty, together with the preceding Twenty-fifth Dynasty, was an epoch of cultural renaissance. The pharaohs of these two dynasties attempted to obliterate the memory of previous foreign rulers by giving their buildings a 'genuine' ancient Egyptian appearance. The masonry of this period is especially carefully executed, artistic and masterly in its craftsmanship. One way in which the Saïtes attempted to be authentic Egyptians was by once again building in the ancient Egyptian necropolises on the pyramid plateau. The cemeteries from the heyday of the pyramid builders had lain there for around fifteen hundred years. Thery, however, the overseer of Pharaoh Psamtik's police, was among those who constructed an elaborate tomb for himself on that venerable terrain. But he didn't build himself a mere mastaba, a simple, rectangular flat tomb. Nor did he commission a rock-cut chamber in the ancient Egyptian style. Instead, he built a tomb that would stand out from those surrounding it.

The tomb held yet another surprise. In the center of its interior court I discovered a shaft leading down into the lower part, the actual tomb chamber. Could it be that Sir Flinders Petrie had overlooked it? In any case, he didn't mention it. Petrie was by no means an exception in his generation of excavators. The veterans followed their curiosity and their lust for finds. They moved huge masses of sand and rubble, but when they failed to turn up anything exciting, they would abandon their digging and documentation. They made do with the publication of sketches and notes that didn't fully describe a site and fail to meet today's scientific standards.

But the reliefs in Thery's inner court claimed all my attention. The walls were decorated with exquisite pictures and texts in bright reds, blues, and greens, altogether in Old Kingdom style. It is not easy to distinguish between the signs of the various epochs and properly date them, but I noticed that it became easier and easier for me to recognize subtle differences. Thery and his wife are seated, while servants bring them food and drink and the couple are entertained by singers and musicians playing a harp and a flute. Reading the texts, and in the midst of these pictures, I felt surrounded by a second family. I became more and more knowledgable about Thery's biography. He was a man who insisted that the names of his second wife and those of their children should also be immortalized here.

The back four chambers of the upper tomb chapel were dark and filled with sand and rubble. Four workers began to remove the debris, always keeping long sticks at hand to keep horned vipers at bay. The venom of these snakes is deadly and works in a very short time. The day we cleared the western chamber, there were suddenly warning cries. Finally Saad al-Abbadi brought out a good-sized cobra. I insisted that he not club it to death but simply let it loose somewhere far away. Unlike horned vipers, cobras are not truly dangerous, and outside there were plenty of mice and other small animals for them to live on. Saad laughed, "We were just about to give it to you so that you could have a nice snakeskin bag made out of it." The snake had hidden in the farthest back corner of the chamber. Saad showed me where it had curled up, and then pointed to the wall. The room was covered over and over with Chapter 146 of the Book of the Dead: the Book of Gates to the Beyond, which describes the journey of the sun god through the twelve hours of the night. We could see a series of gates in which demons stood guard. Painted next to them were texts that Thery would be required to recite so that the guards would grant him entrance to the underworld. He could only pass once he had pronounced each of the gatekeepers' names. The portals of the gates were decorated with rearing cobras. The laborers looked at me meaningfully: How wise of the snake to nest near its symbolic home.

Registering all the reliefs and texts took weeks. Finally there were the shaft and whatever might be found at the end of it. With great care the workers had exposed a rectangular hole roughly 1.6 meters by 1 meter carved out of the limestone. They warned me, but I was determined to climb down into it. My desire to document the tomb completely in drawings and photographs was greater than my fear. I bought a stout rope, a good lamp, and though shaking his head, Saad al-Abbadi tied the rope around my waist and shoulders. While the men mumbled suras from the Qur'an, they slowly lowered me into the shaft. We had previously determined that it was twelve meters deep. After four meters I spotted a narrow side shaft with a skeleton in it on the west side. Apparently a Roman-era burial. When I aimed my flashlight into the niche I saw two large eyes shining at the back of it. Frightened, I screamed and jerked backward. I then saw two large wings lift upward above me, and could hear how the men at the top also screamed as they let go of the rope. I plunged a few meters downward until Saad al-Abbadi managed to grab the rope again. I struck the rock wall, and for a few seconds was almost senseless with pain. The men slowly lowered me to the floor, where I cowered barely conscious. I couldn't feel any strength in my legs, and had to first calm myself. Saad called down to ask if I was okay, whether I was alive. "Al-hamdulillah," the men called. "Al-hamdulillah," I repeated. I lay there for perhaps twenty minutes unable to move. Despite the poor light I could make out that the bottom part of the tomb consisted of two chambers, not one. I discovered a rectangular cavity filled with rubble, probably a shaft leading to the actual tomb chamber. Finally I pulled myself together and called to Saad that we should now try it together. With great effort they pulled me back up the twelve meters to the top, the rope painfully cutting into my shoulders. I arrived completely exhausted. As we all caught our breath, we tried to think how we might get down again safely. Saad explained that a large owl had flown out, a splendid creature that apparently lived in the tomb niche. I confessed to the men that I had thought I was looking into a man's eyes down there, and related that the ancient Egyptians believed that the soul of the dead flies out during the day in the form of a bird and returns to the other world only at night—a bird with the head of the deceased. Again the men looked at me wide-eyed. Then it was the soul of Thery that had flown out, and it would probably only return in the night. I will never forget that experience.

That day Saad al-Abbadi saved my life. I could have broken my neck. That time it was he who was my guardian angel. However, weeks later I was unable to help him. I had not seen him for several days and asked the other *ghaffir*s about him. Saad wasn't doing well, they told me; he was at the university clinic. I drove there that same day and found him lying on a trolley on a wet sheet while his wife sat next to him weeping. He scarcely noticed me and was unable to speak. I called a nurse and asked why the man was having to lie on a wet sheet. The nurse apologized, explaining that there were not enough staff. I pressed money in her hand, left more money with Saad's wife, and promised to look in on him again the next day. When I arrived the next morning the trolley was empty. Saad had died of kidney failure in the night.

I sat in the bus, looked at the people around me, and asked myself, Was it because Saad was a *ghaffir* that he couldn't be helped? Because he couldn't afford to be hooked up to an expensive dialysis machine?

I was certain that Thery's tomb chamber lay at the base of the rubble-filled shaft. I showed the architect of the Giza precinct my cross-section drawings and explained to him that I definitely wanted to clear the shaft. Who knows, maybe it was the original workmen themselves who had dumped stones into it to protect the grave goods. But my colleague advised me against it. "The stone is too friable. The tomb shaft could cave in. You would in any case require ceiling braces and a lifting apparatus for the rubble. Wait until we have better machinery. The tomb isn't going to run away from you."

But I couldn't stop thinking about the stolen relief blocks from the east chamber of the tomb chapel. From the archival documents from 1912, I knew that the crates had been shipped to the museums in Bristol and Brooklyn. I determined to search for the lost reliefs and wrote to the curator of the Egyptian Department at the Brooklyn Museum, Bernhard V. Bothmer. I suspected that the reliefs were possibly lying unused in his storerooms, that perhaps we could get them back and even return them to the tomb. A short time later I received a reply. Bothmer wrote that the museum no longer owned the blocks; the reliefs had been sold to a museum in South America because the museum decided to concentrate on collecting sculptures. Unfortunately, it could no longer be determined which museum it was. I was somewhat astonished that the reliefs had not been returned to their home country, but simply resold. So I set about finding out which museums in South America had Egyptian collections, and wrote to Argentina, Brazil, and Cuba. But I received only negative replies. The relief blocks remained missing—until twenty-five years later when, as director of the Egyptian Museum, I received a Colombian delegation, including the director of the National Museum in Bogotá. She told me that her museum owned a few Egyptian relief blocks, but that they didn't know what period they came from. I pricked up my ears. The reliefs had come from New York a long time ago, my colleague explained, in exchange for other pieces. I asked her to send me photos, and behold, they were indeed Thery's lost tomb reliefs.

Protesters in Tahrir Square; behind them the museum and the burning building of the National Democratic Party, January 29, 2011 (photograph by Didier Lepoivre)

Mariette Pasha, the founder of the Egyptian Museum, and the burning NDP building, 2011

The mosque of my family patriarch Sheikh Hassan al-Diasti in Faraskur, 1880

View of the garden of Abdeen Palace in Cairo

My cousins in Alexandria; my mother Tawhida al-Diasti is standing at the back on the right; I am the second girl, bottom right

From another time: the wedding photo
of my uncle Hassan al-Diasti and his
wife Samiha Fadel

My great-uncle Abdel Rahman
and his daughter Afaf

The water tower in Kafr al-Arab

My older brother Mohamed El Saddik

My father Taha El Saddik

My father (right) with two colleagues in front of the old British dam at Aswan, 1964

My great-grandfather Sheikh Ahmed
al-Gedeli, a theologian at al-Azhar
University, Cairo, and my great-uncle
Abdel Rahman

My mother (left) with her relatives (my
uncle's wife Samiha and my cousins) in
Alexandria, 1938

Egypt's prime minister and Wafd
politician Saad Zaghloul; behind
him on the right, his secretary,
my great-uncle Abdel Rahman

Director of the Boat Museum, still encased in scaffolding behind me, 1979

With my friend Enayat Siena in Aswan, 1972

In front of the Khafre Pyramid during my work with the American excavation mission in the west necropolis at Giza, 1975

A trip to Edinburgh, during my study visit in England, 1978

My first time in Yorkshire, 1978

Thery, overseer of police under Pharaoh Psamtik I

Thery's tomb on the southern hill of the pyramid plateau, al-Gebel al-Qibli

The roughly twelve-meter vertical shaft leading to Thery's tomb chamber

At the Golden Gate Bridge with Mrs. El Sawy, wife of Minister of Culture Abdul Monem El Sawy and Mrs. Hakki, wife of the Egyptian ambassador in Washington, 1977

The excavation at the feet of the cement plant in Tura; the workmen came from the village of Quft, near Luxor, 1978

A skeleton in one of the round graves from the early dynasties; the body, not embalmed, was placed on its back, its face turned toward the east, Tura, 1978

The stone quarries at Tura; graves of the former quarry workers lie right next to the cement plant, 1978

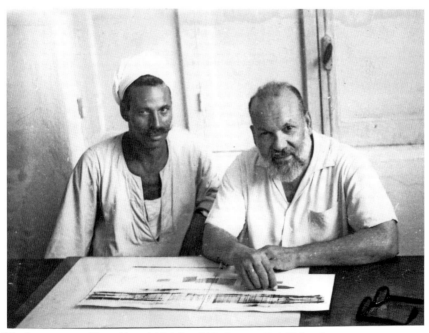

The boat restorer Hagg Ahmed (right) and his foreman Rais Tuhami

In Vienna's Hofburg: Austrian President Rudolf Kirchschläger receiving his classmates

Receiving my doctorate in the festival hall at the University of Vienna, fall of 1983

In the museum built for the 4,500-year-old Khufu boat, right next to the Great Pyramid, 2011

With King Carl XVI Gustaf of Sweden and Queen Silvia at Abu Simbel, 1986

With Queen Margrethe II of Denmark in
Luxor, 1986

The reception with two hundred guests on
the cruise ship *Nile Pharaoh* in Cairo, 1987

The wedding contract: the old sheikh, my father, my brother Mohammed, and Azmy
dealing with formalities in al-Hussein Mosque; the women and men were seated apart;
the husband signs the contract first, then the wife, 1987

5

IN THE BELLY
OF THE BARQUE

"Where?"

"In Tura," I said, and tried to sound as nonchalant as possible, just as though I were speaking of Karnak, Memphis, or Heliopolis, and Tura was simply another standard Egyptian excavation site. But Mother was furious. She couldn't believe her ears.

"In Tura," I repeated. "In the stone quarries."

Now Father stared at me in disbelief. "Child, do you know what you're doing? That's a frightful place!"

Tura was frightful, I knew it. I had heard it often enough in the past few days. The name Tura is notorious in all of Egypt. A few kilometers south of Cairo lies the state prison where political opponents of the regime were tortured and abused, often enough to death. Its inmates were required to labor in the limestone quarries that supplied the nearby cement plant. Even Hosni Mubarak spent time in the Tura prison's hospital after the Revolution. His two sons and a few members of his corrupt regime were also held there—though exempt from forced labor. But the infamous prison was only one reason for the place's bad reputation. The other was Egypt's largest cement plant, with its gigantic furnaces and smokestacks. Day in, day out, black smoke hung over the area, mixed with the dust from the quarries that coated a person's respiratory system and the fine sand blowing in from the desert.

"Tura is my chance," I said. "Who knows when I'll get another one!"

In the winter of 1977 the cement plant wanted to expand. The new building site extended into the ancient stone quarries. Already at the time of the Old Kingdom limestone blocks were quarried there for the pyramids, for the construction of tombs and temples. Greeks, Romans, and Mamluks also mined them for building material, and the quarries were still being worked. But before the extension could proceed, the new site had to be explored for possible archaeological remains and excavations undertaken wherever something looked promising, for the area was still dotted with cemeteries of the ancient quarry workers. My colleague who was to carry out the salvage excavation had reported sick shortly after being appointed. He regretted being unable to direct the project on account of poor health.

When I heard of it, I immediately reported to Nassef Hassan. "Let me take on the dig. I can do it. I'm far enough along. Let me prove that a woman can direct an excavation too!"

Nassef Hassan had not always been well disposed to me, but he clearly wanted to put one over on his colleague in Tura. "What a brilliant idea!" he said. "We'll teach them a lesson." He seemed delighted by the idea. "My colleague will be mortified when a woman shows him what a washrag he is!"

Mama and Papa were long-suffering. They also came to accept Tura. They knew it would have been useless to try to talk me out of it. In fact, in the previous months I had sorely tested their nerves. The memory of my inspection tour to Abu Rawash, which caused them several anxious hours, was still fresh in their minds.

Inspectors working on the pyramid plateau were regularly required to visit the region's archaeological sites as far away as the Bahariya Oasis. I enjoyed those trips by Jeep through the desert with my two colleagues Amani Monier and Mohamed Hafiz. The outings were an exciting change of pace and reminded me of excursions from my student years. So early one morning we set out for Abu Rawash, to sites around the pyramid of Djedefre, son and successor of the pharaoh Khufu. His pyramid is the northernmost one on the Giza plateau, lying some eight kilometers from his father's on a roughly eighty-meter rise that is not easy to reach. The hill serves as a natural base for the structure, which itself reaches a height of only sixty-seven meters, but with the additional height of the plateau it once would have towered into the sky as high as his father's pyramid. It was a gorgeous morning, and we could look across at the three Giza pyramids, looming up in the haze. Unfortunately, Djedefre's tomb monument has been reduced to only miserable remnants of the pyramid's core. It was quarried especially in Roman times. Who knows how many of its blocks were used in the construction of the Romans' fortifications in Cairo's ancient Fustat district?

Umran, our driver, then drove us on to Djedefre's quarries two kilometers away. The car was kicking up sand and dust, so clearly we could have been seen from afar. Nevertheless, as we drove nearer we could see a group of frightened men fleeing from the quarry. Obviously they had been intent on secretly helping themselves to some of the still desirable limestone. It was senseless to pursue them. We weren't police and didn't carry any weapons. We looked to see how much damage they had caused and found only the usual holes and pits. They had had to leave behind their tools and their large water jars. Mohamed Hafiz grabbed a pick and started smashing the jars before I was able to stop him.

"What are you doing? Why are you destroying them? Our guards could have made good use of them."

But Mohamed only laughed and gleefully kept hacking the jars to pieces. "That will be a lesson to them!" he called. "They'll never come back!" I didn't feel comfortable about seeing precious water senselessly spilled in the desert.

Once we were back in the Jeep, our front wheels only spun around in the soft sand. Umran raced the motor, but it was no use. The wheels only dug deeper and deeper. We shoveled them free, regretting that we had failed to bring along any mats or sheets of metal. So we removed the rear seats and shoved them under the wheels. But the Jeep would lurch forward only a short distance before getting stuck again. There was nothing to do but repeat the process, dozens of times. We could make only slight headway. We spent hours at it. With no radio, there was no possibility of summoning help; we simply had to see how to somehow free the vehicle ourselves. The sun was scorching, we were sweating, and I was waiting for one of us to say to Mohamed, "If you hadn't spilled the water, we'd now have something to drink." But we refrained. It was already dusk when the tires finally struck hard ground.

Umran drove off, but in the growing darkness he lost his way. He kept driving in a westerly direction without really knowing where we might reach
a road. We kept driving and driving, and the fuel gauge needle sank lower
and lower. Finally lights appeared on the horizon. "*Al-hamdulillah*," Umran
exclaimed—a sentiment we all three shared. It was the Baramus Monastery
in Wadi Natrun. It stands there like a fortress, surrounded by high walls. We
knocked on the great door. A smaller door in it opened, and a monk wearing
a black frock and black head covering emerged. We explained our situation,
and without hesitation he led us into the guest room. A few minutes later the
abbot appeared and invited us to supper. My colleague Amani was overjoyed.
She was a Copt, and was excited to meet the bishop. It was an extraordinary
experience for me as well. We took our places at the long monastery table, the
monks nodded to us in a friendly way, and we talked about excavations and
about the history of the venerable monastery, which was founded in about
the fourth century. Most of the monks had excellent academic training, were
doctors or engineers. But they had opted for a life in the desert rather than the
city. They were self-supporting and devoted their lives to prayer and work.
They had no telephone.

We left the monastery at about 10 o'clock. I was worried about my parents, who would have no idea why I hadn't come home. On the way I was
saddened to think of all I imposed on them. It was a long ride, but Umran was
happy: He sang, laughed, and smoked. The blue smoke from his cigarettes
filled the car, smelling of mint and a sweetish tobacco that was far from pleasant. I asked Umran what sort of nasty stuff he was smoking, but Mohamed
Hafiz only laughed and Umran giggled. He later confessed to me that it was
hashish—the simple pleasure of simple people. It stimulated their sense of
fun and helped them to bear their miserable lives. It was already past mid-
night when I was finally deposited in front of my door. Father was looking up
and down the street with a worried expression. Mother was kneeling on the
prayer rug upstairs, praying for my safe return. I was incredibly tired and not
feeling at all well after inhaling Umran's smoke the whole trip. He was half
stoned, and we were lucky to get home in one piece.

The closer I came to finishing my work in Thery's tomb, the more dismissive was the behavior of Nassef Hassan and my colleagues. But Ali
el-Khouli, the chief inspector at Saqqara, took an interest in my work and

gave me tips and advice. For that reason I finally asked to be transferred to Saqqara, a dream region for a young Egyptologist. It includes the tombs of kings and officials from the early dynastic Memphite era down to Roman times (with the exception of the Fourth Dynasty). The wind must blow there a bit stronger, for it had swept a new tomb free. In Saqqara Pharaoh Djoser (Third Dynasty, ruled c. 2617–2599 BC) erected his famous Step Pyramid, the first skyscraper in human history and a marvel of construction. Accordingly, his architect Imhotep would be venerated in the New Kingdom as the god of wisdom, and later as the god of medicine.

Once again it took an eternity to get from Tahrir Square to the inspectors' building in Saqqara. I would first take a bus to the Giza station, then an old and extremely slow train that had neither doors nor windowpanes, sitting on wooden benches with workmen and farmers. At Badrashein station I would switch to a donkey cart that took me to the village of Saqqara, below the archaeological site. Often I would be sitting among black-clad village women who were on their way to market with chickens and vegetables on their heads. I always looked forward to their company. They would talk about their village, about everyday events, and would shake with laughter when they saw that I couldn't understand their dialect. They would then explain words to me, and the time would pass quickly. Afterward, I would wait for a passing tourist bus to take me the rest of the way to the inspectors' building.

I dealt with archaeological missions of the British (in the north of Saqqara), the French (at the Sixth Dynasty pyramids south of Saqqara), the Germans (on the approach to the Unas Pyramid), and the Dutch (in the New Kingdom cemetery south of the Step Pyramid). Today there are more than twenty international expeditions actively excavating in the area. But in the mid 1970s there were still only shifting sand dunes west of the Step Pyramid. Notes from the early nineteenth century indicate that beneath them are countless tombs of important New Kingdom figures.

As an inspector I had the advantage of being able to follow the progress of the foreign missions from week to week, month to month, as in stop motion. I could compare the working methods of the various teams and have them explain to me their discoveries and conclusions. The decades-long work accomplished by those missions was most admirable, a precedent worthy of emulation to this day. And if I here focus on the work of a Dutch–British expedition, I by no means wish to belittle the achievements of the more than two hundred other research missions active in Egypt. It is because it was one that to my mind made amends for history in exemplary fashion.

In January 1975 the Dutch–British expedition from the Rijksmuseum van Oudheden and the Egypt Exploration Society set out in search of the lost tomb of Maya, treasurer and interior minister under Tutankhamun. Since 1829 the Leiden museum had owned a few relief fragments from that tomb and a very beautiful double statuette of Maya and his wife Merit. The pieces had been removed at the beginning of the nineteenth century. As late as 1843, Karl Richard Lepsius noted the tomb's approximate location on his map of the precinct. With that plan sketch in hand, the expedition, under the direction of Professor Hans Schneider and Geoffrey Martin, began its search. After a scant four weeks they came upon an astonishingly large tomb complex—not Maya's, to be sure, but rather that of Horemheb.

The team was by no means disappointed. On the contrary. Horemheb is a far more interesting figure. He it was who reversed the political legacy of Akhenaten and restored the 'old order' of Amun worship. Horemheb's interregnum forms the link between the Eighteenth and Nineteenth Dynasties, exciting years of extreme interest to every Egyptologist—and of course to me. Akhenaten and Nefertiti—how often have I lingered before the portraits of the two in the Egyptian Museum, gazed into their serene but so very expressive faces. What a remarkable couple! Their extraordinary historical importance had already been recognized by Karl Richard Lepsius, and would subsequently occupy Egyptologists like Heinrich Brugsch, Adolf Erman, and Jan Assmann, and thinkers and writers like Sigmund Freud, Thomas Mann, and Naguib Mahfouz.

In about 1350 BC Nefertiti and Akhenaten conducted a political-religious revolution from the top down. Against resistance from the all-powerful priesthood in Karnak, they deposed the state god Amun as supreme deity, and in his place installed the sun god Aten. The latter was much older, to be sure, but had meanwhile become only a peripheral deity. The royal couple abandoned Thebes and had a new royal residence constructed in Akhetaten (today's al-Amarna). Theirs was a costly and at the same time breathtaking building program. Much has been written about the reign of the so-called heretic king Akhenaten and his coruler Nefertiti: about the introduction of

the first monotheistic religion and the attempted abolition of Egyptian polytheism; about an apparently androgynous, bisexual pharaoh; about what was
possibly a physically and mentally degenerate ruling dynasty; about an ingenious intellectual couple on the double throne. Much of this is speculative,
much of it false. Egyptian polytheism, developed over the course of millennia, was by no means abolished; even in the new residence in Akhetaten,
people at court were able to continue to venerate their familiar gods. It is
true that with Aten, Akhenaten and Nefertiti imposed on their court a wholly
abstract and blindingly dazzling deity that no longer communicated with
the populace through a priesthood but solely through the ruling couple. The
whole new pictorial language—the Amarna aesthetic—must have struck the
people as puzzling, possibly even offputting. Today it strikes us as being so
very familiar and modern: the many private, even intimate, scenes depicting
the ruling couple and their children tenderly caressing each other; the almost
daring realism with which the rulers are depicted with pudgy bodies so very
unlike the youthful ideal with which the ancient elite normally had themselves represented.

But Amarna was only an episode, one that lasted a brief sixteen years.
Akhenaten's successor Tutankhamun died after only a brief reign at barely
twenty years of age. He was first succeeded by the 'old man' Ay, and then by
Horemheb, who had probably already served as a general under Amenhotep
III, then as commander under Akhenaten, and generalissimo under Tutankhamun. Ay and Horemheb abandoned the still unfinished new residence
in Akhetaten and returned the court to Karnak. When Horemheb became
pharaoh himself, he married a sister of Nefertiti's, but at the same time had
all memory of the Amarna intermezzo erased from the official annals. The
names of Akhenaten and Nefertiti were chiseled out of the royal cartouches,
their statues and temples destroyed. But Horemheb remained childless. The
'generalissimo' carefully selected his successor from among his generals:
Ramses I—the founder of a new dynasty.

Horemheb's tomb is remarkable in many respects. As pharaoh, he was
provided with a tomb among his equals in the Valley of the Kings, so he
abandoned the private tomb he had built in Saqqara while still Akhenat-
en's commander. His two wives, Amenia and Mutnedjemet, both of whom
died young, were buried in the chambers beneath that sixty-five-meter long,

aboveground complex with its columns, interior courtyards, and tomb chapel. Until the beginning of the nineteenth century, the complex was still adorned with hundreds of statues, steles, and relief decorations of epic breadth stamped by the Amarna style. But roughly a dozen illegal art dealers saw to it that today fourteen museums around the world hold objects from the tomb, including the Leiden museum, the British Museum, the Hermitage in Saint Petersburg, the Louvre, and the Brooklyn Museum. One relief is even shared by three museums: One fragment lies in Leiden, another in Vienna, and a third in Berlin. So for decades Egyptologists were required to fit together the pieces of the puzzle on the basis of photographs, drawings, or plaster casts. Often enough it was only chance that revealed that pieces belonged together. Tomb robbers record nothing of the origin and context of their booty. It is perfectly possible that additional fragments from the smashed tomb walls are still lying unrecognized in some museum storeroom or private collection.

The Dutch–British team not only secured and restored the huge tomb complex, but its scientists also set into the walls copies of the scenes whose originals can be seen in the Leiden museum. Then there was also their good fortune as excavators: In 2004 they were able to make sensational identifications on the basis of finds overlooked twenty years before. Previously unidentified sculptures in the Leiden and British museums were seen to be of Horemheb. If all fourteen museums were to make copies of their Horemheb objects available, how wonderfully the tomb could be reconstructed for visitors so that the wounds inflicted in the nineteenth century could at least be partially healed. In addition, the Dutch also discovered the tomb of Maya they had originally been seeking—but only in 1986, eleven years after hitting upon the tomb of Horemheb.

As inspector, on this occasion I remained only an observer, though it was difficult for me not to become involved. It was different with some Italian colleagues who were working in tombs from the Twenty-sixth Dynasty a few hundred meters southeast of the Step Pyramid, including the tomb of Bakenrenef, which was one of the main reasons for my transfer to Saqqara. Bakenrenef was the son of a vizier under Pharaoh Psamtik I, so his tomb dated from the same epoch as that of Thery. Years ago Champollion and Rosellini mentioned the tomb in their notes, and Lepsius was still able to describe it as largely intact. But then tomb robbers struck. Unlike Thery's tomb, Bakenrenef's columned courtyards and tomb chapel were not erected aboveground, but carved out of the bedrock. His tomb chamber lies at the end of a long, deep shaft. I used my inspection visits to compare the reliefs of the two tombs and discovered numerous similarities.

The complex structures of the shaft tombs created in the period following Bakenrenef and Thery are also fascinating. Their shafts extend downward for as much as twenty-five meters, leading into vaulted chambers completely covered with carefully engraved religious inscriptions, portions of the so-called Pyramid Texts. The ancient tomb builders' methods were equally ingenious: Branching off from each main shaft are a series of smaller ones that lead still deeper. To lower the immensely heavy tomb chamber, in which the sarcophagus lay with its mummy, the workmen first filled the main shaft with sand. They would then open the previously sealed side shafts and let the sand from the main channel pour into them. Little by little the chamber with its sarcophagus was lowered to the bottom of the shaft. Such sophisticated technology was not yet in use in Thery's time. Presumably his sarcophagus was lowered with ropes. I would still love to know whether he is lying beneath the rubble of the second shaft. To protect the sunken tomb chamber from thieves, necropolis workers once again filled the main shaft with sand. But sadly it didn't help. The Saïte-era tombs at Saqqara were also already plundered in antiquity. But Bakenrenef's limestone sarcophagus remained on-site—at least until 1828, when modern European plundering began. His sarcophagus was carried away to the Archaeological Museum in Florence. Was Thery's sarcophagus preserved from such a fate? And if not, in which museum might it be standing today?

A highlight for me was the inspection of the famous step pyramid of Pharaoh Sekhemkhet, from the Third Dynasty, who reigned from 2700 to 2695 BC. The pyramid was unfortunately left unfinished, and its eight-meter-tall ruin was rediscovered only in 1952 by my countryman Mohamed Zakaria Goneim. A superb colleague who came to a sad end, Goneim spent decades doing archaeological work in Luxor and Saqqara. When he opened Sekhemkhet's tomb chamber in the mid 1950s, he had every reason to believe he had before him an undamaged tomb. The lid of the sarcophagus was still covered with floral wreaths from the burial some 4,695 years before. Goneim informed the antiquities service and the press. Expectations ran high—and the ultimate disappointment was correspondingly great, for Goneim was to share George Reisner's experience: Sekhemkhet's sarcophagus was empty. Nevertheless, Goneim performed an important service for Egyptology. His book about the discovery was extraordinarily popular. But success creates envy, and it can do terrible damage. An anonymous notice accused Goneim of dealing in antiquities illegally. It was said that he had sold a precious vessel found years before near the Djoser Pyramid. Goneim was repeatedly questioned, and it was impossible to prove any theft on his part. But he suffered terribly from the campaign to ruin his reputation. His friend the French archaeologist Jean-Philippe Lauer stood up for him and initiated a search for the vessel, which he in fact found in the corner of one of the Egyptian Museum's storerooms in 1959. But by then Goneim was already dead. His body was found in the Nile and the cause of death was never explained. Either he took his own life or accidentally drowned. As director of the Egyptian Museum, I often had to think of Goneim. The methods of intrigue and character assassination have not changed greatly in all these years.

I felt very comfortable with my colleagues in Saqqara, and my former boss Nassef Hassan heard about it. He could not stand Ali el-Khouli, the director in Saqqara, and felt that his colleagues in the antiquities administration would assume that I had had myself transferred because of his resentment of him. Suddenly Nassef Hassan insisted that I return to Giza, that I was urgently needed there. I was by no means happy about this turn of events, though I also had to consider the long trips I had to take every day between Cairo and Saqqara. So I tried to think of my return as something positive—especially since I had recently had a dramatic experience.

One morning, instead of the slow train, I took the faster minibus from Giza to Saqqara. The driver sped down the much too narrow road, to the left the Maryutiya Canal, to the right fields and simple mud-brick houses. Next to me sat a farm woman with her small son, who wriggled restlessly on his seat between us. Suddenly I had the feeling that something terrible was about to happen. I grabbed the child and held him close to me. At just that moment a huge camel trotted out of one of the fields on the right and onto the road in front of us. There was no chance of avoiding it, and we struck the camel, rolled over and over, and landed in the canal, in which the water was very low, fortunately, as it was winter. A few villagers immediately helped us climb out of the bus. Miraculously, we were unhurt, only soaking wet. The mother whimpered with joy that nothing had happened to her child. Then the villagers turned to the dead camel. The women began their shrill mourning ululations, lamenting as though they had lost a close relative. I could see how the angry men wanted to attack the driver, who was still in shock. But to their surprise, they discovered that the young man came from their village. Now the mourning was unbounded. I could well understand it, for camels were an indispensable part of their village life. They performed hard work in the fields, patiently lifting the heaviest of weights. Often they were a family's only possessions. On the rest of my way to work the scene kept passing before my eyes like a film loop. Everything had happened in an instant, only seconds separating life and death. I had felt neither panic nor fear.

I had been back in Giza only a few weeks in fact, when I was appointed director of the excavation in Tura. I knew that I was facing a difficult job. The dig was supposed to be carried out in the winter months of 1977–78 and 1978–79. The time was short because the cement plant, which was obliged to pay for the rescue excavation, was pressing. My journey to work was no shorter, to be sure, but certainly less complicated and less dangerous. The excavation site lay right next to the plant, in the shadow of its smokestacks. Through the middle of the site ran a small rail line, and trains roared past our heads several times a day. Yet all this failed to dampen my high spirits.

But I was met by ill-humored and reluctant laborers. They were offended at the prospect of having to work under a woman's supervision. Most of them came from Quft. Archaeologists value the men from that village near Luxor. They are skilled and, best of all, honest. But their pride prevented these Upper Egyptians from willingly following a woman's directions. Still, I managed to work around it. I knew that their natural good nature and humor would soon win out. Unlike my male predecessor, I was reliably punctual, arriving early at the site. The men quickly noticed that I appreciated their work. I would join them at breakfast, ask about their families, their village. Sometimes I would take along pastries from the city. It wasn't long before I gained their loyalty and we became a team. For them it was probably similar to my experience in becoming accustomed to drinking their tea. They would brew it in a rather unsightly black pot that hung over the fire all day. And they kept the water in a dirty canister. They would simmer water, tea, and a huge amount of sugar over the fire for a very long time. Then they would pour the tea into a glass and back into the pot a few times. The sugary glass would stick to my hand. At first I was disgusted by the potion, but after a few days I was addicted to it.

At first they addressed me in the same way as my male predecessor, as Pasha (the same honorific that lower-level workers in the museum would use for me later). Finally they came to call me Princess. Rais Ali, the second foreman after Rais Saleh, felt that that was much more appropriate. Rais Ali wore a splendid mustache, which he was extremely proud of and which he groomed with obvious vanity. But he was also a heavy smoker, and one time, not paying attention, he set fire to his mustache with a match and burned off half of it. What a catastrophe for poor Ali! The young workers were convulsed with laughter, and were met with Ali's angry looks. They frequently sang as they worked, and I noticed how pleased they were that I liked hearing it. I felt truly comfortable among them—and they thanked me with their good temper. When my friend Aisha heard that I was directing a dig, she begged me to let her take part. So she too worked with us for two months—and the men from Quft didn't rebel.

We produced respectable results: The many burial sites we uncovered differed, both in form and contents, according to the epoch from which they dated. Graves from the early dynasties were flat, oval depressions in which the unembalmed bodies lay on their sides with their knees drawn up as though awaiting their rebirth, in a fetal position in the earth as in the womb. Placed next to their heads were clay or stone vessels with food or drink. The following epoch buried its dead in deep, rectangular graves, lying on their backs, faces turned toward the rising sun in the east. Buried with them were vessels and flint tools, simple amulets, sometimes a small *ushabti* figure. Women's graves had more elaborate grave goods: necklaces and armbands of ivory, pearls, and semiprecious stones, especially amethyst, which was native to the region. Above many of these burial sites we also found graves from Roman times. Since they were exclusively graves of commoners, they had not been plundered in antiquity. It probably didn't pay—or the grave robbers, poor themselves, respected the resting places of their peers. In any case, the area lay before us like an open history book. It told us about the simple quarry workers and poor populations of various epochs. My excavation workers recognized that immediately—here lay their own kind.

Then we discovered a more elaborate tomb chamber, apparently that of a foreman: an undisturbed shaft grave. I let myself down into the vertical shaft some three meters deep, at the end of which I found a small room with undecorated walls. Before me lay an embalmed mummy. Since there was no coffin and there were no inscriptions of any kind on the walls, the deceased remains nameless. I found a few simple vessels, some modest jewelry, and in a wall niche the untouched canopic chest with four very beautiful jars of fine limestone. I knew that the lids of early canopic jars were adorned with four heads of deities. That was also the case here, so it was clear that I was dealing with a grave from the Middle Kingdom, around 1900 BC. Only in a later period, at the beginning of the Nineteenth Dynasty, did the decoration change to correspond with changed funerary customs. The four heads stand for the four sons of the sun god Horus, the patron deities responsible for assuring the proper function of the organ in the given jar. The baboon god Hapi guaranteed the function of the lungs; the jackal-headed god Duamutef that of the stomach; the falcon-headed god Qebehsenuef that of the intestines; and Imsety, with a human head, protected the liver. The heart was left in the embalmed body.

In January 1979, on the very last day of our final excavation season, when I had given up hope of finding any more graves, we made a truly lucky find. Our budget had been exhausted, and on the previous evening I had instructed the workers to strike the tents the next day. When I arrived at the Tura railway station that morning, Saleh was already waiting for me. The rais greeted me with a broad grin, and I immediately knew he had good news.

"We've found something, Princess! We dismantled the tents, and under the dust and sand we found steps that must lead to a tomb. Everybody's waiting for you."

I raced to the site. The workers greeted me euphorically, pointing to a few steps leading into the rocky ground. My heart was racing with excitement, and I begged them to dig deeper. While doing so they sang the song they would always strike up during heavy work: "Praise to Allah and His Prophet." After more steps a broad stone block came into view. We lifted the block and found a skeleton beneath it.

"A thief!" the experienced Saleh cried. "A tomb robber. He tried to get in, but the stone that he had raised up behind him fell on him and killed him. Just look!"

I had probably read of such tales in novels, but never had I thought to see such a thing myself. Before me lay the skeleton of a young man. That was something else I had learned during this dig: the ability to determine the approximate age and gender of a skeleton based on the size of its pelvis, skull, and teeth. We removed the skeleton and finally came upon a wall whose surface was completely covered with a thin layer of clay.

I couldn't believe my good fortune. The entrance was sealed with an intact layer of clay! My heart was pounding so hard that Rais Saleh and the workers must have heard it. An intact clay layer means an undisturbed tomb chamber. At that moment I knew how Howard Carter must have felt when he knelt in front of the sealed door of Tutankhamun's tomb. We removed the clay completely and found the tomb chamber in precisely the state in which it had been left by the deceased's mourning relatives thousands of years before: There stood clay and stone vessels and plates, and a wooden headrest that was sadly in very poor condition. As was customary in tombs from the First and Second Dynasties, the walls of the chamber held no writing. There was no sarcophagus. The body of the deceased had not been embalmed, and at that time canopic jars were not yet customary. Yet some of the vessels were sealed with clay stoppers. Unfortunately, nothing was left in them. Their liquid contents, presumably wine, had long since evaporated. But the clay stoppers bore the impressions of seals. To Egyptologists intact seals are more important finds than gold. I couldn't believe my eyes: One seal bore the names of King Hor Aha and King Djer—the first two kings of the First Dynasty. That meant that the tomb chamber had been sealed for more than five thousand years. The early-period First Dynasty is still only a vague epoch in Egyptological research. The seal confirmed the royal succession of the two kings, something that was by no means certain in 1979.

I notified the antiquities service, and a short time later Said el-Feki, the inspector from Saqqara, and my colleague Michael Murphy from the British Saqqara mission came to join us. They knew the seals Flinders Petrie had found in Saqqara at the beginning of the twentieth century. Murphy had significant information about seals of the archaic period, and I was delighted that the antiquities administration allowed him, together with me, to document and decipher the inscriptions and seals. He called my attention to details of the impressions that I had not been able to identify. The names of the two kings stood above a sign called a serekh: a rectangle containing the stylized façade of a royal palace. And the image of the Horus falcon seated on a donkey repeatedly appeared. It symbolizes the triumph of Horus over the evil god Seth, represented by the donkey. The king's name Hor Aha means Horus the Victor. In addition, there were depictions of plants as symbols of the Delta region. Up until the reign of Pharaoh Hor Aha, Egypt was divided into southern Upper Egypt, symbolized by the falcon, and northern Lower Egypt, symbolized by the plants. The Horus falcon had thus triumphed over the Delta. The seal documented that the unification of the kingdom was only completed after King Narmer, whose famous Narmer Palette is displayed in the Egyptian Museum in Cairo.

Murphy advised me to publish this important find in one of the Egyptology journals. But I had not yet written a scholarly article, and I begged him to write the article with me. From him I learned something else: the craft of scholarly writing and publishing. In September 1979 I was actually invited to present the Tura excavation at the International Egyptology Congress in Grenoble. In Grenoble! The birthplace of Jean-François Champollion, the founder of Egyptology. I was still a student, and now I was supposed to appear before the dignitaries of the profession! I was the youngest participant, and terribly nervous. In the front row sat the brother of the emperor of Japan (the uncle of the present emperor)—a man who took a great interest in Egyptology. I began with a weak, unsteady voice, but several of the people in the audience encouraged me with their gazes, so my voice became firm and clear. At the end there was great applause. The Japanese prince congratulated me, as did some of the highly respected archaeologists. It had all gone well. I sat through the rest of the conference relaxed and with no more anxiety.

After the conclusion of my excavation work in Tura, I wrote to the head of museum affairs within the antiquities administration, Dr. Diaa Eddin Abu Ghazi. She was already quite old, but still a vital and extremely well-educated woman from an influential Egyptian family. Her uncle was the well-known artist and sculptor Mahmud Mukhtar, creator of the statue *Egypt's Awakening*. Her brother was minister of culture under Nasser. Diaa Eddin never married; she had devoted her entire life to science. At that time she was like a role model for me. She tended to bully her subordinates, but she was very kind to us students once she confirmed that we were serious. Her office was in the library wing of the Egyptian Museum, and I found the small, frail woman between towering piles of new books she was entering into the inventory. All I could see was her shock of gray hair. I think she first read every book herself before she added it to the inventory. Their authors took the place of a family of her own. I asked Diaa Eddin whether the Egyptian Museum would accept the clay seals in its collection. Naturally I was eager to have an object I had excavated displayed there next to all the famous treasures of the great archaeologists. Nothing could have been a greater honor for me. To my joy, Diaa Eddin immediately agreed. But for form's sake she would first have to obtain the approval of the head of the Department of Pharaonic Antiquities. At that time Egypt's antiquities administration had three divisions: one for pharaonic antiquity, one for Islamic antiquity, and the Department of Museum Administration. All three were overseen by the antiquities administration's director. Since then the so-called Project Department has been added, responsible for renovations, restorations, and new research projects.

The Director of Pharaonic Antiquities declined his colleague Diaa Eddin's proposal without any explanation. It was known that the man could not stand seeing other people successful. He looked on their achievements with envy, and generally referred to them dismissively. Self-importance and arrogance only provoke my pride and sense of justice. I had not been put off by two generals, why then by this small-minded man? I wanted him to explain to me in person why the seals couldn't be included in the collection. The director scarcely looked up from his papers and said in a condescending tone, "Oh, stop bothering me with such trifles!" The man was not only an ignoramus, he was a boor, which really roused my temper.

"You haven't even read my report? If you had looked at the photographs, you would have seen that the seals are remarkable. Also, you didn't even come to the excavation, although that would have been part of your job. And now, without reviewing the case yourself, you block the judgment of your colleague?"

I was so steamed up that I stormed out of the office without waiting for his response. How could it be that we had people sitting at the top of our antiquities adminstration who made their decisions on the basis of personal prejudice, resentment, and mere whim? The director couldn't stand Diaa Eddin Abu Ghazi—she was a woman, for one thing, and he suffered from an inferiority complex. Years later I learned that the seals and a few other objects from the Tura tomb had been incorporated into the displays of the newly erected National Museum of Egyptian Civilization (NMEC) in Cairo's old city, Fustat. I was greatly pleased. The graves in the Tura stone quarries have long since disappeared. Today the cement plant stands on top of them.

The news of my work in Tura soon got around, and not only in the antiquities service. *Al-Ahram* wrote that for the first time a young Egyptian woman had directed a very successful excavation. My example encouraged some of my female colleagues. A few years later there were as many as five women in the Giza precinct working on Egyptian digs. And by now native female Egyptologists are digging in every region of the country, even in the most remote desert areas. It has become routine practice. But today we women are once again having to defend the practice.

During my time in the quarries a small tempest was brewing within the antiquities administration. Hagg Ahmed Yussef, the conservator and restorer of the famous Khufu boat, had reached retirement age—but he flat-out refused to surrender the keys to the museum and its storeroom to an inspector. Very few people had heard of Hagg Ahmed in the West, but in Egypt he was a veritable national institution. For twenty-five years he had captained the oldest complete wooden vessel ever discovered, found in 1954 in a pit behind the Great Pyramid. It was a worldwide sensation: disassembled into 1,254 wooden pieces, 95 percent of which were cedar imported from Lebanon, it lay in the pit in thirteen carefully stacked layers, the deposit concealed by large limestone blocks, each weighing roughly fifteen tons. It is the ship that brought the sarcophagus containing the body of Pharaoh Khufu down the Nile to the quay in front of the pyramid's valley temple forty-five hundred years ago.

The sensational find presented the antiquities administration with a quandary. It needed a restorer and expert in the field of the conservation of ancient wood, someone who would take on the proper restoration of the separate pieces and then put the boat back together again in its original form—a mammoth task that would occupy a team for a period of years. In addition, the boat's so carefully sorted pieces posed riddles: They were not held together with nails, but with a complex system of ropes—a barque 43 meters long and 5.6 meters wide with a large cabin, captain's tent, and long wooden rudders, all fitted together and secured by nothing but ropes.

The choice fell on Hagg Ahmed. In an exemplary manner he had previously restored the tomb furnishings of Queen Hetepheres, the mother of Khufu. That tomb had been discovered in the 1920s. He had also done excellent work on the wonderful reliefs in the tomb chamber of Queen Nefertari in the Valley of the Queens. So in 1954 Hagg Ahmed began removing the wooden pieces, restoring them in a temporary structure next to the pyramid, and putting them together piece by piece. That took him until 1969. In the late 1970s the structure that is now the Boat Museum was completed, and Hagg Ahmed then took the boat apart again and reassembled it in the adjacent new museum building. In those twenty-five years he had devoted himself solely to this task. The boat was his life's work, and he couldn't simply walk away from it. His authority was so undisputed that he had to be asked for permission whenever an exalted state guest or crowned head expressed the wish to see the wonderful barque. And he by no means let everyone in.

Hagg Ahmed Yussef lived with his wife in a rest house belonging to the antiquities authority on the Giza plateau south of the Khufu Pyramid. They had a servant who did the housework and shopping for them, and lived a withdrawn and contented life near 'their' boat. I had known them both since my student days, when Professor Mohamed Abdel Qader had taken us to Giza. Abdel Qader was a close friend of Hagg Ahmed and his wife Hagga, as everyone called her. I think very few knew her real first name. In any case, Abdel Qader always looked forward to such excursions because Hagga would serve him and his students a delicious meal. Hagga was like a figure from a Tolstoy novel; she somehow seemed to belong to a different time. She was a good-hearted, touchingly naïve little woman who was automatically loved and respected by everyone. She was totally devoted to her Hagg—with a loving care that had nothing to do with submissive self-sacrifice. The two couldn't imagine a life anywhere else. For that reason, too, Hagg Ahmed didn't want to leave his job. But pressure from the antiquities administration was increasing. He simply could not stay on forever.

When I became an inspector in Giza, I saw the couple regularly, but I was totally surprised when I learned that when asked who he could imagine as his successor, Hagg Ahmed had given my name. I didn't know what was happening. I had no idea how much Hagg and his wife had taken me to their hearts, that they thought of me as the daughter they had not been able to have.

The antiquities administration wanted to finally settle the matter and asked me whether I could picture myself as director of the museum, which was not to be opened to the public until 1980. I said I could, but only on condition that Hagg Ahmed stay on as the boat's custodian. I certainly didn't have the expertise, and ultimately there was no one in the entire antiquities service who had such comprehensive knowledge as he. I wanted to use the time with my predecessor learning as much as I could from him. Hagg Ahmed was naturally very taken with my suggestion. He could continue to live in the rest house near his boat and with his laboratory and his library.

In June 1978 I assumed my first director's post—one for which everyone who had ever seen the boat must have envied me. The first time I stepped bare-foot into the belly of the barque was a magical moment. I carefully touched the cedar planks that were more than forty-five hundred years old. There were tears in my eyes, and a shudder ran through my whole body. In awe I entered the sacred cabin, which was adorned with carved palm-tree columns. And in the belly of the boat there were the hieroglyphs inscribed by the builders so that the ship could be reconstructed in the afterworld. I could see the waterline on the outside of the hull, the indentations left in the wood by the ropes. They left no doubt about the fact that the boat had once actually been used, that it was not simply a 'sun barque' built solely for the symbolic journey into the beyond.

In 1954 Kamal el-Mallakh dubbed the barque 'Solar Boat.' In the early 1950s the young architect had been commissioned to clean up the area on the south side of the pyramid. Mountains of debris up to twenty meters high had to be removed where a road was to be built. But it was not el-Mallakh but the antiquities inspector Zaki Nur who discovered massive limestone blocks under the debris and the ancient boat pit. El-Mallakh worked as a journalist for *al-Ahram*, and although there were many witnesses who knew better, he announced in its pages that he himself was the discoverer. And in order to imbue the boat with a somewhat poetic, religious aura, he named it the Solar Boat, a designation that caught on with the public. Since that time it has been erroneously thought that the boat was never actually used, that it had had only a ceremonial function. On closer study, however, it is easy to see the signs of use. Moreover, the boat had highly sophisticated climate control. Together with the ropes, plant-fiber mats were found in the pit; they had covered the cabin and crew space. The mats were soaked with water to mitigate the heat. The cabin had a double roof, and in the intervening fifteen centimeters a partial vacuum was produced thanks to the wet mats above. They thus provided for a pleasant circulation of air.

Hagg Ahmed introduced me to every aspect of his research and opened his huge photo archive that he guarded like a treasure. He had documented every detail of his work as he raised the heavy sealing stones with the laborers, removed the parts of the boat, restored, sorted, and fitted them together. In the reconstruction he followed the guides left on the pieces by the ancient boatbuilders so the boat could be correctly rebuilt in the afterlife. We spent most of our time documenting the boat's condition, setting the temperature and humidity level in the new museum and monitoring them. Each part of the boat was cataloged. Again and again I could only marvel at the extraordinary state of preservation of the organic materials more than forty-five hundred years old.

Hagg Ahmed asked me to translate for him the books being sent to him from all over the world as tokens of esteem. He knew no foreign languages himself. It was a lot of work and time-consuming, and at first I felt it an imposition. I was an Egyptologist, not a translator. But then I came to realize how much I was profiting by reading and translating the various articles and books. They made me familiar with the current state of scholarship regarding ancient boatbuilding—and that was precisely Hagg Ahmed's intention. I became so fascinated by the subject that I made a trip to England. In the National Maritime Museum in Greenwich and in the Mary Rose Museum in Portsmouth, I researched the subject of ship restoration. I dreamed of one day rescuing and restoring the sister boat that was also discovered in 1954 in a pit a few meters west of the Khufu barque.

Today that project has been entrusted to a team of Japanese scholars under the direction of Professor Sakuji Yoshimura from Waseda University. I am following their work with great excitement. They have raised the stone blocks above the pit and removed samples of the wood. Unfortunately, it is not in good condition. In the next few years these Japanese colleagues will nevertheless restore that boat as well, and I hope to live to see the day when it stands before us once again.

Within a matter of weeks Hagg Ahmed and his coworkers had become like a family to me. Most of them, like the excavation laborers in Tura, came from the village of Quft in Upper Egypt. Since I was already familiar with many of their customs and traditions, I was invited to their celebrations. The men lived with their families in simple mud-brick houses hidden on the plateau behind the mastaba tombs. I became friends with the foreman, Rais Tuhami, and his wife and children. At the same time, however, I was also introduced to an entirely different world. As director, I led state visitors through the Boat Museum, among them royalty and presidents. A number of them impressed me greatly. President Jimmy Carter because of his calm, kind manner; Queen Margrethe of Denmark and Helmut Schmidt for their attentive interest.

In the summer of 1979 I was unexpectedly awarded a stipend from the Austrian government. I was invited to be an observer for five months in the Egyptian Collection of the Kunsthistorisches Museum in Vienna. It was a chance to finally get more done on my master's thesis on the Thery tomb, and Hagg Ahmed advised me to accept. But that was not the way I had wanted my time in the Boat Museum to end. For one thing, there was the little booklet I had written about the Khufu boat. The director of the printing shop in the antiquities administration saw to it that my name didn't appear on it. The privilege of being credited on an official publication was reserved for others. The lady was a cousin of the minister of information, Safwat el-Sherif, one of the most influential men in Egypt (incarcerated along with Mubarak since 2011, because, as reported in the press, he is said to have enriched himself to the tune of LE700 million, among other things). And there was Mona, a classical archaeologist who on the recommendation of a high-level official in the Ministry of Culture was assigned to the museum and on my departure became its new director. It had long been rumored that she was a protégée of the influential Kamal el-Mallakh, the self-proclaimed discoverer of the 'Solar Boat.' Scarcely had Mona become director than she cancelled the contract with the aged Hagg Ahmed. A few months later the grand old man of the antiquities service died—and I have often wondered whether I could have prevented that if I had listened to my parents.

"And you're not going to Vienna!" Mother insisted. She was anything but enthusiastic. "You've achieved everything you wanted. You've led an excavation. You're the director of a beautiful new museum in Giza. If you absolutely want to earn a doctorate you can do that just as well in Cairo."

Actually it wasn't about Vienna. They were concerned about something else: I was twenty-eight years old and had still not made any preparations for marriage and starting a family like my two sisters Nur and Safaa. Mother complained, "You'll become an old maid!" After all, my female student friends had all been married a long time. "But you only keep digging around in cemeteries."

Father tried another way of keeping me at home. There was an empty apartment in my sister Safaa's building in Giza. An ideal location. From the window I would be able to look out at the pyramids, and the Sphinx was only a ten-minute walk away. Papa and Mama drove with me to Damietta, where we even bought furniture—for an apartment I would never occupy.

The apartment raised my parents' expectation that I might now finally accept one of the men my family had stubbornly, and altogether with the best intentions, introduced me to. On weekends one or another of my brother Mohamed's friends would visit us; brothers of my sister Nur's women friends would stop by, or the son of one of Papa's friends. On one occasion my parents announced that a university professor and his family were coming for a visit. Mother told me to make myself attractive and be nice to the people.

"He's a fine man," she said. "You should give him a chance!"

I had no idea who they were and didn't want to know. I wasn't feeling well and did not appear to welcome them. That evening my parents and I had a serious quarrel. Papa was furious. What was I thinking of to be so impolite? The man had felt humiliated in front of everybody.

"And what about me? Am I just some kind of merchandise at a bazaar?" The accusations flew back and forth until we finally had nothing more to say and grew silent. Then I explained as calmly as I could, "I'm not yet ready for marriage. I haven't met the right man." I simply wanted to continue my studies. "Can't you accept that?" There was still plenty of time for marriage.

Mama finally threw up her hands. "Do what you want!"

But Papa remained obstinate. "You're not flying off to Vienna. Not with my blessing!" It was our tradition that without my father's permission I couldn't go. And Papa wouldn't allow any further discussion of the matter. But naturally word of our quarrel got around within the family. A few days later my uncle Mohamed was sitting in the living room with my father. He was then vice president of Cairo University and responsible there for the training of outstanding students and the awarding of stipends. "You have to let Wafaa go," I heard him say. "The Austrian government awards two stipends each year to directors of Egypt's antiquities administration—a generous gift. The antiquities service is unable to come up with such assistance out of its own funds. We work very hard to provide stipends for our students. If Wafaa has been awarded one, she has to accept it. We cannot afford to refuse such an offer." Furthermore, he had every confidence that I would make a success of myself in Vienna. "If you won't allow her to go, I'll adopt her. Then she can go with my permission." Papa gave in.

On June 5, 1979, I landed in Vienna for what proved to be much longer than six months. I would be living in a student residence hall, the Jägerhorn, in the 1st District. It would be the first time I had ever lived on my own, and it was my first student dorm. At first I was concerned. I had heard that the rooms were very small and dark, also that students were housed two to a room. But it turned out to be very different. The residence hall was one of the university's oldest, a venerable structure from the late nineteenth century: a lovely, large room with a parquet floor, high ceiling, several windows, very bright and pleasant. My assigned Cypriot roommate had chosen to live with her boyfriend, and kept the room only as an official address to give to her parents. So I was doubly fortunate: I had a very beautiful room for myself and had to pay only half the rent.

The six-story residence hall was a whole new world for me. The director, Herr Manafi, was a political exile from Iran. My fellow residents came from all over the world, including Syrian Kurds and Iraqis and other fugitives from tyranny at home. They would talk a lot about politics, and naturally Anwar Sadat's name would come up. They couldn't understand why the West courted such an autocrat. To them Sadat had betrayed the Palestinians with the peace treaty. And in Egypt as well, the rage and discontent were unmistakable. It was almost palpable that something was brewing against Sadat. He himself was behaving with increasing nervousness, was arresting intellectuals, journalists, and writers like Mohamed Heikal. After the news of Sadat's assassination, some of my fellow residents declared their relief: "One less Near Eastern tyrant!"

There were also scholars from China and South Korea, from India, Nepal, Latin America, Ethiopia, Jamaica. Contacts in the dorm, our shared time cooking in the kitchen, our evening get-togethers, and our visits to Vienna's wonderful coffeehouses greatly enriched my understanding of different peoples, customs, traditions, and political conditions. Whenever I would talk to them about Egypt, I would get homesick. And it was too expensive to talk to my parents and siblings in Cairo by telephone very often. But there were people who comforted me. Two were Dr. Motaza Khater, the director of the Cultural Department of the Egyptian Embassy, and cultural attaché Ferial Saker, both of whom I met in their offices on my second day there. We instantly bonded. In the coming weeks, months, years, they fussed over me like siblings: whether I was eating properly, getting enough sleep, and how was my work progressing.

I first met Professor Helmut Satzinger in the Kunsthistorisches Museum. I first saw only his feet. He was lying in his gray smock under a display case that he was apparently repairing in the best of spirits. I heard him call, "One moment, please, I'm almost finished." I was puzzled. A museum director in a laborer's smock—and under a cabinet? What a contrast to our directors at home, who lived behind closed office doors. Satzinger relished his work, tackled things himself, and maintained a relaxed relationship with his team. How very different from our own supervisors, who lorded it over everybody. I learned a lot from Satzinger, not only professionally, but also about how to deal with colleagues and workers. During my time at the Egyptian Museum I tried to follow his example, and not without success, I feel. In any case, I could see the astonishment in the eyes of my fellow directors, who were being shown that you can achieve things quicker if you get involved yourself, and that it can be fun as well.

As it happened, I didn't get off to a particularly good start with Satzinger. I was supposed to be an observer in his department for five months. Satzinger was an institution, a very busy Egyptologist with an international reputation. He spoke fluent Arabic and knew various Egyptian dialects in addition to a number of ancient and modern languages. When I introduced myself to him, he said, quite formally, "How nice to have you here. I hope you enjoy your time with us. But unfortunately I won't have much time for you myself."

I had been euphoric about coming to Vienna, and now I had suffered a first letdown. "Very well, I'm here to study. As far as I'm concerned, I can start right away." I later learned that it was because Satzinger hated to be bothered by Egyptian stipend scholars needing something translated. My colleagues had overly exploited his kindness and his knowledge of languages.

I spent my first few days in the museum's library. It didn't escape me that I was being observed by Satzinger and his assistants. Finally, he took a seat next to me and asked me about my work. I showed him my notes on Thery's tomb and my studies comparing it with the Saïte-era tombs on the Giza plateau. That appeared to interest him. He fetched various books, led me to display cases in the museum, and devoted attention and time to my studies. One day I asked him what he thought of the idea of writing a comparative study of several tombs from the Twenty-sixth Dynasty in the Giza area. He was taken with the idea. I told him that my Cairo certificates would be recognized by the University of Vienna, that there was no reason why I couldn't do my doctoral work there. Satzinger replied that the acceptance requirements also imposed other conditions. He asked whether I was prepared to learn Latin, for example, for without Latin, I wouldn't be allowed to take my examination. I would also have to present two additional minor studies. If I were willing to take all that on, he would be happy to serve as my 'doctor father.' I should think it over. I don't need to, I told him. But what I needed was a scholarship. When Satzinger saw that I was serious, he helped me fill out the many application forms. He wrote a recommendation, and in a surprisingly short time I was assured by the Austrian Ministry of Education of a two-year doctoral scholarship. I was exultant: two years in Vienna! And now I had to console my parents with an explanation of my extended absence.

When I now look back on my total of four years in Vienna, they seem to me endlessly filled with memories and experiences. It was an exciting, intense, and very strenuous time. At first I had money for only two years and hoped to finish everything within that time, so I couldn't waste a minute or dawdle. In addition to my major subject, Egyptology, and my Latin courses, I enrolled in seminars in two minors: philosophy and Arabic. Why had my mother urged me to speak and read standard Arabic if it was not going to help me pass my minor examinations without a lot of effort? But I hadn't calculated on Professor Arne A. Ambros. Ambros, originally a physicist, taught Arabic with the meticulousness of a scientist, and it was no walk in the park. I came to recognize that I had no notion of Arabic. In fact I was studying a completely new language that was as complicated as quantum mechanics. I didn't allow myself any time off, which was unwise, for I wore myself out, and several times landed in a clinic. Johanna Holaubeck, from the Institute for Egyptology, touchingly worried about me, and to this day she is like a sister to me. I finally was incapable of finishing in two years. My health simply wouldn't allow it.

There were wonderful moments in Vienna, like the joy of the first snow. When I stepped to the window one morning I looked out at a transformed, somehow radiant darkness. White flakes were drifting downward, dancing in front of my window, and landing on roofs, trees, streets, and sidewalks. In the night a thick, soft layer of cotton had settled on the 1st District, and all the street noises were muted. I remembered Father's telling us about snow when as children we would play in the soft, white mountains of cotton. I stuck my hands into the first snow of my life. Up to that time I had known snow only from movies or television. It was unbelievably beautiful, and what I most wanted to do was immediately phone my parents and my siblings: "Snow! Just imagine, it's snowing!" But then I realized that in my Egyptian shoes I wouldn't even make it to the nearest telephone office. My toes were already freezing. My excitement about the snow didn't last so very long. I froze miserably in those winter months. I was soon yearning for the sun above the pyramid plateau.

Vienna is an open-air museum. I loved the city, and I learned to know it much better than my budget would have permitted. Motaza Khater asked me whether I would like to occasionally accompany guests of official Egyptian missions around the city. She knew that I had some experience in dealing with state visitors. So I got to experience Vienna's cultural offerings: the Burgtheater, the Opera, the museums, all the wonderful historic buildings, palaces, and parks. With several Egyptian summer visitors I drove to Salzburg and Innsbruck. We visited cities and villages in Upper Austria, and I was awestruck by the mountains: Grossglockner, Hoher Dachstein, and the turquoise-blue lakes in snow-covered mountain landscapes. I went ice skating on frozen lakes, explored ice caves, and marveled at icicles that looked liked giant church organs. I enjoyed all those outings enormously, and think of them still today as precious gifts.

In Vienna I had a small, but to this day very devoted, circle of friends. There were my professors and colleagues in the museum and in the Institute for Egyptology. But there were also my two Egyptian friends in the residence hall. What a pair! Adiela el-Saadi was from a village near Luxor and was studying chemistry. She spoke the southern Egyptian Saidi dialect. Menu Raghib couldn't understand it. She spoke more French than Arabic, came from Alexandria, and was studying music. The two were too funny: It was as if a native Berliner were trying to make himself understood by a native Bavarian. I would translate for them, and we would spend delightful weekends together, often doubled over with laughter. Adiela became a professor at Aswan University and later dean of the Chemistry Faculty. Menu became a music professor at Cairo's Art Academy.

The residence hall was scheduled for renovation, so for a few months we had to evacuate. I sublet a room from a Frau Pflegshörl, an elderly lady and former opera singer who loved to tell me about her father, Emperor Franz Josef's personal physician. She lived near the Belvedere Palace in a beautiful old building on Goldeggasse. Not a day went by without classical music. Frau Pflegshörl placed great store on etiquette, including at mealtime. She set the table with old silver and fine porcelain. She never lapsed into Viennese dialect, so I too spoke only High German. She liked telling me that everything had been better in the past. "Children simply had greater respect for their parents." She spoke of her mother as Frau Mutter and her father as Herr Vater, and naturally she had addressed both of them formally. "I don't at all like hearing people use 'Du' with each other so soon. You know that it is much easier to come out with '*Du* fool' than with '*Sie* fool.'" But a shadow lay over Frau Pflegshörl's life. Her only daughter had suddenly left home twenty years before and had never written to her since. It was as if she had simply vanished. There were some days on which Frau Pflegshörl spoke very little, yet others on which I clearly sensed how much she thought of me as her substitute daughter. She was extremely saddened when I moved back to the residence hall. She tried to talk me into staying: I could continue to live with her for nothing. She did not understand that I simply couldn't concentrate there. If I was reading, she would stand next to me; if I was writing, she would say something. It nearly broke my heart to have to do it to her, but it simply didn't work. But I would visit her regularly and take her dog Blacky for walks in the palace park. Once I was back in Egypt I invited her to visit us, and she actually came and stayed for four weeks. When my older son Tarek was born in Cologne she wanted desperately to see him. But by then she was very old and sick. Her caretaker warned me that the trip to Cologne could be too much of a strain on her. It could even kill her. So I was supposed to tell her not to come. But I couldn't simply disappoint her, so she came, very old, very sick, but overjoyed at being able to see Tarek and me. Frau Pflegshörl died a few months later. We never addressed each other as "Du."

I would regularly attend cultural events at the embassy, even at the express wish of the diplomats. One day the cultural attaché begged me to write him an article on ancient Egypt on the occasion of the opening of a presentation, which I was glad to do. The evening of the opening I was astonished: My text was read by the ambassador. The cultural adviser had assigned the lecture to the cultural attaché, who in turn delegated it to me, but without telling me so. I had to laugh. There in Vienna I was encountering the Egyptian system that I had so often observed in the antiquities administration and would do again later in the governmental bureaucracy: The lowest official does the work, which his director passes on to the minister, who submits it to the prime minister, who ultimately presents it to Mubarak as his own. I often noticed work that wasn't credited to the person who had originated it but was rather adorned with a false signature.

Going to the university in the morning and back home at night, I would meet other Egyptians: young men in thin clothing and a plastic overcoat emblazoned with the name of the newspaper they were selling mornings or evenings on a breezy streetcorner. They would stand there shivering in thin shoes. Seeing them made me sad and thoughtful. Each of them had his own history. Each of them was trying to put Egypt behind him, yet carried it with him into exile. Often several of them lived together in a tiny apartment, sharing beds in shifts, one using it during the day, the other at night. I later encountered the same faces elsewhere. In New York they stand on street-corners selling hot dogs. In Rome they move from restaurant to restaurant with roses—young men, some of them engineers, doctors, lawyers. Egypt strikes me as a country that expels its children. We lose its best minds. For many under Mubarak their only chance at a better-paying job was to pay a bribe to a contact. And in that way people poorly qualified but with money managed to get positions. Others put themselves and their families hopelessly in debt. They then had to exploit their jobs to somehow recover the money. Thus the floodgates were wide open for corruption.

Other experiences impressed me, given that Austria is so fixated on titles and protocol. In Vienna, and later in Germany, I saw how people treated each other with respect, regardless of their social status or professional position. For me, and for many of my fellow residents in the dorm, this was by no means a matter of course. For example, Austria's president, Rudolf Kirchschläger, came to the philosophy lectures I was attending. Without any security guard, he would sit among us students, listen attentively, take notes, and after the lecture chat with us completely without ceremony. He would even invite foreign students to the Hofburg, guide us through its rooms, and relate delicious anecdotes from the time of the empire. I too got to talk with Kirchschläger.

"Where are you from?" he asked.

"I'm from Egypt, from Cairo."

"And what are you studying here?"

"I'm studying Egyptology."

Kirchschläger laughed and clapped his hands. "An Egyptian woman studying Egyptology with us here in Vienna? *Donnerwetter*!"

"Yes," I replied. "You not only have an outstanding professorship, in the Kunsthistorisches Museum you also have an extraordinary Egyptian collection."

Kirchschläger was very well informed. "And do you know what's the best thing about it? It all came to us perfectly legally. Archduke Maximilian had been given it. We didn't steal it." Kirchschläger was altogether unpretentious and modest. I found Federal President Heinz Fischer, whom in later years I would guide through the Egyptian Museum in Cairo with his wife, to be the same. On the occasion of the opening of the Tutankhamun exhibit in Vienna, they invited my husband Azmy and me to the Hofburg. We were thrilled to recognize that they had extended the invitation in all sincerity.

I always enjoyed telling my friends and acquaintances at home about such encounters whenever once again thousands of security police and soldiers would block off Cairo's main traffic arteries for Mubarak, for the prime minister, or one of his many ministers. That was by no means uncommon; they were constant nuisances with which the population of Cairo and Alexandria were humiliated. To the regime it was totally immaterial that people regularly died in ambulances because they had to wait for hours for a convoy and couldn't get to the hospital on time; that women had to give birth to babies in taxis because Mubarak's caravan of limousines made them wait. You could write a book about all that happened or failed to happen because of, and during, such endless waiting: unrealized chances lost, difficulties unnecessarily encountered because you were stuck in a government traffic jam.

My Vienna stipend wasn't enough; I also had to make money. Professor Satzinger offered me a job in the museum's storeroom. As a scholarly assistant I helped with the storeroom inventory and documentation of its holdings. As an inspector I had worked at excavation sites, and in the Boat Museum gained documentation experience, but I did not yet have practical experience in how an important collection is maintained. In Tura I had dealt with canopic jars from the Middle Kingdom. But now there were vessels from every epoch. I came in contact, in every sense of the word, with precious antiquities that I measured, described, and cataloged. During that time I gathered important experience that would be of great use to me twenty years later in the huge depot of the Egyptian Museum.

Finally there was the traditional closing celebration in the Great Hall of the university. I had slogged through Arabic, crammed in Latin, written examinations, and faced orals—but nothing gave me greater jitters than the few Latin phrases I was supposed to recite before the university rector as he passed out diplomas to the new doctors. I learned the sentences by heart and could recite them in my sleep, yet the idea of having to deliver them in front of all those people made me incredibly nervous. I calmed down only once I saw that all the other students around me were just as nervous. We were twenty graduates, Austrians and foreigners. The dean and his assistants were wearing their historic academic robes. The hall in which such ceremonies had been celebrated for centuries was filled with professors, students, their families, and friends. Among them was my father. He had come from Cairo and was very proud. There was Frau Pflegshörl, who smiled most aristocratically. And there was Helmut Satzinger, who nodded at me in recognition. There were Motaza Khater from the Egyptian Cultural Office, and her colleagues from the embassy, people from the Kunsthistorisches Museum, and Johanna Holaubeck from the Institute for Egyptology. They arranged so many congratulatory parties that my room in the Jägerhorn came to look like a flower shop. One piece of news made me especially proud. I received it shortly before my departure for Cairo: The University of Vienna was going to publish my doctoral thesis.

I know that readers quickly skip over acknowledgments and dedications in books and dissertations. Many see them as only thanks an author is obliged to extend to his or her sponsors and supporters. I felt then, and I still feel today, more than thirty years after my studies in Vienna, extreme gratitude to my host country Austria, to Helmut Satzinger, and to my professors Manfred Bietak, Dieter Arnold, and Dorothea Arnold, later director of the Department of Egyptian Art of the Metropolitan Museum in New York. Why have we become who we are today? Where would I be today? Who would I be had there not been people at that time who encouraged and supported me? I had the good fortune to meet people who took me seriously without regard to my country of origin, my religion, or my status. Without them and the Austrian stipend, my life would have taken a different course. It is always a lovely feeling to return to Vienna and once again see the people who have become my friends. Each visit only reminds me to do what I can to see that other young people have a similar experience.

6

THE TOUGH WOMEN
OF LUXOR

I had been in Vienna for four years. In late November 1983 I returned to Cairo. I was thirty-three years old and looking forward to seeing my family, my friends, and my colleagues—and the sun. But Cairo gave me a chill. The people had changed, as had my views about Egypt. In four years the atmosphere had palpably worsened. I would open familiar doors and encounter different people. Everywhere there was a different spirit.

Hosni Mubarak had been in power since October 1981. At first he had announced reforms, and even allowed greater freedoms to the opposition and the press. But the people's hopes were soon crushed. Mubarak continued the so-called liberalization course imposed by the International Monetary Fund and the World Bank as a condition for the credits that shored up his regime. At the same time, Egypt's markets were opened to a flood of foreign goods, which meant that domestic products were either scorned or could not compete in price—in 1990 manufacturers in the former East Germany would have a similar experience. But those who managed to obtain marketing and production licenses for international consumer goods were cleaning up.

Years before, in one of his speeches, Sadat had proclaimed that anyone who failed to get rich under his aegis never would. But he surely hadn't meant enrich yourselves—at your countrymen's expense! Sadat had gone on to say that only those who were ready to work harder would gain wealth. Under Mubarak that clarification was completely forgotten. Quite the opposite became the norm, especially for young people born since 1981—and today they are two-thirds of Egypt's population: It isn't by working that you can rise out of your social misery, but by being shrewd and unscrupulous. Corruption—a contempt for justice, legality, decency, and dignity—came to be seen as a ruthless recipe for success. Anyone who couldn't sit inside the limousines roaring ever onward with the successful ones had to lie and dissemble if they wanted to get ahead, or at the very least ride on the running boards. Because a person could see from others' success how deeply mired he or she still was in the swamp, people lost respect for each other: a creeping but dangerous process of social erosion.

You quickly learn to recognize shiftiness and greed in the eyes of the person you're talking to, in the corners of their mouth, even in their laugh. I had seen how this spirit had spread over the decades, in ministries, administrations, courts, the police and security services, in private enterprise. It infected all classes, the nouveaux riches as well as the little people, in whom this national sickness produced the sour stench of fear, bitterness, and aggression. This is the true legacy of the Mubarak era—a poison that corrupted entire peoples.

Father related how his good nature and readiness to help had lost him a piece of land. A farmer had begged him to be allowed to skip his rent payments for a while because of poor harvests and his financial straits. Father was kind enough to accommodate him for a few months, just as his father had done in similar situations. But the man used the time to falsify papers and to claim to the authorities that the land was his own—based on the fact that the owner had for so long failed to exercise his right to rent from it that he had thereby forfeited it. Father was not so upset about the loss of his land as about the farmer's wickedness and the compliance of the judges who allowed him to get away with it.

And then there was Mona, my replacement in the Boat Museum. I had made an agreement with the antiquities administration that after my return

I would resume my role as director. But she—and her husband—had no intention of surrendering her position. She underscored her importance by flourishing a doctor's degree, the authenticity and source of which, astonishingly, no one in the antiquities service bothered to question. I decided to fight for my job.

I presented myself to Ahmed Qadri, the new head of the antiquities administration. I had not yet met him, but had heard of him. Like so many former military men who made careers in the civil administration, he had the reputation of being a hot-tempered, unpredictable man. In 1952 Qadri was the youngest of the Free Officers around Nasser. Like Hosni Mubarak, he had been an Air Force pilot and was accustomed to issuing orders in a commanding tone. But I was surprised: Qadri's office was in a rather modest apartment building in the Bab al-Luq quarter. His predecessors had lived at luxurious addresses, shielded by an entourage of security and office personnel. Qadri employed only a receptionist. His greeting was cordial. He congratulated me on my doctorate.

After an exchange of civilities, I got to the point. "I want my old job back."

Qadri showed no surprise, but gently responded with a counter-suggestion: "I would like to make you another offer. I can't see you in the Boat Museum. I see you here at the head of the antiquities administration's Museums Department. But I leave the choice up to you. Alternatively, I'll offer you the post of director of the Egyptian Museum. Now what do say?"

I was almost speechless and initially had no idea how to respond, but I held firm in my frontal attack on Mona: "I'm sorry, I can't accept either offer. I want to be back in the Boat Museum!" Qadri was annoyed, and gestured that he didn't understand. I said, "I'm still too young for either position, too inexperienced. Also, in Vienna I prepared myself for the direction of the Boat Museum. I studied the problems of restoration and developed ideas about a new museum concept. I want my old position back."

I then got to experience what others had warned me about: Qadri, the man with the hot temper. All of a sudden the man who had previously been so gentle became angry and loud. He screamed at me, "You can't be serious. I offer you the directorship of the largest and most important museum in the country, oversight over all the museums in the antiquities service, and you insist on a little museum with only a single object. That's childish! Sheer stupidity!"

I stubbornly replied, "That object is as important to me as the Egyptian Museum."

Qadri jumped up and, red with rage, told me our appointment had ended. He would consider how to proceed.

Depressed, and with my whole body trembling, I made my way home. I had lost all along the line. I had disappointed the head of the antiquities administration. I had made myself impossible, and Mona had won. I then had the sudden suspicion: Qadri is somehow covering for Mona! I began to imagine all manner of conspiracy scenarios—but finally caught myself and decided to reconsider carefully what Qadri had said. Why would he offer me two responsible positions when at worst he could have simply humiliated me and made me Mona's assistant? Suddenly it came to me: Qadri was right. From his point of view a colleague who had continued her education abroad for four years would have been misplaced in a position that actually required a restorer like Hagg Ahmed instead of an archaeologist. I phoned Qadri the next day. I thanked him for his offer, and asked for time to consider it. Qadri sounded conciliatory. We scheduled a new appointment.

As a returning stipend recipient, I was allowed some time off before I had to get back to work. I needed that time to make a number of trips to the administration and to rest, for the weeks leading up to my Vienna exams had exhausted me. Moreover, something was waiting for me at the port in Alexandria: my car! On the advice of colleagues, in Vienna I had bought a small second-hand Peugeot. As a student I could import it duty-free. I had sent the car, packed full of books and souvenirs, to Genoa, and it had been shipped from there to Alexandria. Now, finally, there would no longer be tedious bus and train rides out to Giza; I could drive myself.

I turned to my brother Mohamed, who had acquaintances in Alexandria. One of them advised engaging a professional agent to take care of customs clearance at the port. That would shorten the bureaucratic process. But first we showed up at the customs office in Alexandria ourselves. The car wasn't there, we were told, and we should come back later. We returned to Cairo empty-handed. We then phoned the agent, who reported back a week later: The car is now there, we should come to Alexandria immediately.

I naturally had no idea of how customs affairs are conducted. So Father and I drove off, fully assuming that I would be back that evening with my own car. It was a rainy day. Father took the Agricultural Road, for the faster Desert Road was known for its high risk of accidents—farmers simply crossing the road with their herds. It took us five hours, and we reached Alexandria only in the afternoon, too late to show up at the port customs office. We drove on to my uncle's summer house, which was right on the sea near Sidi Bishr. The wind was blowing hard, and the waves were pounding so loudly that on that December night we hardly slept. The next morning we set out early. Again an overcast, rainy day. The sea was crashing against the cliffs and water splashing up onto the coast road. At customs we met our agent, carrying a number of files under his arm. It was clear that we were not his only clients. The man gave us our papers back and instructed us to wait at the quay where ships from Genoa docked. He would meet us there in an hour. He asked for his fee and trotted off. Father suggested that paying him in advance was perhaps a mistake.

The port is a world of its own, a city for giants. The tall cranes, the towering hulls of ships from all over the world, the air reeking of gas and benzene, the ground an oozing, oil-shimmering, muddy, rainswept tract. The perfect setting for a gangster film, with policemen chasing after bands of smugglers and other riffraff. Father and I were freezing. Two hours passed. Then our agent reappeared. Nothing could be done today. The ship wasn't yet completely unloaded. We would meet again at the same time the next morning. Before we had a chance to ask any questions, the man raced away. We never saw him again.

We spent another sleepless night in the summer house, the wind roaring outside, and the next day appeared punctually at the quay. We waited for four hours. Our man was nowhere in sight. Instead, we had to witness an increasingly vociferous and aggressive quarrel between the dockworkers. It turned into a fistfight, and some of them even drew out knives. We stood to one side, frightened, until the men finally separated, threatening and cursing each other. Finally a customs official showed up, but he claimed not to know our agent. Other customs officials were hurrying about with businesspeople. Father felt that it was clear that here it was the parties with deep pockets who were handled first. Apparently it was only possible to speed up your own case with an attractive baksheesh.

"I won't pay a bribe," Father said. "Absolutely not."

We stood there and waited, dejected, and with no idea what to do next. Suddenly a police officer confronted us and asked if we had a problem. I explained to him that our 'agent' had left us in the lurch, that we now had no one to talk to and had no idea how to proceed. The officer took my papers and handed them to a subordinate, who immediately went to the customs official. They stared over at us suspiciously. Apparently they thought that the officer was an acquaintance of ours or a relative; in any case, the papers were promptly stamped. Now things moved quickly: The officer disappeared, but soon returned and asked me to identify my car among those standing on the quay. I recognized it from afar. My light blue Peugeot! *Al-hamdulillah*! But my joy was soon squelched: Everything I had packed into the car, except for the books, was gone. Even the car's battery. What remained was only the car's skeleton. Everything that wasn't welded or bolted down had been stripped off. It had all happened in Genoa, we were told. The officer saw how shocked I was and explained—small comfort—that this sort of thing happened there every day. I should now at least sign the papers so I could take possession of what was left of my vehicle. I was supposed to trust him and come back early in the morning.

Father and I spent a third sleepless night in a cold summer house next to a stormy sea. The next day the officer was actually waiting at the appointed time and at the spot agreed upon—with my fully restored Peugeot. The man laughed. "Here at port customs there are any number of cars standing around. Their owners have never shown up." Presumably those owners no longer had the money to pay the import duty. In any case, among them was another Peugeot from which the port staff had helped themselves. I should just check to see that everything had been replaced, even the battery. I could drive away immediately. Father and I were speechless. But before we could thank the man he had disappeared. We didn't even know his name. Father insisted on waiting until he showed up again so he could properly thank him. But our officer and gentleman was gone. I have often had such experiences: There are truly many decent, helpful people. But their help only confirms the general rule, that nothing can be done without connections.

After all that I didn't really get any pleasure out of my car. For years I had been driven by Father, then by Umran, had been swept through traffic in taxis or buses. In Vienna I had passed my written and road driver's tests—but at home I failed miserably. Other vehicles would cross in front of me only millimeters from my hood, pedestrians suddenly pop up in the middle of my lane, unlit donkey carts loom up in the dark of night. No one used turn signals, everybody honked, sped up, suddenly stopped, held me up, squeezed in front of me. There were no rules; only the most brazen had the right of way. Every trip affected my nerves, which are sensitive at best. Sometimes my hands would be swollen from having gripped the steering wheel so tightly. Barely a year later I sold the car to my younger brother Kamel. Since then I have never again sat behind the wheel of a car in Egypt.

My nerves truly were affected. I would react to stress and noise with shortness of breath. Doctors and friends advised me to take it easy. Dear colleagues of mine told me, "Maybe you shouldn't get so upset about everything that has happened here, and accept a scholarly position at the university or in the museum." When I showed up for my second appointment with Ahmed Qadri, I had a splitting headache. But Qadri was sympathetic. "I know how much you love the Boat Museum and the pyramid plateau, but I need you for a more important job. How would it be if you were to take over the direction of the scholarly office in the antiquities service? I need someone to edit our magazine *The World of Archaeology*. We had to discontinue it after only two issues. Apparently it was too much for our people."

Basically I was prepared for anything, but please not an office right next to Qadri, a loud man with a temper. "I'd really like to excavate again. I'm somewhat run down. Working in the sun, in the fresh air, in contact with our workers, would be good for me."

Qadri didn't explode this time; instead he smiled. "I'm not offering you an office job. You won't be simply sitting around here. You'll travel all around Egypt and follow every dig from a scholar's point of view. I've been wondering for a long time who I could entrust such a job to, and I'm convinced that you're the right person. You learned a great deal in Vienna. You know foreign languages. You'll whip the magazine into shape. So what do you think?"

It was a wonderful offer. Qadri again gave me time to consider it, and I quickly determined that it was a dream job. I would travel all over Egypt from the Mediterranean coast down as far as Abu Simbel, from the Red Sea to the oases in the Western Desert. I would get to know places in parts of the country completely unknown to me, inspect tomb complexes closed to the public—tombs full of snakes and scorpions, with plundered mummies and jumbled piles of bones. I would write articles about the work of Egyptian and foreign missions. *The World of Archaeology* would reach all the Egyptologists in the antiquities administration and keep them informed about excavations, research, and restoration projects. It was the first Arabic archaeological journal. I would translate synopses into English. I would be working as an archaeologist and as a journalist—just as I had always wanted to.

And I got to know Ahmed Qadri better. The former pilot had given up a promising military career in order to study ancient Egyptian, Coptic, and Islamic history. He had earned his doctorate on the armed forces of ancient Egypt. But the medication he was taking for his advanced diabetes must have needed adjustment. That was why his behavior was occasionally rude and violent, for which he would always humbly apologize. From my office next door I would often hear him loudly railing at somebody. I had little contact with him myself; he let me work. I got to know Qadri as a man who couldn't be intimidated by either ministers or military men, not even by his former flying colleague Hosni Mubarak. Qadri's apartment was a meeting place for intellectuals, journalists, and scholars, and I knew that he had made dangerous enemies with his impulsive way of saying openly what he thought of someone. It had already brought him prison time under Nasser.

There is no question but that Qadri can be credited with being the first antiquities chief to recognize that ancient sites needed to be protected against environmental pollution, urbanization, and mass tourism. He introduced immediate measures. We are indebted to him for any number of preservation efforts carried out with international know-how and money he enlisted. Qadri's name will always be linked to the restoration of many Islamic and Coptic monuments, among them Salah al-Din's Citadel in Cairo and the Qaitbay Citadel in Alexandria. Many hundreds of young people were given employment in those projects. They learned to invest themselves in their cultural heritage. Qadri also had their work documented on film and aired on Egyptian television, which helped to increase the population's appreciation of ancient sites.

I had the good fortune of being allowed to inspect many of those restoration measures. I remember the beautiful fortress on the Gezirat el-Faraon,

Pharaoh's Island, in the blue Gulf of Aqaba, one of the most beautiful places I know. Or an evening stroll near Saint Catherine's Monastery at the foot of Mount Sinai. Anyone who has ever gazed up into the starry sky above the Sinai knows that it is a place where heaven and earth meet. I can understand why Anwar Sadat used to go there to meditate. He loved the peace and seclusion of the place. His successor Mubarak preferred the seaside resort Sharm el-Sheikh.

Qadri asked me to oversee the restoration of tomb TT 34 in Luxor—the tomb of Montemhet. TT 34 stands for "Theban Tombs No. 34." It is the second-largest private tomb complex in al-Assasif, the projecting mountain range on the west side of the Nile. The antiquities administration wanted to clear the interior of sand and debris and restore the wall reliefs. The inhabitants of the famous village of Qurna, which stands atop the tombs of al-Assasif, refer to the tomb as Bab al-Affena. Bab, or gate, because of the round-arch entrance in the first of its imposing aboveground pylons, and al-Affena because of the absolutely unbearable stench in the tomb's interior. Bats nested in it for centuries and left behind the choking smell of ammonia from their guano. The stench is so strong that it kept even the inhabitants of the village at bay—but not the desecrators of the tomb. The treasures of Thebes's wealthy administrators from the time of the Twenty-fifth and Twenty-sixth Dynasties were too tempting.

Montemhet was the mayor of Thebes and the fourth priest of the god Amun under the Kushite king Taharqa. He directed the construction of the Nubian pharaoh's additions to the Temple of Karnak. Even during the Assyrian invasions under King Asarhaddon, he seems to have had the territory around Thebes firmly under his control. A cylinder seal from the reign of King Assurbanipal calls him 'Lord of the God's State,' which at that time presumably extended from Aswan in the south to Hermopolis Magna in the north.

His tomb consists of an upper structure with gigantic mud-brick pylons and a large underground complex: a forecourt with tall columns, a large atrium, and roughly fifty chambers and corridors. The atrium walls are decorated with exquisite lotus blossom reliefs. But the restoration of the tomb complex was a mammoth task. Like many other tombs in al-Assasif—for example the huge neighboring tomb of Petamenopet, TT 33—Montemhet's complex had suffered greatly from earthquakes and intrusions of rainwater. Many of the seemingly endless wall reliefs had blistered or been chiseled out by tomb robbers. They cut scenes apart in order to be able to sell them more readily. For that reason Montemhet's reliefs can now be seen in many of the world's museums and private collections. Our most important job was to remove the debris and carefully sort through it for any remaining fragments of the ceiling and wall decor, which needed to be replaced in the reliefs. I marveled at the resourcefulness of our workers, watched how patiently they collected even the tiniest pieces, identified their original positions on the walls, and restored them to their proper places. It was a giant puzzle, but our people seemed to enjoy it. Especially as they saw that with me as Qadri's representative, their work was being scrupulously inspected. Today the tomb is one of the most beautifully restored monuments in al-Assasif, even though its restoration is by no means finished.

Once while feeling my way through the dark corridors of the labyrinth and waiting for my eyes to adjust to the gloom, in a side room I suddenly felt something strange beneath my feet. Something was being crushed under my shoes. A worker rushed over and shone a light on the floor: I was standing in the middle of a mass grave. Dozens of skeletons! Apparently in later epochs the tomb was used as an ossuary. Perhaps even after wholesale deaths from an epidemic? I felt terrible. When I entered the tomb again after a lunch break, I suddenly lost my balance, tripped, and broke my right foot. For weeks I was confined in a plaster cast in Cairo, but the workers regularly called me, wishing me a swift recovery.

One day during my weeks in Luxor, Sheikh Abdel Sattar came to me. He complained that the antiquities administration wanted to tear down his shop in Qurna, which stood on the way to the Tomb of Vizier Ramose. But he made his living from it, selling cold drinks and souvenirs. I explained to him that I could be of no help; he had built his shop in an unauthorized spot, and there was nothing I could do. I was lying encased in plaster at home in Cairo when my father once came to me and announced, "There's a man from Luxor out there. His name is Sheikh Abdel Sattar, and he says you wouldn't help him with the building of his mosque."

"What kind of mosque? It's an illegal shop!"

The sheikh from Qurna was seated in the living room. He explained that he had built a small mosque around his shop. No one can tear down a mosque, he said, and if I didn't help him now Allah would punish me! When I explained that I saw no possibility of supporting him, he left our apartment in a rage.

Father looked at me uncomprehendingly. "How can you consent to the destruction of a mosque? Where are people supposed to pray?"

"But Papa, the man is a charlatan. The people will pray outdoors as they always have, and go to the great mosque on Friday. He only built it so we couldn't tear down his shop!"

Back in Qurna I visited Abdel Sattar's new house of prayer. It was empty, no worshippers at any hour. But the clever fox had prevailed.

The village of Qurna is legendary for its tomb robbers. For centuries, possibly even millennia, its farmers and cowherds have lived at the edge of the fertile bank of the Nile, on which they have tended to their fields. They built their houses mainly atop or inside ancient tomb complexes. Often enough they lived in tombs' spacious corridors and vaults, cooked and slept in their chambers, and in the hot summer months sheltered their flocks in them. They would dig in every direction beneath their houses into adjacent tombs, whose treasures they then plundered and sold to tourists and collectors. Their houses had neither electricity nor running water; they were shabby, but also picturesque. They have been captured in countless historical paintings and photographs. Many of their houses, even the entire village ensemble, could rightly have been placed under monument protection or listed as a World Heritage Site. But under Luxor's governor Samir Farag, the houses were torn down and the people resettled, just as in Luxor's old town, to be able to uncover the ancient avenue of sphinxes between the Karnak and Luxor temples so as to create a mile-long promenade for strolling tourists, a swath was cut straight through the city. It was a part of the city that was no showplace, to be sure, but people had their homes there. The ruthlessness with which Luxor's governor carried out this 'redevelopment program' and his resettlement of people with inadequate compensation hurt any number of families, and only sowed rage and hatred.

In the winter of 1984, Ahmed Qadri asked me into his office. He wanted to introduce Diane Smith, an attractive blonde American, well-to-do, a go-getter and lover of Egypt who, together with a group of other women, wished to finance and undertake an excavation in Karnak. Qadri explained to me in Arabic, "You are to direct the project. Pick another two or three female Egyptologists." The team was to be made up solely of women. The American laywomen would only use electromagnetic sensors, and we would make selective excavation soundings. I asked where and what was to be excavated in Karnak. A French mission was working in the Amun Temple, Karnak's great main temple; archaeologists from the Brooklyn Museum were digging in the Mut Temple; and next to them were Canadians. The terrain seemed fairly crowded. Qadri told me that they had selected a site in south Karnak, an area of roughly eight hectares between the Amun and Mut temples that could be easily seen from the Amun Temple's tenth pylon. In 1984 that area next to the avenue of sphinxes was actually terra incognita in terms of archaeology. In front of the temple's gate there were still the remains of two colossal statues of Amenhotep III, the father of Akhenaten. Qadri felt that it would be interesting to discover what the twenty-meter quartzite colossi had looked down upon around the year 1360 BC, what was hidden beneath the surface.

In the spring of 1985 I came to know the other four women from Aspen, Colorado's famous ski resort: Mary Martin, a painter and art dealer; Audrey Topping, a photographer and writer; Betje Carlson, a former skeet-shooting champion; and her sister Gypsy Grave, previously a riding teacher and now director of a private archaeological museum in Florida. Diane Smith was the most glamorous of the five, a former *Life* and *Time* cover girl, television starlet, and member of the Rockettes, the famous dance ensemble at Radio City Music Hall in New York City. She was a friend of Ronald Reagan, had danced with Fred Astaire, and could tell wonderfully glamorous stories about her encounters with Dean Martin, Frank Sinatra, and Bob Hope. They were five power women who had pulled strings to get permission for the first all-female archaeological mission. They set up the private Nile Foundation, for which they collected roughly $100,000 in sponsors' money by way of charity and fundraising events. They were hooked on ancient Egypt, which they knew very well from many visits, and even believed they had lived in Egypt in some former life. Diane was convinced that she had been a temple dancer. Gypsy was the only trained Egyptologist in the group. She had brought along from America a mathematician, a surveyor, and an archaeologist—all women—for technical support. In Aspen the five women had had to listen to all manner of ridicule—it was only sandbox play, reincarnation non-sense. Qadri had to protect himself. The concession for the project had been obtained through the American Research Center in Egypt, and the standing committee of the antiquities administration had approved it only with the stipulation that it be strictly scientific. Before the Nile Foundation appeared on the scene, I carried out an investigation, and the subsequent surveying and digging of test trenches would also be overseen by colleagues from the antiquities administration in Karnak. There was nothing that could go wrong. Today one would say that it was a win-win situation for all concerned, for the Aspen team's high-tech equipment was more than welcome to us.

We were quartered in the antiquities administration's rest house, an atmospheric structure right on the bank of the Nile not far from the Karnak temple and surrounded by a garden with old trees and tall palms. That building would later fall victim to Luxor's 'urban development project'—but it could have told plenty of interesting stories from the rich history of Egyptology starting in the nineteenth century. Our rooms were on the ground floor next to a glorious terrace; above us were the apartment and offices of Luxor's antiquities chief, Mohamed el-Saghir, an elegant and very popular man who lived there with his wife and two sons. We were ten women, and had to make do with three bedrooms and a single bathroom. At first I doubted whether the spoiled American women would accept three-bed rooms. But everything went smoothly, and we got along very well. Kamal and Abu Saadi cooked for us; we had two housekeepers, four guards, and a driver—all men, for in Upper Egypt women are not allowed to work as domestics. Even hotels are staffed exclusively by men—with the exception of Aswan, where there are hotels employing women. Although we could walk to the site, we needed the car for all our gear, and early mornings were still cold in January. In the morning we would put on multiple layers of clothing that we could later remove, layer by layer, in the afternoon sun.

Our investigation site was an untouched field of ruins strewn with thousands of clay shards, with remnants of mud-brick structures and massive squared stones rising here and there out of the sand. In two months we surveyed the entire area, pacing it off, strip by strip, with the magnetometer. From its readings we obtained a computer-generated map showing what lay beneath the surface: remnants of mud-brick walls and massive stonework.

Even while pacing off the surface we made small finds. We collected any number of little faience amulets, tiny votive figurines of nude women, a maternal symbol that played a role in the cult of the mother goddess Mut, consort of the state god Amun. In ancient Egyptian, Mut meant 'mother,' and her temple lay directly to the south of us. Could it be that the buildings whose foundations we were reading once belonged to the priests of Mut? Our test digs at the end of the season confirmed that that was the case. We searched the map for a spot that at one time had been densely built up. Together with our workers we dug a test trench that led us into the remnants of a kitchen. We found a baking oven, jars, even traces of foodstuffs. We photographed, drew, and documented everything accurately and delivered our finds to the depot of the antiquities administration. The ladies were by no means divas; they worked hard and with concentration, and our results earned the respect of colleagues with whom we compared notes in the famous Chicago House, in the Americans' archaeological mission.

Inhabitants of the nearby village of Karnak would come to visit us. They all wanted to know exactly what these women were up to; they feared that our surveying was possibly in preparation for the resettling of their village, which lay next to the avenue of sphinxes linking the Amun and Mut temples. But we were able to put their minds at ease. Even better, Diane, who ran a ballet school at home, was able to coax the children into learning a few dance steps with her. She would dance for them, and the children would clap their hands with delight. It was very moving to see those children from the most miserable of circumstances so happy as they copied Diane's steps. While some of us were standing with the children and others were busy surveying, behind our backs some goats trotted into our excavation tent and ate everything they could find: papers, tent patches, surveying cords, even nails.

After work there was enough time to explore the vast temple area of Karnak, of which only a small portion is accessible to the public—mainly the temples consecrated to the state god Amun-Re. To the uninitiated visitor Karnak is a labyrinth of walls, pylons, columns, and sculptures that appear to have grown into and alongside each other through centuries of construction. Roughly thirty pharaohs added to the complex, dedicated to countless deities, from the Middle Kingdom down to the time of the Ptolemies: processional streets with chapels and shrines for the sacred barque, thousands of square meters of reliefs and paintings on stone 'papyrus' columns and temple walls, obelisks, and colossal statues. For centuries a highly active cult was established there, even after the year AD 323, when pharaonic temple services were abandoned after Rome had accepted Christianity.

I learned a lot about Karnak in those months, but also about Luxor and its inhabitants. In fact, the people in the surrounding villages were not living so very differently from their predecessors in the time of the pharaohs. Although Copts and Muslims, their traditions and beliefs were still greatly influenced by those of ancient Egypt. I would see women talking to the Nile, complaining to the river about their hard lives, and when one of their children had fallen sick, for example, begging it for help. And I would see women in the temple of the goddess Hathor in Dendera beseeching the goddess of motherhood for their long-desired offspring. Standing alone in the great hall of the Amun Temple in the evening, sometimes a temple guard would cautiously approach me. In the dusk, while the stars rose magically above the columns, he would describe his temple nights: how white-robed figures would stride before him through the columned hall toward the sanctum; that under a full moon a splendid barque could be seen gliding across the Sacred Lake. And he would ask whether I had seen the big vulture that lived on top of the second pylon. In fact I had regularly seen a vulture shortly before sunset. It nested near a relief of the goddess Mut—whose symbol was a vulture. Cats roamed everywhere through the precinct, and it was forbidden to mistreat them. Our servant Gad also believed that twin babies turned into cats at night and ran around until sunrise. Gad had had twins, but they had died shortly after birth. He was firmly convinced that they turned into cats at night. Then there was my colleague Ibrahim Soliman, at that time inspector in Qurna and the Valley of the Kings. Ibrahim had grown up in Qurna, and related how as children, when the Nile flood still rose up to the edge of the village, he and his friends would sail around the Colossi of Memnon in a little boat. That was before the building of the High Dam.

And there was Sheikh Hafiz, an old man who was supposed to help us with the excavation. I never saw him do any work. People called him sheikh because he was a kind of conjurer, one who knew how to make the djinns, or spirits, subservient to him, and had produced a number of miracles. He once called me over to him and showed me an amulet he had made specially for me: a folded piece of paper on which he had previously written spells. It would protect me, he assured me, but I mustn't ever open it. He pressed it into my hand. I still have it—and have never been tempted to open it.

I can't write about our work in Karnak without telling about Radi. Radi was a simple laborer when he started with the antiquities administration—a donkey driver's helper, a boy who ran behind the animal keeping it on the right course with a stick. In earlier times archaeologists would transport all their equipment to their digs on donkeys, and even today donkeys carry water canisters into many a station in al-Assasif. When I first met Radi in 1985, he was the director of the Luxor's Department of Public Works and a member of Mubarak's National Democratic Party. Nothing could be done without Radi. He even organized the laborers for our exacavations, recruiting them exclusively from his own village. His younger brother functioned as an overseer. The workers told me that Radi would collect LE5 from each of them every day. I was hesitant to believe that, but I regretted my good faith when I saw Radi's villa, to which he invited us one evening. He found it undignified that the American ladies were lodged in the cramped quarters of the rest house, and insisted that they needed to be provided with a house of their own—and it must be nothing less than, needless to say, his own villa, which he was willing to turn over to the Americans at a bargain price. The women were greatly surprised to see what grand properties a minor official might acquire in our country.

The man was crafty, a smooth public relations professional. He had any number of tricks. One operated as follows: If a state visit to Luxor was announced by Hosni Mubarak or his wife Suzanne, during the public appearances he would maneuver himself as close as possible to the prominent guests. A photographer he had engaged especially for the occasion took pictures in which it actually looked as though he was a privileged, even intimate, member of the highest circles. He could be seen, at least by visitors to his office, in countless such photos. And because everyone believed he was powerful, he became so. It was a case not of clothes making the man but photographs. So he would organize activities and events in Luxor, always in specific hotels that paid him handsome commissions. He even managed to get into the photograph taken at the conclusion of our excavation. It would not be the last time I saw him.

Above the forecourt of the tomb at Bab el Affena rises the gate that gave the tomb its name

Tarek and Hadi in the village of Qurna after the Islamist attack of November 17, 1997

Restoration work
in the Tomb of
Montemhet: piece by
piece the fragments
of the tomb relief are
being fitted together
again and placed
on the pillars in the
forecourt, 1985

The forecourt of the Tomb of Montemhet, Assasif, Luxor

The "tough women of Luxor": the team of the Egyptian–American excavation mission, financed by the Nile Foundation, Aspen, 1985

The arrival of the Aspen Ladies at Luxor Airport, 1985

No excavation without tea: our workmen in Karnak provide us with their strong, sugary, but wonderfully delicious tea, 1985

Our exploratory work in the south of Karnak on the expanse between the Amun and Mut temples, 1985

Late and all-too-brief happiness
together: Diane Smith and
Ahmed Qadri, 1986

Beneath palms next to the Nile: our excavation house in Luxor, which sadly fell victim to
"urban renewal"

Hadi on the lawn of the Mena House Hotel in Giza, 1994

With my son Tarek in Luxor, 1989

Tarek and Hadi on horseback in front of the Khafre Pyramid, Giza, 1995

My husband Azmy in Cologne's Dom-Apotheke

The Egyptian Museum, unchanged for more than 110 years, built in the neoclassical style after designs by the French architect Marcel Dourgnon

The laying of the foundation stone of the Egyptian Museum at Tahrir Square, April 1897

The museum's atrium; here the main displays are sarcophagi weighing many tons, and huge statues of the great pharaohs

With Queen Rania of Jordan and her daughter Salma in the museum, 2006

Royal visitors to the museum: Charles, Prince of Wales, and his wife Camilla, Duchess of Cornwall, were particularly fascinated by the famous mummy portraits from the Fayum, 2004

Sabah and I searching in the museum's cellar for objects in need of restoration, 2005

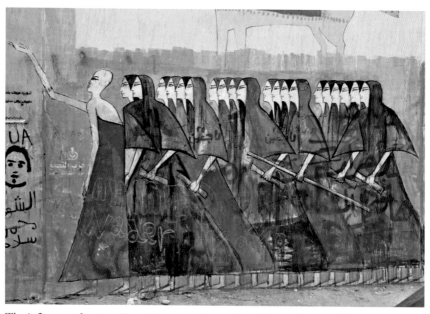

The influence of ancient Egyptian art on the murals of the revolution, February 2012; photograph by Vincent Euverte

Egyptian graffiti artists arranged a "No Walls" protest; they painted this spectacular, eye-deceiving mural on the Sheikh Rihan Street wall, Tahrir, November 2012; photograph by Mia Gröndahl

The ceremonial finale of our spring program for the blind in April 2010; the Egyptian Museum was unsuited for the appearance of the blind orchestra Nur wa Amal ('Light and Hope'), so it performed in the Cairo Opera House

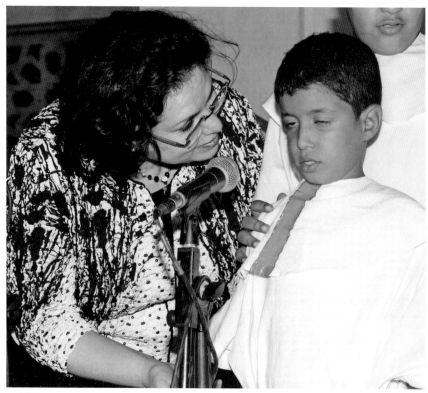

A blind boy appearing in a play, 2011

Blind children learning by touching a Lego statue of the Sphinx at the Children's Museum, 2010

The legendary house of Andraus Pasha in Luxor

With the colossal copper statue of King Pepi I (2332–2287 BC) at the Children's Museum, 2010

Naturally we also used the free time to visit the Assasif tombs over on the west side. Sometimes before sunrise we would climb to the top of the mountain above the Valley of the Kings, in ancient Egypt named after the goddess Meretseger—'She Who Loves Silence'—a woman with a serpent's head, occasionally depicted as a sphinx with a serpent's head. She was especially venerated as a patron goddess by workers in the Valley of the Kings. From the top of Meretseger we would then proceed on foot to the Temple of Hatshepsut in Deir al-Bahari. There we would watch the sunrise over the east side of the Nile. It was ice-cold, and we froze miserably, but the sight made it worthwhile: the awakening of the colors, the first spark of light over the Nile, the mist above the desert. The guards would bring hot tea up to us and invite us to have breakfast with them later in front of Hatshepsut's temple.

That is how I got to know Shahat, a guard at the Temple of Hatshepsut. He was in his forties, a portly, well-fed man who looked like the Sheikh al-Balad, as the well-known wooden statue of Ka-aper in the Egyptian Museum in Cairo is called. Shahat also told us about his odd experiences in the temple, that sometimes at night a voice would call to him that he would follow into the moonlit temple courtyard, from where he could see up on the mountain the figure of a woman, the goddess Meretseger. In the mountain massif one can in fact make out the outlines of a seated woman. He also assured us that at night he would see the Amun barque, borne on the shoulders of priests in the flare of torches. His stories were similar to those told by the guards of the Karnak Temple. And is it any wonder that in this nocturnal atmosphere, this magical silence, pictures on the temple walls come to life? All those figures interested Shahat a great deal, and he wished he could understand their meanings. He would have loved to become an Egyptologist, like the scholars who arrived in winter to study the tombs and temples. But his father had been poor, and had not even been able to send him to school, let alone the university in Cairo. But working as a guard for the antiquities administration, he had learned a lot about the history and architecture of the temple from the archaeologists of the Polish mission during its restoration work. "I know that at one time there was a luxuriant garden here, with incense trees and a beautiful rest house in which Queen Hatshepsut would stay during the Beautiful Valley Festival." The Beautiful Festival of the Desert Valley was celebrated each year in September, at the end of the Nile's flooding. Festivities were held throughout the necropolis on the west side of the Nile. Priests crossed the river with the Sacred Barque and proceeded to the tombs in a long procession. There relatives of the deceased would gather and together celebrate a kind of funeral feast, a 'Tomb Celebration,' a 'Day of Inebriation.'

Shahat died on November 17, 1997, during the attack by six Islamic terrorists. Sixty-eight people were killed. On that day Shahat gave his life trying to protect others. In 1997 I was already living in Germany, and learned of the massacre only from the television news. Over the Christmas holidays we traveled to Luxor with the children. We had heard of Shahat's death, and knew that he had left behind a wife and seven children. It did not take us long to find the martyr's house. I knocked on the door, and a woman dressed in black, not more than forty years old, opened it; behind her was a girl as pretty as a picture, possibly sixteen, also in black and with a baby on her arm. I could see their tear-stained faces. The woman was unprepared for our visit, and hesitated to let us in. Aside from her relatives and neighbors, she had had no visitors since the attack, not a single representative from the antiquities administration. Mubarak had gone to Luxor immediately after the incident to speak with groups of visitors in front of the cameras—but he didn't bother with the relatives of his dead countrymen. Five Egyptians were the first to be shot, among them Shahat and two of his colleagues, a policeman, and a tour guide.

Shahat's wife finally let us in, after I explained to her that I had known her husband and had come to express my sympathy and, if possible, to help. But the woman sat there apprehensively, saying nothing. The tension was only relieved when the children came in, having learned of our visit. It was a simple house with a clay floor, around us chickens and doves. I was glad that Azmy and my two boys were with me. In Germany their friends were all well-to-do, and they had no knowledge of such a world as this.

Finally Shahat's widow began to speak, interrupted by spells of crying. She had heard the shots at home. When a neighbor had rushed over to tell her that her husband was wounded or even killed, she had raced to the temple. "There was blood everywhere! Shahat was lying on the ground near the gate, surrounded by people waiting to carry him to the ambulance. But there were so many dead and wounded." One man had told her that Shahat had refused to leave the temple and had tried to block the terrorists. "They screamed at him to get away from the gate, but he wouldn't leave."

Then they shot at him with a machine gun. "I said to Shahat, 'Why didn't you run like all the other guards and policemen?' And he answered very softly, 'I am responsible for protecting the temple and its visitors.' Then he died in my arms."

The next day I went back to see her alone. The presence of my husband and children had intimidated her. Her name was Fatma; the people in the village called her Umm Mohamed. She began to tell me her history, and I immediately wrote it down. It is the story of one woman from Upper Egypt, and her fate is shared by many women in my country.

*

When I was a little girl I would often sit next to my father while he read the newspaper he had borrowed from our neighbor, the teacher. I so wanted to be able to read the paper too, to go to school and learn to write. But we were poor, and Mother said I didn't need to go to school, I would get married like all the other girls in the village and stay at home. So I played with the children in the street until I was ten years old. Then Mother forbade me from playing any longer with the boys. A girl's place was at home, where she could learn to bake and cook, tend to the poultry, and feed the animals in the stable. Girls had to stay at home until they had a husband.

*

Fatma was not yet twelve when she was married. Shahat was twenty-two. As was the custom in Upper Egypt's villages, the marriage was arranged by their two families. Traditionally, the first 'choice' for a man was a daughter of his paternal uncle. If that uncle had no daughter, then the daughter of a maternal uncle. Shahat was therefore Fatma's cousin. "He was my savior! I was very happy to escape from the prison of my family and all the arduous work at home. I felt so safe with him, and he meant everything to me. For the first time he gave me the feeling that I too mattered as a person. And he taught me to read the newspaper; he had learned to read from another boy. I was so afraid in the dark when Shahat spent the whole night at the temple, I would often go over to my parents-in-law's room and crawl under their coverlet."

At fourteen she had her first child. By twenty-four she was the mother of seven children, at thirty-four a grandmother for the first time. Two of her three daughters were married at sixteen and had their first children at seventeen. "I had sworn to myself that my daughters would go to school, even attend university. But I faced great resistance from the family. My two oldest girls had to leave school at fifteen. But the third, my Eida, I was able to save. She managed to graduate." And still had to marry at eighteen.

After Shahat's death no one from the administration or the ministry was ever seen by Fatma or the families of the other guards. The government paid sizable compensations to the relatives of the massacred foreign tourists, but relatives of the Egyptian victims got nothing, no pension payments, no survivors' assistance. I encouraged Fatma and her family to go to the authorities and make a claim. But she feared being punished for inconveniencing the officials. I always visit Fatma whenever I'm in Luxor. Her four sons are graduating from university, and I was able to arrange for jobs in the antiquities administration for two of them. Fatma is a tough woman, and we are dear friends to this day.

Evenings I was drawn again and again to the Luxor temple on the Nile. It was delightful to sit there next to the sphinxes in front of the pylon. I asked Ahmed Qadri why we didn't use such splendid settings for evening performances, and he was immediately supportive. I presented myself to Abdel Moneim Kamel, the director of the Cairo Ballet Company, associated with the Academy of Arts, to ask if he would be interested in presenting his ballet ensemble Osiris in front of the temple in Luxor. He was greatly intrigued by the idea, and within a few weeks he had put together a program. His dancers performed in the temple's columned courtyard, a stylized piece suggestive of antiquity. It was as if the ancient Egyptians had come alive again. Two years later, in May 1987, a professional concert agency put on a colossal performance in front of the temple: *Aïda*, performed by the Verona Opera, with Maria Chiara in the title role and Plácido Domingo as Radames. It was a grandiose extravaganza, with vast numbers of supernumeraries: 600 Egyptian soldiers in Radames' triumphal march, 50 ballet dancers, a 190-voice choir, a 200-piece orchestra, chariots, elephants, horses, even a lion and a black panther paraded in front of the first pylon, from the top of which fanfares blared. A huge spectacle—enjoyed by a high-paying audience seated behind Queen Sofía of Spain, Princess Caroline of Monaco, and Suzanne Mubarak. At afternoon tea, when I was sitting beneath the tall trees in the garden of the Winter Palace Hotel, I could hear Plácido Domingo warming up in his room, and that alone was a thrill.

Before my excavation with the women of the Nile Foundation, I had already guided Queen Noor, the wife of Jordan's King Hussein, and Suzanne Mubarak across the pyramid plateau. Everywhere there were security people and television teams, which made me nervous at first. But as soon as I began to talk about history and archaeology, I forgot them. I tried to use simple terms, burdening the ladies with as few numbers, dates, and names as I could, avoiding anything specialized that would prove tiring to a non-Egyptologist. I led the ladies to the pyramids and to the Great Sphinx, and on the next day to Salah al-Din's Citadel, where we had lunch. Queen Noor was simply but elegantly dressed. She had a pleasant, charming manner, and I immediately had the feeling that we were old friends. I told her about my friend Sahar Kattan in Amman, whom I first got to know at age ten as a pen pal while at school, and then met personally when she visited Cairo with her family. We were teenagers then and in middle school. Queen Noor was overjoyed. But of course, she knew Sahar's family, one well known in Amman's aristocratic circles.

Minister of culture Mohamed Abdel Hamid Radwan and Ahmed Qadri were very pleased with me, and wanted me to accompany the royal visitor to Luxor as well. I had apparently passed muster with Suzanne Mubarak; it was well known in the antiquities service that she would become angry if a guide seemed uncertain or spluttered nervously. That visit was to be the first in a whole series. After our Karnak excavation, the Danish ambassador asked me to put together an itinerary for Queen Margrethe II and her consort, Prince Henrik. The queen had already been to Egypt as a young princess, had wonderful memories of it, and wished to visit some of the most interesting excavation sites. I put together a program for Saqqara and Karnak, the Montemhet Tomb in al-Assasif, and the Polish mission's restoration work on the Hatshepsut Temple in Deir al-Bahari. When we were standing before the wall paintings in the tomb of the vizier Ramose, from the time of Amenhotep III and Akhenaten, Margrethe interrupted me. "Could you please stand next to the wall? I find that you look amazingly like Ramose's wife. You must be from Luxor!" While we were enjoying a picnic in the Temple of Dendera, she drew something on a sheet of paper and handed it to me. On it was a sktech of Queen Margrethe in front of the temple, with a cigarette in her hand issuing a great plume of smoke. A lovely caricature of herself that still today serves to remind me of a lovely day. Margrethe got angry at the many press and security people who hounded us, but she had a plan. She wanted to buy fabrics in the bazaar, and when after dinner the crowd of hangers-on had finally drifted off to their rooms in the Winter Palace, we sneaked out by way of the front steps. I still remember how some of the photographers hung out of their windows above, then in no time at all dashed out of the hotel lobby half dressed. We hadn't been able to escape them, and I was very sorry for Margrethe and her husband.

It is possible that Queen Margrethe told her cousin Carl XVI Gustaf of Sweden about her visit to Egypt. In any case, a few months later the Swedish royal couple wished to have me guide them across the pyramid plateau. In the Boat Museum, Carl Gustaf suddenly interrupted my explanations with a dismissive shake of his head. This boat couldn't possibly be forty-five hundred years old, even older than the oldest Viking ship. Queen Silvia clearly saw me raise my eyebrows for a moment in response to her husband's brusque and disrespectful behavior. Since she knew that I had studied in Vienna, she spoke to me in German and encouraged me, with a smile, to continue with the tour. That evening I had to reconsider whether I should accompany the two to Abu Simbel. But at the evening reception for the royal couple, even before dinner, the Swedish ambassador took me aside. The king was awaiting me in a side room, where he and his wife were personally greeting a number of people. With extreme courtesy the king declared that he had very much enjoyed my tour and would be very pleased if I would also serve as their guide in Upper Egypt. The next morning we flew to Abu Simbel and saw the two rock temples of Ramses II and his consort Nefertari. I told them about UNESCO's rescue operation between 1963 and 1968. At that time, with international assistance, a number of temples were dismantled and rebuilt at a safe distance from the new reservoir, including the two rock temples at Abu Simbel. I was delighted that for that visit we were joined by a Swedish architect who had been involved in the operation. He explained how the two temples were cut into more than a thousand limestone blocks, each weighing thirty tons. It was a race against the rising waters of the Nile, and they worked day and night. The four colossal

Ramses statues were cut up with hand saws and carefully transported to the new location, sixty-five meters higher up, by tractor trailers. There an international consortium had constructed two gigantic concrete shells—at the time the largest reinforced concrete domes in the world. The concrete for them had to be chilled, as it was so hot at the site. In front of the domes, the two temple façades were reconstructed, and beneath them the temple interiors were reconstructed down to the last millimeter. Today the two temples stand there as if they had never moved. Even the sun miracle still occurs on schedule. Twice a year, on February 20 and October 20, a shaft of morning sunlight pierces through the temple's interior and illuminates the face of the state god Amun on its back wall, sixty-four meters from the entrance.

From Abu Simbel we proceeded to Aswan and to the famous island of Philae, with its main temple of the goddess Isis. That temple complex was also threatened by the rising reservoir and dismantled. Today, seemingly perfectly unchanged, it stands on the neighboring island Agilkia. And naturally we made a stop in Luxor, visited the Valley of the Kings and the Hatshepsut Temple. Carl Gustaf was especially intrigued by the naïve paintings on the façades of the houses in Gurna. The paintings later disappeared with the rest of the village. All my arguments in favor of saving the village from the bulldozers of the antiquities service failed to be of any help.

I also remember Margaret Thatcher, whom I guided together with her husband Denis and her daughter Carol in 1986. It was the middle of August. Thermometers in Cairo stood at 42 Celsius (108 Fahrenheit), in Luxor at 48 (118 Fahrenheit). I asked Qadri whether the English people knew what they were in for, but Qadri assured me that nothing could be done, the British ambassador had specified these dates. The Karnak Temple was scheduled for midday, when the sun stands high above the ruins. I tried to change the time, but the prime minister was expected that same afternoon by King Hussein in Amman. So we stood in the Karnak Temple under a blazing sun. Everything was radiating heat and dazzling light: the temple walls, the pylons, the sky. But Margaret Thatcher said not a word about it. Around her, members of her entourage fled into any patch of shade they could find, no matter how small. I then understood why she was called the Iron Lady. She was friendly, focused, and very well informed, and it was a joy to be able to guide such a refined woman through the temple complex.

My contact with the Aspen ladies didn't end with our joint excavation. Something had clicked between Diane Smith and Ahmed Qadri, and they married. Diane wanted him to live with her on her ranch near Aspen, but Qadri could not desert his antiquities preservation project, and had no wish to. He stayed in Egypt.

Only weeks after their wedding in 1986, Diane called me. "Are you sitting down? You'd better be, as I have bad news. I have cancer. The doctors tell me I have six months."

I was shocked. "I'll come immediately. I'll help you."

But Diane refused. No, on the contrary, she was coming here. "I want to die in Egypt."

Qadri was devastated. He was touching in his care for her. She died at only forty-nine. Qadri, who also developed cancer, followed her three years later. I had lost two wonderful friends.

The antiquities administration had put together an exhibition about women in ancient Egypt to be shown abroad: *Nofret, the Beautiful*. Qadri wanted me to accompany it to Hildesheim, Germany. That was in the summer of 1985. A year later he asked me to supervise the installation of the same exhibition at the Josef-Haubrich Kunsthalle Museum in Cologne as well. But I didn't want to. I knew that the northern December climate was hard on me. "I don't want to go to Germany in the winter. Besides, I have to finish my work in Luxor." But fate willed otherwise.

Qadri huffed, "And who, may I ask, should I send to Germany instead? Who else is there who speaks German?"

I had no choice. No sooner had I arrived in Cologne than I caught a cold. Hansgerd Hellenkemper, then the director of Cologne's Römisch-Germanisches Museum and the man responsible for the Nofret exhibition, recommended that I try the Dom-Apotheke, only a few steps away, assuring me that the owner was also an Egyptian. "He'll surely have something to make you feel better." So I got to know Azmy el-Rabbat. My cold lingered on. During the next two weeks Azmy would come to the exhibition every day and ask how I was feeling—actually it probably wasn't the cold that interested him. Toward the end of my stay in Cologne, he asked me if I would marry him. I explained to him that I had never thought really seriously about marriage, that I was too busy with my work in Egypt and had no intention of abandoning it. "I also don't think I would make a good housewife." Later that same evening I got a call from Cairo. I was to return immediately. Ingrid, Queen Mother of Denmark, was coming to Egypt and I was to accompany her. The antiquities administration would sent a substitute for me to Cologne. "I have to go to Luxor," I told Azmy. "Perhaps it's for the best. Then we'll both have time to think everything over." But shortly after I arrived in Luxor, I was sitting with Queen Ingrid in the garden of the Winter Palace when Azmy came walking down the path toward us. I introduced him to the queen, and asked her if he might accompany us in Luxor for a bit. She laughed. "But of course!" The queen was accompanied by her physician and his wife. When she suddenly developed throat pains, Azmy gave her some drops that gave her immediate relief. The queen then joked about her physician, whose medications hadn't helped at all. The queen and the two of us spent lovely days together. And she and I corresponded up to the time of her death in November 2000. Her letters and Christmas cards were always handwritten. Sometimes she enclosed photographs of her family, sometimes only of the children. She was a fine lady, and I liked her very much.

The bond of familiarity Azmy and I felt for each other surprised me. We had known each other only a few weeks. In Luxor he again asked me if I would marry him—and I said yes. But I asked him to follow the traditional route and officially ask my parents for my hand. So Azmy visited us on Abdeen Square. My parents had lots of questions: why he had stayed in Germany after his studies, whether he was now thinking of returning to Egypt, whether he knew how devoted I was to my work in Egypt. Azmy told them about his family, which came from Banha, a city north of Cairo. His father Mahmud el-Rabbat had been a well-to-do businessman there who had donated to his quarter a mosque, a school, and a few shops in the best location to finance the madrasa. His parents were buried in a marble tomb inside the mosque. In the early 1950s three of their sons had left for Germany, where they studied mechanical engineering and pharmacy in Würzburg and Cologne. But only Azmy, the youngest, had stayed on, as he had been given attractive offers of employment in Germany. From job to job he postponed his return, until finally he was given the chance to take over the Dom-Apotheke in Cologne, and he settled in for the long term.

After Azmy's visit my parents huddled in indecision. It had been easy with Nur and Safaa. They had married within the extended family; my parents had known their daughters' husbands since they were children. But Azmy was a stranger. That same day Father drove out to Banha—without telling me. It was time for the Isha prayer, the last of the five daily prayers, and he went into a mosque there. After prayers he asked a man where he might find the mosque of the el-Rabbat family. The man explained that he was standing in it. It turned out that Father had spoken with Azmy's brother Mohamed. Father came back home reassured, and the next day Azmy was given his consent.

We married according to Islamic law on April 7, 1987, in the al-Hussein Mosque—the mosque of the Prophet's grandson and one of the patriarchs of my mother's family. It was a large ceremony arranged for us by the director of the Islamic Department in the Ministry of Culture. It was conducted by an ancient sheikh. My brother Mohamed joked, "If they had known you were an Egyptologist, they would have hired Ramses." The old man actually resembled the great pharaoh's mummy. The men sat in the large hall, the women in the women's section. Azmy's brother Faiz brought over a marriage contract and I signed it. In the afternoon we had a small celebration at home. The major celebration was the next day. My brother Mohamed, at that time the manager of the Oberoi hotel chain in Egypt, had reserved the *Nile Pharaoh* for us, a ship restaurant that plied between Giza and Cairo. Uncle Mohamed drove us in his large American limousine, decorated with exquisite flowers, followed by a long column of cars. We were greeted by fanfares from *Aïda*. More than three hundred guests, including ministers and ambassadors, among them Ahmed Qadri, attended the festivities. He was as happy as if he had married off his own daughter. On the *Nile Pharaoh* my brother had arranged for the staff to dress in ancient Egyptian costumes. Enas, my assistant at the excavation in Karnak, sang traditional wedding songs. Mohamed had also engaged a belly dancer. Papa left the deck: A half-naked woman embarrassed him. But Mohamed retorted, "An Egyptian wedding without a belly dancer? Who ever heard of such a thing?" Mother had stayed home. The confusion was too much for her. I think she wanted to be home alone in order to pray in peace for my happiness. After the party we went to the Mena House Hotel, where Mohamed had booked the royal suite for us for three days. As tradition dictated, the next day we received all the well-wishers in the suite's sitting room. Our honeymoon took us to Aswan and Luxor, where we stayed in rest houses belonging to the antiquities administration. In the evening we enjoyed *Aïda*.

Azmy and I had agreed that we would first go to Cologne for a few months, then come back to Cairo so I could continue to work in the antiquities administration. I took an unpaid leave. "Aha! Then watch out during Carnival!" my colleagues at the German Archaeological Institute warned me in farewell.

7

AT THE BASE OF
THE CATHEDRAL

In Cologne we lived in an apartment above the pharmacy, right around the corner from the cathedral. I often visited it. The grandiose edifice reminded me of the pyramids. Although erected thousands of years later, it, like the pyramids, is an amazing testament to the power of faith. I would wander about, each time focusing on a different detail, the wonderful windows or the underground excavations. Although at first I didn't know anyone besides Azmy, I never felt foreign in the city. The cathedral and the Rhine, the museums, and the Philharmonic kept me from becoming homesick, especially since I kept telling myself, "I've only switched rivers. In a few weeks we'll be back in Egypt." The few weeks turned out to be sixteen years.

The situation in Cairo's antiquities administration was becoming increasingly unpleasant. Ahmed Qadri and the new minister of culture, Farouk Hosni, were at war with each other. Hosni had previously served as the director of the Egyptian Academy in Rome. He was a close friend of then prime minister Atef Sedki. When Sedki restructured his government in 1988, he brought Hosni into his cabinet, against the protests of many Egyptian intellectuals, among them Ahmed Qadri. Sedki and Hosni wanted to get rid of the critic Qadri, but he was doing all he could saving monuments. Up until his public repudiation by Hosni, Qadri was the hero of the press. It praised his commitment; even Mubarak had laudatory things to say about him. In 1988 Qadri was preparing for the opening of the Military Museum in Salah al-Din's Citadel in Cairo. He had published the catalog, for which he had written the foreword. But shortly before the museum was to be officially inaugurated by Mubarak, Qadri was dismissed, his name erased from the catalog and his foreword removed. The reason: A block of stone from the restored shoulder section of the Sphinx had come loose.

Up until his early death from cancer in 1990, Qadri saw it as a bitter betrayal. Journalists who had praised him so highly only a short time before had switched over to the Hosni camp. He could handle the fact that they crucified him in print, but what hurt him up to the end, as he told me, was having been betrayed by a man with whom he had worked so long in the antiquities service. He had considered him a friend, but he had turned out to be a Judas.

In 1982 Qadri had become the head of the antiquities administration, after the premature departure of his predecessor. The reason: A block of stone had come loose from the Sphinx. Now six years later, in 1988, once again it was a block of stone from the Sphinx that prematurely ended Qadri's tenure. He refused to be removed so easily, and provoked a public scandal. He declared that the stone could not have loosened by itself; someone had pried it loose in order to get rid of him, and had had accomplices in the antiquities service.

Qadri was extremely hurt by his dismissal, and depressed. He accepted an invitation to Waseda University in Japan, grateful to be able to teach once again, and worked on a new book. Already at that time he urgently needed a second cancer operation. Relatives of the deceased Diane Smith had him come to America. But it was too late. Ahmed Qadri died in October 1990, and was buried in his village in the eastern Delta. More than thirty thousand mourners attended his funeral.

But the group seeking out and dealing with those they considered enemies within the antiquities administration didn't stop with Qadri; they also went after those who had worked closely and amicably with him. It was highly probable that if I had returned, I too would have been badly treated. I soon enough accepted the idea that I would not be going back for the time being, and decided to continue my commitment at long distance. In Hildesheim and during my earlier brief stay in Cologne, I had admired the

educational programs the museums had developed to accompany our exhibition *Nofret, the Beautiful*. I was especially fascinated by the educational
offerings for children, and had enthusiastically written to Qadri about them.
Then I met the archaeologist Beate Schneider from the Cologne museum's
education department, and we immediately clicked. I registered in one of her
workshops, and so came to know the Cologne artist Renate Friedländer, who
had worked for the department for many years and had written a whole series
of catalogs for children. I was particularly intrigued by the way she presented
the museum's holdings to blind children and young people. Though unable to
see the objects, they were able to appreciate their histories and importance.
Their delight and gratitude impressed me.

Watching those children, I recalled the exhibition *Dialogue in the Dark*
that I had visited in the United States many years before and also an encounter I
had had in Minya, near Akhenaten's residence in al-Amarna. That too had been
long ago. On the Nile ferry a woman with three blind children spoke to me. She
had apparently heard someone call me "Doctor." Her name was Umm Said and
she wondered, since I was a doctor, if I could help her. I explained that I was
a doctor of archaeology, but she didn't understand. A doctor for stones? She
told me that her children had been born perfectly healthy, but that all three had
gone blind only a few months later. Yet both she and her husband had perfectly
good eyesight. She wanted so badly for her children to be able to learn to read
and write. I thought of my blind fellow students in the Literature Faculty who
read and wrote in Braille. Some of them were by then quite successful. There
was Mamduh el-Sharqawi, for example, who had studied linguistics in Vienna
and earned his doctorate. He was widely regarded as a genius. So I wrote down
Umm Said's address and later asked my colleague Samir Wanis in Minya's
antiquities administration whether there was a school or foundation for blind
children in the region, and he happened to know of one. In fact a foundation did
take in Umm Said's children. But in Egypt, especially Upper Egypt, there are
so very many blind people.

In Cologne I suddenly knew that I wanted to work on museum education
programs, especially for children and the handicapped. There were no such
programs in Egypt, and today it might seem odd that I should have responded
to the very idea as a kind of revelation. Today education departments are
standard museum features in many countries in Europe and in the United

States. But twenty years ago their success was by no means acknowledged. At that time the original meaning of the term *pedagogy*, guidance of children, was redefined: how, with what, and why were children supposed to be guided through our museums. Up until then, to children museum visits were something boring their parents did on Sunday to pass the time. That was still the case in Egypt as well in the early 1990s. Cairo's Egyptian Museum was no place for children. School classes were directed through museums in single file and were not allowed to ask questions or linger anywhere. They were supposed to disturb the tourist traffic as little as possible, for foreign visitors were our museums' main source of income.

Until the 1980s Egyptians were not really interested in their cultural heritage. Many children in Arab countries never visited antiquities museums at all. To conservative Sunni Muslims the pre-Islamic world was a heathen epoch—one reason why ancient sites were underappreciated. Should a country whose unique, thousands-year-old history excites interest and enthusiasm everywhere in the world have scarcely any notion of its cultural heritage itself? Should young as well as adult museum visitors stand before objects from the past without really understanding them or being able to place them in the past? Museum visitors from all social classes ought to be able to perceive the beauty and aura of an artifact directly, but their meaning needs to be explained. Such objects come alive only once one learns about their history.

"You only see what you already know and understand. Frequently one does not see for many years what more mature knowledge and education allow us to appreciate about an object with which we are daily confronted." Goethe's words, provided here in the translator's own version, have lost none of their validity, and they aptly describe the dilemma of many Egyptian museums: They are unprepared to convey knowledge and education to their countrymen, to help them to see, to make connections. They are magnets for visitors from all over the world, who as a rule bring with them greater knowledge of what they are seeing than Egyptians themselves.

In a country like Egypt, with its many young people, museum education also actively promotes the preservation of its treasures. For how is Egypt to protect its heritage and preserve it for coming generations if the majority of those who one day should be expected to finance such efforts fail to understand and appreciate it? A primary task of museums, especially in Egypt, is the education of the populace, especially its poorer segment. That is accomplished not only didactically, but more importantly through direct experience, through the emotions. Museums should make it possible for children and young people to think of the acquisition of knowledge as an adventure. Museums are 'treasure houses,' but also learning places, information centers, meeting places, promoters of processes of discovery.

I recognized this in Cologne and in Hildesheim, where I saw how schoolchildren, young people, and art-loving teachers and adults were invited to engage in creative activities. I accepted that invitation myself, and attended seminars and conferences not only in Germany but also in Belgium, where I met my colleague Marie-Cécile Bruwier, a scholarly director at the Musée Royal de Mariemont. But how was I to manage to convince my colleagues in Egypt's antiquities service of such an innovation?

Once again fate played into my hands. In the spring of 1988 I received a call from Helmut Danner, the director of the Hanns Seidel Foundation in Cairo. He had heard that I was interested in museum education. Would I be willing to prepare a study on the establishment of a children's museum in Egypt? The foundation would finance it. Naturally the offer was greatly welcome. I wanted to do something for children in Egypt, and a children's museum would be wonderful. At the time I was pregnant with my son Tarek, and it could not have been mere coincidence that his offer came to me when it did.

I was doubly fortunate. Azmy engaged a housekeeper, a good-hearted soul named Maria Meneses. She took care of the household and the baby so that I could work on the study without a guilty conscience, for Tarek, and later Hadi too, loved Maria. They called her Mama Mia. I wrote to museums all over the world—in the United States, Venezuela, England, Japan, France, and Germany. Anne Reuter-Rautenberg, the director of the Staatliche Kunsthalle Karlsruhe, and Renate Friedländer were a great help to me. The two women would be the first professionals to teach my museum colleagues in Egypt. But that would be a long time in the future.

From 1988 to 1991 I worked on the study about an Egyptian children's museum, writing it first in Arabic, then in a German version, which I could not have managed without my friend Beate Schneider. After the book was published, Helmut Danner sent a copy to Suzanne Mubarak, hoping that it might have an influence on her private foundation planning to establish a children's museum in Heliopolis. Danner asked me whether I wouldn't rather present the book to Mrs. Mubarak myself, but I politely declined. "And what if I were to fly to Egypt especially and the first lady didn't happen to have time for me? No, thank you!"

Even then I had reservations about a children's museum set up by the most powerful woman in Egypt. For in addition to conveying knowledge, museum education programs seek to promote democratic goals: Even the lower classes should be inspired to explore their own artistic creativity, to think of themselves differently within a group than they do in school, where they are under pressure to achieve, under constant oversight and the paternalism of teachers, imams, parents, and state authorities. In such programs children develop a different sense of their own worth, their critical faculties are encouraged, their eyes opened to their place within the family and society. Anyone who dreams and plays develops his own perspective on life, formulates his own desires and needs. I could not then, and cannot now think that it was a sincere desire of the Mubarak system to effectively promote such qualities and virtues.

My sons Tarek and Hadi were five and two, at a wonderfully playful age. Naturally I also had children's books about the pyramids, the Sphinx, and the young pharaoh Tutankhamun. But those picture books were outclassed by an exhibit we visited in Cologne in 1993: *The Secret of the Pharaohs*, built entirely out of Lego bricks. Tarek, Hadi, and their friend Maximilian were wide-eyed; I couldn't tear them away from the large, colorful structures and ancient building sites, the war chariots and Nile barques. They spent hours in the play area, building their own temples, pylons, and palaces. I asked the exhibition's director whether he thought that Lego might also send the exhibit to Egypt, assuring him that it was wonderfully educational. He was pleased to hear this from an Egyptian Egyptologist, of course, and gave me an address in Denmark. I learned from the company that the exhibit was scheduled to travel through Europe for a few years, and after such continuous exposure might no longer be suitable for display in Egypt. I kept the correspondence and the documentation about the exhibition—little suspecting that I would one day become the director of the Egyptian Museum.

I had lived in Vienna for four years, had accompanied exhibitions to Germany, and was therefore perfectly familiar with life in central Europe.

Azmy had a large circle of friends and acquaintances in Cologne, and our contacts with museum people, Egyptologists, university professors, teachers, and many educated and interesting people in that uncommonly socially active city made it easy for me to find a place in a circle of people similar to the one in which I had moved in Cairo. Perhaps it would have been different had I conformed to the cliché of a head-scarf-wearing Egyptian Muslim woman. I also got to know Egyptian women who would complain to me that they felt excluded, in part because of their head scarves and modest clothing. I, by contrast, had the good fortune of immediately rousing interest as an Egyptologist. But it was above all the children who made it easy for me to feel at home in Cologne. In their kindergarten and school I was chosen to be the parents' spokesperson, which made it possible for me to talk to teachers about their methods. Only once, on a parents' night, did I witness a mother complaining with alarm that there were three foreign children in her child's class. She demanded that the school's directors not admit any foreigners or children with a background of migration, but the other parents protested. Through my children I came to know new and very dear women friends, whose predictable birthday calls I always looked forward to back in Egypt.

So Cologne wasn't foreign to me, but occasionally strange. My colleagues at the German Archaeological Institute in Cairo had jokingly warned me: "Watch out for Carnival in Cologne!" I experienced my first one right in the eye of the storm. We were still living above the Dom-Apotheke, near where the Shrove Monday parade ended. I stood at the window, watching the Carnival floats at eye level. If we had kept the windows closed, they would have been shattered by the boxes of pralines, oranges, and candy being thrown about. It was a bizarre picture. I gazed out at a swaying, dancing, singing crowd, and when I looked closely I could make out Bedouin sheikhs, belly dancers, pharaohs—a whole colorfully costumed Orient. Though sensitive to noise, I was greatly amused. But I am probably not revealing anything new when I add that the whole affair gets out of hand and takes on Dionysian aspects that may be interesting from the perspective of a cultural anthropologist, but leave much to be desired. Since I don't drink alcohol, I find the public consumption of it incomprehensible and disgusting. In later years I naturally went with my boys to the children's Carnival, to watch the schools parade, those of the separate districts, and the Junkersdorf street fair. I was delighted for the children, scrambling for candy in their colorful costumes. But at the sight of such wasteful bounty I couldn't suppress my memories of earlier experiences. Street sweepers would follow behind the parade, cleaning up all the chocolate bars, sticks of gum, popcorn, and gummy bears that had been trodden underfoot, and I had to think about all the world's hungry children.

A true shock awaited me when friends invited Azmy and me to Garmisch-Partenkirchen. We set out for a walk beside a lake and unknowingly happened upon a nudist beach. It was appalling. I had never in my whole life seen naked people behaving with such nonchalance. Such permissiveness is absolutely unthinkable in Egypt. I was helpless, I simply didn't know where to look. But at the sight of the incredible Alpine landscape we soon put the experience behind us.

My mother died in June 1994. We were then living in Cologne-Junkersdorf, and Tarek and Hadi were taking up all my time. But I remember that 12th of June very clearly. I had had an odd feeling the entire day. I felt that something wasn't right in Cairo. Since his heart attack my father was bedridden and in need of care. I was always afraid of getting a call from my siblings telling me that Father had died. I couldn't eat or sleep, and I called home. But no one answered. I called Safaa and asked how Father was. Has something happened to him? No, he's fine. I explained that I had such a bad feeling and wanted to come to Cairo.

"Yes," she said curtly. "Come home."

But she didn't reveal what was really wrong. Azmy had already been told, but had been asked not to tell me. He bought me a black dress without saying anything about it. He had also arranged for plane tickets. At the Düsseldorf airport the director of Egyptair received us in his office and promptly expressed his deepest sympathy.

I was shocked. "What has happened to my father?"

I could see the man's eyes tear up. He apologized profusely, he had made a slip. He had read the death notice in the newspaper that had arrived that morning with the first plane. It was a tense flight. Safaa and her husband met us at the Cairo airport. Safaa was wearing white. I asked how Father was. Then she started to cry.

"It's not Father. Mama died on the 12th of June."

I fainted on the spot. At home I couldn't say a word, but only cried. Mother had always been healthy. Never had I dreamed of losing her before Father. My siblings explained to me that I shouldn't dress in black, for Father still hadn't been told. But when he saw the two of us he burst into tears. Mother had already been buried. We visited her grave in Fariskur and saw how sympathetic people there were. The cemetery guard whispered that our mother must have been a saint, for at night there was always a light around her grave. My siblings told me that she must have sensed she was dying. Days before, she had thoroughly cleaned the apartment as though wanting to prepare for the mourning guests in the coming days. On the day she died, she gave her clothes to her servant woman. She gave her front door key to my sister Nur with the words "look after your father." She had fasted and prayed all day, and died in the evening. My father passed away two years later, also without suffering. I was not in Egypt when he died either, or when my brother Mohamed died. I bitterly reproached myself. But in my dreams all three comforted me: They were now in a better place. My mother often spoke to me, especially when I was facing problems in the museum.

We traveled to Egypt several times a year, in part because I wanted to present my museum education proposals to the president of the antiquities administration. But he scoffed at me. "But that's childish. We have neither time nor money for such nonsense. Museums aren't kindergartens." My colleagues in the Egyptian Museum responded in much the same way. I had arranged with Helmut Danner that we might invite colleagues, especially directors, to a museum education seminar and explain to them the importance of working with schoolchildren, young people, and the handicapped. In the spring of 1995, the foundation issued invitations to an international workshop in Luxor. The antiquities administration had a new president, Abdel Halim Nureddin, an open-minded scholar who welcomed such cooperation. Helmut Danner suggested holding it in the foundation's Nile Center, but Luxor's mayor and the director of its public relations department turned that down. They insisted that the workshop required the amenities of a five-star hotel. It was I who turned that down. I knew that public relations man only too well. "Why should we spend so much money when the foundation's rooms are at our disposal for nothing?" The mayor explained that colleagues from abroad should not be expected to look at torn-up side streets. I assured him that he shouldn't worry, our colleagues were accustomed to that. But the man explained to me that he was absolutely certain that the function wouldn't take place at the Nile Center. The next day the street in front of the center was obstructed by a bulldozer; there was no getting around it. We had no other choice: We had to move to the recommended hotel. The seminar cost the Egyptian antiquities service a great deal of money. I was shocked. But the public relations man only laughed in my face.

Only a year later we were able to offer a six-month training course. Many of my colleagues from Egyptian museums took part in it. Anne Reuter-Rautenberg, Renate Friedländer, and Regine Schulz, then the director of the Roemer- und Pelizaeus-Museum in Hildesheim, came from Germany, and Marie-Cécile Bruwier came from Belgium. The course was a great success. The Hanns Seidel Foundation financed stipends allowing six curators from Cairo and Alexandria to go to Cologne, Karlsruhe, and Munich. But when Helmut Danner left Cairo for Kenya, that assistance was cut off; there was no money for either courses or practical experience abroad. And after the attack on the Hatshepsut Temple the Supreme Council had no more funds available for museum education. Even so, we were able to send two colleagues to my friend Marie-Cécile in Belgium; there just wasn't any money for Germany.

One evening we were invited to friends of ours in Junkersdorf. Also there were Regina Doffing, the pastor of the local Protestant church; her husband, the judge Wolfgang Raack; and Jürgen Ibach, former director of the German Protestant School in Cairo. Azmy and I told them about the situation in Egypt, and that we wanted to establish a society through which we could continue promoting museum education. Wolfgang Raack reminded us that in Germany only seven people were needed to found a society, and five were already sitting around the table; two more could easily be found. And in fact on March 13, 1999, a small circle of roughly twenty friends and acquaintances established CATS, the Children's Alliance for Tradition and Social Engagement. Over the next few years CATS organized events for children, especially those from socially disadvantaged classes, for street urchins, for the mentally and physically handicapped, and for children with cancer, in Cairo, Luxor, Aswan, and other museum cities. The children made pottery, built models, put together *ushabti* figures, temple layouts, and mummy masks, and in doing so learned to observe closely, and were for a short while completely caught up in the world of ancient Egypt. We could see how strict museum guards would at first look suspiciously over their shoulders, then hang around with growing curiosity, and finally show up with cardboard boxes, paper, and paints so the children could keep working. Operating solely with donations, CATS managed to conduct regular workshops in Egypt and arrange for hands-on training for Egyptian curators at German, Belgian, French, and Portuguese museums, and we helped them establish education departments at their own museums.

In Germany we maintained close contact with the successive Egyptian ambassadors and their cultural and press departments. Interest in ancient Egypt culture was intense. I was asked to give lectures on Egyptology and archaeology, and through them we soon made many interesting contacts with German–Egyptian societies in various cities. My school-age sons also led me to offer museum visits and week-long projects focusing on Egypt or Islam in kindergartens and schools.

One day ambassador Ihab Muqbil invited me to meet the German engineer and Egypt enthusiast Rudolf Gantenbrink. In March 1993 he had steered a remote-controlled miniature vehicle he had constructed himself up into one of the two air shafts of the so-called Queen's Chamber of the Khufu Pyramid. By means of a small camera he had filmed the shafts and thereby provided a glimpse of an otherwise inaccessible part of the structure. But the shaft ended at a stone slab that was apparently fitted with two copper pins. His robot mission ended there as well. Gantenbrink visited us at home in Cologne. He was a calm, soft-spoken man who obviously had a problem with Zahi Hawass. In fact there could be no greater contrast between any two men: here the seemingly introverted technician, there the energetic, grandstanding antiquities chief. Gantenbrink wanted to continue his mission with a new robot, but could not get permission from Hawass. I had heard about it. Gantenbrink had made one mistake. He had gone to the press with the results of his investigation alone, thereby angering the antiquities administration and naturally Zahi Hawass himself. In the world of Egyptology, of which Hawass saw himself the custodian, you don't abuse your host's publicity privilege lightly.

"That wasn't all," Gantenbrink related. "Hawass believes there's nothing to be found behind the slab, that further investigation is senseless."

I too had read Zahi Hawass's remarks in the *Guardian*: There's no mystery waiting to be discovered, none that still needs to be solved. He had carefully studied Gantenbrink's film material, and been unable to discover either a crack or a narrow opening in the so-called door through which one might look behind the stone. "That means that we have no possibility of looking behind it." Gantenbrink was convinced that he could find out more about the 'space' behind the 'door' by new exploratory methods. But Hawass refused to permit it.

I explained to the engineer that I shared Hawass's scholarly opinion: The two former air shafts of the Queen's Chamber end some sixteen meters short of the pyramid's outer face and are not a structural mystery. They were features of an early phase of the original construction that was then abandoned. The pyramid was first meant to be smaller, and in that initial structure the Queen's Chamber was intended to be the pharaoh's tomb chamber. But then came a change of plan. The pyramid was to become considerably larger. A second and final tomb chamber, the present one, was created in the core of the structure, with two new air shafts that actually led to the outside. One of them is oriented toward the star Sirius, for in mythology Osiris, the god of the dead, is associated with Sirius—the deceased pharaoh's soul needed to be able to leave his tomb every night through this shaft. In fact, it also provided ventilation. I had often breathed the fresh air in the chamber in the early morning, before it grew stale from the many visitors. "But I have no objection to further exploration," I explained. "Provided that it does no damage to the structure. I could even picture your robots deployed in other tombs. They could provide us with insights we could otherwise obtain only at great expense." That was the way things were left in March 1998.

In the summer of 2002, Zahi Hawass came to Germany on a lecture tour organized by the Egyptian Tourism Office in Frankfurt. During the tour he also stopped in Cologne. We spent the day together, attended his evening lecture in the Römisch-Germanisches Museum, and were invited to the dinner afterward in the Dom Hotel. At that time Zahi was not yet secretary general of the antiquities administration, but he was already absolutely certain that he would get the job. I was surprised at the zeal with which he was preparing for his tenure as secretary general, and that he already occupied important posts. That evening he explained in the presence of the journalists traveling with him that it was time for me to return to Egypt and once again actively work for the antiquities administration. In front of the journalists he declared, "She's a born leader!" I chose to believe that he seriously meant it. Naturally I had heard one thing and another about him from friends in Egypt, but I myself had no particular reason to distrust him, and after all, our working relationship dated back for many years. I was also delighted with his offer: "Would you like to be director of the Egyptian Museum?"

I explained to him what I had already explained to two of his predecessors: Yes, I would love to work again, I would be very happy to be director of the Egyptian Museum, but I have a family here in Cologne. My children are still in school here, my husband has his business here. "Even if my family agreed to it, we would need at least a year in which to arrange for our return to Cairo."

Zahi Hawass was in the most generous of moods that evening in Cologne. "Take your time, Wafaa. I stand by my offer."

A few weeks later, in September 2002, I read in the newspapers about a scientific spectacle the new antiquities chief was preparing with *National Geographic* at the Great Pyramid. It was to be carried live on worldwide television. A robot that was obviously inspired by the vehicle Gantenbrink had made was to head up one of the ventilation shafts in the Queen's Chamber. With astonishment I read of Zahi's suddenly altered view of things: The shaft's terminal stone could well be a door, behind which undiscovered mysteries might be hidden, for example an unknown manuscript by Pharaoh Khufu, possibly a kind of diary, possibly a papyrus scroll whose content could finally perhaps provide information about the riddle of the pyramid's construction. The door could have had a religious function and led to magical spaces, resting places for the deceased pharaoh's soul.

As yet no books or papyrus scrolls have ever been found in any pyramid. There are the so-called Books of the Dead, to be sure, but only beginning in the Middle Kingdom, and the Book of the Two Paths, which has been found on coffins. The Book of the Dead also appears on papyrus scrolls found next to the deceased, but only in the New Kingdom. I spent the pyramid night in front of the television—a TV special scheduled for prime time in America and broadcast to more than one hundred countries worldwide. The robot *Explorer*, equipped with a stone drill, rolled sixty meters up the shaft and drilled a hole in the mysterious 'door.' A hollow space became visible, and behind it another stone slab. That was it. This was immediately followed by much speculation about the significance of the hollow space. A sacred precinct? A secret chamber of the god Thoth, the guardian of wisdom?

The next day the telephone never stopped ringing. Friends and journalists wanted to know whether that was the kind of Egyptology we practiced in Cairo? Was that the way the antiquities administration was treating the country's cultural heritage? Why would an antiquities chief permit such a spectacle? How much would *National Geographic* have made from the worldwide TV broadcast? It was clear to me that as antiquities chief, Zahi had aligned himself closely with the promoters of tourism, so important to Egypt's finances. But I was disappointed that the scholarly reputation of our native Egyptology was being demeaned in such manner, and was unsparing in public criticism of the undertaking.

8

IN THE MUSEUM

W as it a mistake to go back to Cairo? To impose the city on my two sons? There were moments when I had no answer to such questions. Blessedly—I have to say this before anything else—I would be compensated for all my anxiety many times over. By the miracles that revealed themselves to me in many forgotten corners of the museum; by the loyalty and friendship of magnificent colleagues; and by the gratitude I was able to see in the faces of so many children when we opened to them the gates of that gigantic treasury.

In the summer of 2003 we packed our bags. Azmy and I had decided. I was almost fifty-three years old. With Zahi Hawass my generation had moved into management positions in the antiquities administration. Now it was our turn. In ten years a younger generation could call the shots. If I still wished to accomplish something, now was the time. Before Zahi Hawass, the previous directors of the Supreme Council of Antiquities, Abdel Halim Nureddin and Gaballa Ali Gaballa, had both offered me the post of director of the Egyptian Museum in Cairo, and I had turned them down. Were I to decline once more, there was a good chance that no one in Cairo would ever consider me again. According to Egyptian law, I was still an employee of the antiquities administration, on unpaid maternity leave with the option to return. I wanted to work as an archaeologist again.

There was also the fact that Azmy wanted to give up the Dom-Apotheke. He wasn't enjoying it any longer. Instead, he wanted to concentrate on the subject of medicine in ancient Egypt. "I think I'll take early retirement." Moreover, we wanted our sons to get to know what life in Egypt was really like and to acquire a command of Arabic as if it were their mother tongue.

We were looking forward to a new chapter in our lives. But there were moments, especially in the first months of my seven-year tenure as director, in which I regretted one thing: my naïveté. I was prepared for hard work, tough negotiations, resistance, and plenty of tests of my patience. I had known the antiquities administration and the dark side of that mammoth bureaucracy with its thirty thousand employees for decades. The mills of bureaucracy grind slowly, and in authoritarian systems, I knew, they also crush people. I thought I was prepared for that, yet I had no idea what it would mean to have to stand up to that machinery every day. I couldn't imagine, or chose not to, that there would be people who were only waiting for me to make a mistake and have to ingloriously resign in ignominy.

We had the great good fortune of finding an apartment in Dokki, a district in the center of the city favored by businesspeople and foreign diplomats. The red tape and formalities associated with my move from Cairo to Cologne had been a bagatelle compared to the time and effort required in making the return journey. It was clear to us that we would have to live near the German Protestant School. We didn't want to expose Hadi and Tarek to hours-long school bus rides through Cairo. But it had not been easy to get them admitted, for there were plenty of Cairo families better off than us who also wanted to place their children there. A regular Egyptian school would have been out of the question—our boys would not have learned anything and only felt uncomfortable, especially since our younger one was constantly reproaching me, Why had I taken him away from all the friends in Cologne he had known since kindergarten? Why had we exchanged our lovely apartment with its large garden in Junkersdorf for a high-rise apartment in Dokki? "For what? For this town?" In those first weeks I had no reasonable response to Hadi's complaints. I sat at home for three weeks and had already abandoned my dream of being museum director.

As soon as our affairs permitted, I made an initial visit to the museum. Its director was Mamdouh Eldamaty, a young, bright colleague who, like his predecessor, had been called away from his chair at the university to take over the directorship. Eldamaty had always impressed me as a committed, serious man, and I had not counted on the fact that he would resign his office, normally renewed each year, so very soon. I had not made my return to Egypt contingent on my appointment as director, certain that I would be able to find some sort of suitable employment. I had greatly looked forward to seeing the museum again. I presented my antiquities service identity card, nodded to the security police at the entrance, and entered the great hall. Immediately I felt a rush of familiarity: the loud echoes of countless voices and footsteps, the warm light falling in through the upper windows and washing across the heavy sarcophagi, steles, and statues of black basalt, pink granite, quarzite, and porphyry, also the chirping of the guards' walkie-talkies, the multilingual cacophony of the guides, and in between the voice of a little girl—and that of my mother.

"Mama, were all the pharaohs so big?"

"No, they weren't. They were normal size, perhaps even a little smaller than people today."

"Then why are they all so gigantic?"

"Because the ancient Egyptians believed that their pharaoh was very powerful, for it was he who guaranteed order in the world. If the pharaoh was big and strong, Egypt was also big and strong. That's why they made colossal statues of their rulers."

I was eight years old the first time Mama took me to the Egyptian Museum. We had just moved to Cairo from Kafr al-Arab. Everything was outsize in this city: the royal palace, the pyramids, the museum, and the colossal statues inside it. I still clearly remember standing with Mama in the great hall in front of the double statue of Tiye and Amenhotep III.

"But how did they transport them?"

Their heads nearly reached the second-floor cornice, twelve meters above me. The couple dominated the wide atrium, even dwarfing the figure of the striding Senusret III, which was hardly small, and the huge stone sarcophagi at their feet. I'm sure that even today all the eight-year-olds' necks hurt when they gaze up at Tiye and Amenhotep III.

"They're a lot bigger than the main entrance! How did they get them in here?"

Mama explained that the statue, found in Luxor in 1889, had been broken in pieces. When the big new museum was built around 1900, archaeologists fitted the fragments together and restored the missing ones (some of which are still being found in Medinet Habu to this day) in the still empty hall.

"The queen is the same size as the pharaoh!" I cried. "In the other statues the wife is much smaller."

Mama said that Queen Tiye played an important role at her husband's side, and probably helped him rule the country.

More than four decades later, at almost fifty-three, I was once again standing in front of Queen Tiye. Even as a student, my first visit had always been to her. My favorite seminar papers had been the ones about Tiye, the mother of the pharaoh Akhenaten, and about the brief but so fascinating Amarna epoch. Later I liked to show Tiye's statue in my lectures on the role of women in ancient Egypt, on the great royal consorts and women rulers like Hatshepsut and Nefertiti. It was to the latter that I paid my second visit that morning—the most beautiful portrait of the queen. An unfinished head study from the workshop of Thutmose: a work in ocher-colored quartzite in which the master sculptor traced the eyelids, nose, and mouth as though with the finest eyeliner. It is impossible to express in words the effect Nefertiti's face has on me, and supposedly on most visitors as well. The German archaeologist Ludwig Borchardt discovered the workshop of Thutmose on December 6, 1912, and I feel he was absolutely correct in remarking, after he and his excavation worker Mohamed el-Senusi had freed the famous bust from the desert sand after more than thirty-three hundred years, "Description is of no use. Just look at it!" His words still apply today, and not only to the piece Borchardt took back to Berlin with him. They also suit perfectly the magical version in Cairo. In my opinion the woman's coy and distanced noblesse is expressed even more transcendently in the Cairo head than in the bust in Berlin. Nefertiti isn't smiling. On none of her portraits or those of Akhenaten do they wear the gracious, happy smiles with which Amenhotep III and Tiye greet visitors in the atrium. There is something else in her expression: a wisdom that looks beyond everything commonplace. I would often visit her in the evening, after the gates were closed, in order to restore my strength. Our woman-to-woman chats always did me good.

I then proceeded to the second floor, to Yuya and Tuya, Tiye's parents. Yuya was the commander of charioteers under Amenhotep III. In 1907 he and Tuya were the first star attractions of the still-new museum—it was only their grandson Tutankhamun who stole the whole show a couple of decades later. But I was shattered. Yuya's gold coffin was in terrible shape! Everywhere there were deep cracks in the wood that was overlaid with heavy sheet gold. It was still in the glass case in which it had been placed after the discovery of his almost fully intact tomb in 1905. Ever since then, beneath the ordinary glass of the display case, virtually unprotected, the treasure had been exposed to heat and cold and seasonal humidity changes. Even worse: Yuya and Tuya's mummies were still lying in their coffins. Yuya's corpse lay there, swathed in cloth, just as it had been 3,390 years ago, his head still covered with thick, henna-tinted hair. He looked as though he had only just fallen asleep. To me he is the most impressive personality of the museum, which is also a cemetery in which the prominent dead are on public display. This was always anathema to my mother.

I was also shocked by the miserable condition of the museum itself. In western travel guides it is said, at times dismissively, that the Egyptian Museum resembles a storeroom bursting at the seams. It is true, the most priceless artifacts are crowded close together. But when the French architect Marcel Dourgnon designed the structure at the end of the nineteenth century, he could not have known that within only a few years an ever increasing number of archaeological missions would make more discoveries and finds than in all the years since Auguste Mariette.

The first collection of Egyptian antiquities, virtually wrenched from the hands of zealous European collectors, had still been quite manageable. It had taken considerable skill to convince Muhammad Ali Pasha that he too ought to have a collection of pharaonic masterworks. The first antiquities were gathered together from about 1835, and in 1848 they were housed in a storeroom in the Azbakiya Garden, then in 1851 in the Citadel. It was only in 1858 that Mariette was able to set up the first public museum, which was then enlarged little by little, in Cairo's Bulaq district. But even while it was installed in former storage sheds next to the 'Beautiful Lake'—the quarter took its name from *Beau Lac*—it was perceived that the rapidly growing collection would soon require a presentable structure of its own. In 1890 the art treasures were moved into forty-six splendid rooms in the palace of the Ottoman viceroy in Giza. But there too it was already clear that the palace was only a temporary solution.

At that time Cairo was considered the Paris of the East, and the viceroy wanted an Egyptian 'Louvre.' Inasmuch as the antiquities service had been the domain of the French since Muhammad Ali's days, it is not surprising that of all the designs submitted it was ultimately that of the Frenchman Marcel Dourgnon that won the architectural competition. In 1897 the cornerstone for the neoclassical structure was laid in a huge open space near the British army barracks. Five years later, on November 15, 1902, the building was dedicated with great pomp. At that time it was the first structure in the East to have been built specifically for a museum.

Gaston Maspero, its first director, oversaw the transport of five thousand wooden crates from Giza and other antiquities depots. The huge cellar rooms served as a central warehouse for all the excavation finds to which the country was entitled. In 1902 the museum's inventory book, the Journal d'Entrée, listed roughly thirty-five thousand objects—today it numbers some one hundred sixty thousand. The museum could not keep up with the crop of finds from the following years; the large, spectacular tomb openings presented particular space problems. First there were the almost complete tomb furnishings of Yuya and Tuya, then came the five thousand treasures from the tomb of Tutankhamun, for which a whole wing of the museum had to be cleared on the second floor. Then in 1940 Pierre Montet sent the gold treasure from Tanis. Again space had to be created for the gold mask of Psusennes I (Pasebakhaenniu), for the sarcophagus and silver coffin, for display cases with hundreds of the most intricate pieces of jewelry. In the 1950s and 1960s the legendary third Nubian campaign—the first two had both taken place before the old British Aswan dam had been constructed and later heightened—became the greatest challenge to the building's capacity. An international excavation and research action on the part of UNESCO probed and excavated ancient sites in Nubia, which would otherwise have been irretrievably submerged in Nasser's reservoir, among them dozens of Nubian cemeteries, hill tombs, and settlements. In short, the hundred galleries of the Cairo Museum became increasingly tightly packed with display cases. Hundreds of mummies, coffins, precious palace furnishings, papyri, jewelry, and statues from all epochs of Egyptian high culture crowded into the building, and now cover nearly every square meter of its wall and floor surfaces. The library in the museum's left wing had to vacate a number of its spaces; storerooms were built into the galleries themselves; curators were forced to abandon their workrooms. The attic floor, not accessible to the public, became a storeroom for stacks of coffins and mummies—and for decades truckloads of wooden crates filled with excavation finds were crammed into the cellar.

Yet the basic concept of the building hadn't changed since Maspero's time. The collection was still presented as an old-style scholarly teaching collection. But meanwhile the display cases had become so full that many visitors found the sheer abundance overwhelming. Many joked that the galleries were at the same time probably the storeroom, and they were right. With the museum's treasures one could easily supply five to ten additional antiquities museums in Egypt—and since then that development has indeed happened.

But for me the antiquated feel of the building was its special charm. The structure in Tahrir Square, more than one hundred years old, is itself a museum piece—in the middle of a rapidly expanding city in which less and less of the former magic of the Paris of the East survives. For years I stubbornly refused to have the old glass display cases from the Bulaq museum, some of them 150 years old, simply junked. When Berlin's Neues Museum reopened in 2009, I noted with gratification that the Berliners had restored the ruins of the neoclassical Stüler building at great expense, and in many galleries refurbished its original furnishings, including the historic wooden display cases and cabinets. To me this was proof that our museum also urgently needed to be upgraded, with modern fire protection and air conditioning, but that its concept and furnishings were altogether à jour.

It was not only the battered state of the historic furniture that moved me that morning, not only the dust and the largely antiquated, even inaccurate, vitrine labels, some of which dated back to Maspero's time. It was most of all the recognition that in the years I had been away it was obvious that nothing had been done. I had to wonder whether my predecessors couldn't see what I was seeing. Perhaps they were too absorbed in scholarship, perhaps they were used to the more modest academic apparatus of their universities but unable to cope with a museum staff of more than three hundred and the extremely complex hierarchy within the antiquities service. But where had all the money gone that was spent on the museum's centenary the year before? After all, the museum's income is enormous.

The Egyptian Museum is the antiquities service's main source of funds. A hundred years ago perhaps 500 visitors strolled through its rooms and galleries every day; in 2003 there were as many as 5,000, and some days at the end of my tenure as director in 2010 there would be up to 12,000 visitors—roughly 2.5 million people annually. I knew for certain that we could count on roughly LE1 million a day—which before the Revolution converted to $172,400—from entrance fees. In good years the museum thus produced annual revenues of roughly $50 million—in addition to entrance and loan fees from exhibitions abroad. In 2003 this was in contrast to the museum's petty budget of LE2,000 returned from the tills of the antiquities service. I learned this from Mamdouh Eldamaty.

"Two thousand pounds a day?" I asked, appalled.

"Two thousand pounds a year!" Or less than $350 for all repairs, painting, installations. Egypt's most important museum generates millions, but via the Ministry of Culture those millions flow into the coffers of the Egyptian government. It is true that a new coat of paint was applied to the façade. But I later discovered that for the jubilee the antiquities service also had gold medals minted for distribution to guests and members of the government. I found a few of these valuable medals in the museum safe—at a time when I didn't know how I was supposed to pay my staff. A record of their original number and their recipients was nowhere to be found. I immediately had those that remained entered into the inventory lists.

On that morning I once more called on Mai Terade, the museum's factotum. No one knew exactly how old she was. I had known her since my student days in the early 1970s. Mai came from Lebanon, was an Egyptologist, and for more than thirty years had probably spent every day in the museum and assisted any number of prominent Egyptologists from around the world with their research projects. The museum was her home, and no one knew the historical registers and collection catalogs as well as she did. Wherever I would visit museum colleagues outside the country, they would inevitably ask, "How is Mai doing? Is she still at the museum?" Today, sadly, no longer. After the 2011 Revolution she returned to Lebanon. Mai lived near Tahrir Square. The tumult kept the old woman from venturing out of the house, and the noise and the tear gas affected her health. She could no longer manage the few meters' walk over to the museum. I miss her greatly. She was the soul of the museum.

I can still see the little woman quite clearly before me. She needed a cane, to be sure, but her eyes darted about in a lively way; nothing in the building escaped her.

"I've been waiting for you, Wafaa," she said. "I've always known that you would come. Now everything will be fine, *in sha' Allah.*"

We greeted each other like mother and daughter, and in the following years simply knowing that Mai was in the building gave me confidence. The old woman introduced her closest colleague to me: Sabah Abdel Razeq. "Sabah is the most industrious curator of all," Mai said, and a friendly smile lit up the Nubian woman's beautiful face. Sabah was just forty years old, and like Mai she was married to the museum. Also probably single because Nubian tradition would have required that she marry a member of her family or her tribe. Sabah became my closest colleague—reliable, loyal, and end-lessly active. In the next few years she would accomplish huge amounts of work, and even in critical situations never lose her concentration and inner composure.

Mai hooked her arm in mine and we went out into the museum garden, where we strolled about between its fragments of a granite obelisk of Ramses II, the remnants of his colossal statue, and a sphinx dating from the reign of King Thutmose III. I loved that garden, its pond with lotus and papyrus plants, symbols of Upper and Lower Egypt. But the lawn and plantings were neglected and untidy, the pond completely clogged with algae.

"I'm sad and angry, Wafaa," Mai said. "Over the past year they've spent great sums of money, but nothing has stayed in the museum. They've squandered all of it."

"I know, I saw that on television. That's why I didn't come for the celebration."

The antiquities service had placed me on the program of the conference "Museology in the 21st Century," for which I had prepared a lecture on museum education. But then friends told me by phone that seasonal workers, the poorest of our temporary employees in the antiquities service, hadn't been paid for weeks. The money was apparently being used to finance the centennial events. So I refused to take part. My colleague Ula el-Ugazi, a professor at Cairo University, delivered the lecture in my place, and I then followed the several days of centennial celebrations in December 2002 via satellite on Egyptian television.

A festival tent capable of holding several hundred guests had been set up in the green space in front of the museum. For security reasons, all the flowerbeds and hedges had been removed, for Suzanne Mubarak was expected as the honored guest, and they were potential hiding places for bombs. A few rooms in the cellar had been cleared for the special exhibition *Hidden Treasures of the Egyptian Museum*—which created hopeless disorder in the remaining vaults. Crates and boxes had simply been shoved at random into the neighboring spaces, which were already overfilled. To the guests arrayed around Suzanne Mubarak—the directors of world-famous museums including those of Paris, London, New York, Vienna, Hildesheim, Boston, and Oslo—Zahi Hawass then presented his vision for the Grand Egyptian Museum on the Giza plateau, on which planning had begun in early 2002. Of the seventeen hundred submissions to the architectural competition, twenty proposals were already in the final selection stage. The construction cost, estimated at $450 million, was to be financed by contributions secured by a fundraising organization under the direction of the minister of culture. The new museum would exhibit only 'masterpieces' from ancient Egypt like Tutankhamun's tomb treasure. The famous royal mummies would in future be placed in the Museum for Egyptian Civilization in Fustat, or Old Cairo. There were also already plans for a museum in the resort city of Sharm el-Sheikh.

What was announced on the hundredth birthday of the Egyptian Museum would thus be its demise. Its most spectacular holdings were to be sent to Giza, and other prominent artifacts divided among other museums around the country. The old building would be left with only its huge mishmash of lesser artifacts. It was immediately clear to me that the streams of visitors would thus be redirected from Tahrir Square to Giza, where tourists might visit the major draw, Tutankhamun, as well as the pyramids. Virtually no one would bother to travel into the city anymore. The words with which my Hildesheim colleague Arne Eggebrecht had greeted me struck me as an admonitory motivation: "There are many museums of Egyptian art around the world, but only one Egyptian Museum. And it has stood in Cairo for precisely one hundred years."

I took my leave from Mai, and after our conversation I was utterly depressed. The next day I called on Zahi Hawass and explained to him that I saw no sense in assuming the directorship as long as the antiquities administration was unwilling to do something for the old museum. Zahi listened attentively, then nodded. Yes, he knew that certain things were in bad shape there, I was perfectly right. We would discuss them in due course. "You have my full support, Wafaa. But you know that here everything takes time, in the antiquities administration and in the ministry."

"I'll take on the directorship only if I'm given an authoritative promise of adequate funding."

There was plenty to do, reorganizing our family life and mitigating Hadi's homesickness. At the end of September there were a few days with no school, and we drove to Luxor. After the stress of the move, we deserved a break. Again I followed my long familiar routes across the temple complexes, to the Hatshepsut Temple, to the Valley of the Kings. Next to the Amun-Re Temple in Karnak I surveyed the excavations by colleagues from the French–Egyptian Center for the Study of the Temples of Karnak, and what I saw saddened me. Our young Egyptian inspectors were idly watching while their French counterparts went about their work. I spoke to one young woman and asked why she wasn't working as well.

"Because they ignore us," she explained. "They shove us aside and won't let us work with them. Even though the mission is supposedly a joint venture."

I read the sign on the excavation hut and noted the difference between the Arabic and French versions of the mission's name: In Arabic it read "Egyptian–French," in the French translation "French–Egyptian." So it was clear who was playing first fiddle.

"The Frenchmen also prevent us Egyptians from doing our own digs here in the temple," the young woman complained. "They still treat Karnak as their own colony."

Since the 1960s an official protocol had been in place between the antiquities administration and the French. It specified that the excavations in Karnak were to be cooperative ventures.

"My colleagues and I have complained in Cairo, but we have received no response from the antiquities administration," she said.

Had nothing changed since my own time as an inspector? "Come with me," I said. "We'll see about this."

At the dig I searched for the French director, introduced myself as a member of the antiquities administration, and reminded him that his mission had been granted an excavation permit from our country, and thus the favor of being allowed to dig in one of the most important spots in the history of Egyptian high culture.

"If you continue to refuse to include your Egyptian colleagues in your work, you are in violation of our agreement. If you continue to treat my colleagues this way, you will have to leave the site. I'll see to it!" I made certain that the dig's director understood my every word.

Ten years later, as I write this, I read in the issue of *al-Akhbar* for December 1, 2012, an article that makes me furious. It reports that Egyptian inspectors have complained about the attitude of the French mission in Karnak.

While I was still talking with the inspector about her problem, a few Egyptian excavation workers approached me, one of whom had apparently recognized me. None of them had been paid for three months. I refused to believe it at first, but their foreman confirmed it.

"These men have children who were supposed to start school last week. But they can't go to school because their fathers have no money for school uniforms. There's not even money to feed their families."

I promised to speak to Zahi Hawass about it immediately. I called him and explained the situation in Karnak. Zahi promised to take care of it immediately. At the hotel I was unable to eat dinner, thinking of the hungry children, and during the night I had nightmares. The next morning Azmy said, "Come, let's go to Karnak. I have some money for the workmen." He couldn't stand seeing me refuse to eat. Back in Cairo I discovered that Karnak was not an exception, but the dismal rule. Where were the workers' wages going? When would these people man the barricades?

In October 2003 Zahi Hawass phoned me. "You have to take over the directorship of the Scientific Bureau. I need you to be my assistant." I accepted the position that I had already occupied under Ahmed Qadri. I looked forward to getting back to scholarly work; I would have a free hand, and I had plenty of ideas. Collaboration with international excavation teams had to become truly cooperative. But Zahi asked me to first make contact with a man I'll call, out of consideration for his family, Ali Fahmi. Fahmi would explain which undertakings were of concern to the Scientific Bureau. I didn't know the man, he was not a member of the antiquities service. When I mentioned his name to Azmy, he was surprised. "I know him. He's an acquaintance of my friend Kahul, the director of the sports club in the Nile Hilton. I've played tennis with him there a few times. I'll tell you what, I'll come along to say hello." So we drove to the address Zahi had given me, and I was astonished: Fahmi was the owner of a travel agency. He received us quite cordially and chatted with Azmy about mutual acquaintances. Fahmi was about fifty. On the walls of his office hung historical photographs of Egypt. He related that he owned a large collection of rare and very beautiful photographic plates and that his second hobby was the enjoyment of fine wines, an indulgence that was clearly registered in his face. I was surprised to see next door various high-ranking colleagues from the antiquities administration discussing various official matters and apparently receiving Fahmi's instructions. He had no specific instructions for me; it appeared as though he first wanted to size me up. "Firstly, please write me an outline of what you propose to undertake in the Scientific Bureau. It would be nice if you could let me have it in a week."

I was shocked. Why should I provide access to internal matters to an outsider? I made inquiries among friends and colleagues. Who is Ali Fahmi? I was told that after Zahi Hawass, Fahmi was possibly the most powerful man in the antiquities service. I drove to Zamalek and Zahi's office. We're friends, I thought, we can talk openly and honestly about everything.

"Who is Ali Fahmi?"

"A friend. An adviser. A man I can depend on."

"But he operates a tourist and travel office! Since when do we work with private travel agencies?" There was an unwritten rule in the antiquities service: no collaboration with commercial travel interests. "Why should an outsider make decisions about matters that are supposed to be managed by us alone?"

But Zahi responded, "Do what he says. He's a businessman. He knows how to resolve problems in a professional manner."

"You know that he also has an antiques store."

"Don't worry, Wafaa. Everything is in order."

Fahmi soon learned how I felt about him. Working in Zahi's office was a woman—who later became Fahmi's wife—I will call Amal out of respect for her family. Two floors above Zahi was another Fahmi confidant: Abdel Aziz Mansur (again not his real name), chief architect to the Supreme Council.

Weeks passed, days in my office, the long days of Ramadan. We gradually became accustomed to the rhythm of life in this city again, to close contact with my siblings and good friends old and new. Tarek and Hadi found new friends in the German school. I enjoyed my work in the Scientific Bureau. Then in January 2004 Mamdouh Eldamaty resigned his office prematurely.

Friends called me. "Now you have to become the director. The people in the museum need you, Wafaa. Go to Zahi!" Ali Radwan and Shafia Bedier, both university professors, got in touch. "Make me happy and take over the museum," Ali Radwan said. "It needs your help so desperately." Shafia Bedier even appealed to my patriotism: "Do it for Egypt!" Finally Mahmud Mabruk was on the phone, the director of the Museums Department in the antiquities administration. "Dr. Wafaa, I can assure you that you will be given all the support you require."

Zahi Hawass summoned me to Zamalek. "We all want you to be successful. That's why I summoned you back to Cairo after all. Now you can take on the directorship."

If I weren't able to obtain definite promises of adequate funding then, I surely wouldn't later. So I explained to Zahi that I would by no means take over the museum under the conditions imposed on my predecessor. The antiquities administration would have to allocate an appropriate, separate budget.

"Mere patchwork has to finally stop. I have no desire to have to beg for months for every pound."

Zahi could hardly believe that the museum's annual budget was only LE2,000. He promised to change that. In fact, in the coming years he always promptly approved the funds I asked for. Zahi was truly interested in the fortunes of the building—though at the same time committed to the building of the Grand Museum.

"Wouldn't it be possible to take the Egyptian Museum away from the Museums Department?" I asked. "Treat it as an independent institution?"

Zahi hated the bureaucracy too. "Wafaa, in the museum you'll have a completely free hand. I promise you that. But the law wouldn't allow special status for the museum. That I can't change."

I believed him, but finally made it absolutely clear: "No intervention in the affairs of the museum. I don't want Ali Fahmi or any other outsider telling me what to do."

At the end of January I visited Mamdouh Eldamaty at the museum. I was eager to learn what he could tell me about the working conditions, what tips and advice he might give me, and what unfinished projects he was leaving behind. I found him already packing. His office was filled with cardboard boxes, stacks of books and journals ready for the move. He greeted me cordially, but he made no secret of his bitterness.

"To be frank, my dear colleague, I've had it. I'm truly happy to be getting out of here and being able to return to my chair at the university. Shall I show you something?" Eldamaty reached for a thick file folder. "This is my correspondence with the antiquities administration. In it are only a portion of my appeals for modernization of the museum, for urgently needed repairs and new projects. But wouldn't you think I might have received a response from the Museums Sector, if only a notice that it was under consideration? Nothing. Nothing was dealt with." That was mainly the fault of the director of the Museums Department. "You'll get to know him too."

I felt sorry for Eldamaty as he proceeded to pack his briefcase. Would I one day leave the building the same way? Not on your life, I swore to myself.

In February 2004 I assumed the office of general director of the museum and director of the Committee for Exhibitions Abroad. In the museum's hundred-year history, I was officially the first woman to head it. At first I was paid LE750 a month, or around $120. I was surprised, for as director I was being paid far less than a great number of my colleagues at the Supreme Council's headquarters in Zamalek. I was making less than my cleaning woman. Our rent in Dokki alone amounted to LE6,000. Without Azmy's German pension we could not have paid it, to say nothing of Hadi and Tarek's school fees and of course the ordinary household expenses. I then learned that I was entitled to additional honoraria, so that I at least received LE2,250, or roughly $365. I had little more than nothing to lose.

On my very first day I asked the curators, the director of the restoration workshops, the chief of police, and the head of the security personnel separately into my office. The police were responsible for security outside the museum, and were appointed by the Interior Ministry. The 160 or so members of the security service worked for the antiquities administration. They saw to security in the museum's interior, protecting against theft and enforcing regulations like the ban on smoking, eating, and taking photographs. In addition, the museum was under surveillance by a number of cameras—the video room was right next to my office. The police chief politely left me immediately: his unit's location was changed every three years, and he was to be reassigned in the next few days. He wished me good luck. The head of security made no bones about his reluctance to take directions from a woman. He had himself transferred.

I met with the curators, most of whom I didn't yet know. Each of the museum's six departments was overseen by a chief curator and his or her deputy, and employed three assistants, so there were thirty curators in all, 90 percent of them women. A few months later I would establish two additional departments. Sabah Abdel Razeq became the head curator of the cellar project and was assigned five assistants. I also added the registration project, with eight female employees, charged with creating a digital database. The laboratory employed twenty-three restorers. Four Egyptologists were in charge of the museum's audio guides. In addition, we employed eight administrative assistants, two photographers, four publicity people, six electricians, two exhibition architects, three cabinetmakers, three painters, three plumbers, two garden architects and sixteen gardeners, two doctors and three doctors' assistants, eight firefighters with two fire trucks, twenty laborers for handling heavy objects, four storeroom workers—all in all, a staff of more than three hundred.

The curators were responsible for all the objects in their collections. It was up to them to appraise the artifacts' condition and if necessary have them restored; they were also responsible for the illumination, cleanliness, and security of objects both displayed and in storage, and they assisted outside scholars with their research projects. Among other things, they were also responsible for the vitrine labels, which were supposed to convey to visitors briefly and accurately the current state of knowledge about each piece displayed. But those were in bad shape. I therefore explained to my colleagues that in the coming months we needed to revise the case labels, making them bilingual, English and Arabic. Most of them, long since yellowed, were handwritten in French, and dated back to the time of the museum's found-ing. No Egyptian visitor could decipher those hieroglyphs. I knew that it was a challenge to produce brief, up-to-date descriptions of several thousand objects, but little by little we managed to modernize at least the most import-ant ones.

It would take a while before we trusted each other; I could see that during our initial conversations. Most of the curators were frustrated after long years of bad experiences. Finally, during the centennial celebrations they had had to see what enormous sums were spent on festivities while they had strug-gled in their separate departments for years. Curators and the director of the laboratory earned even less than I did; the younger curators, security people, and workmen made not even LE200 a month, or $32. With less than $1 a day they could hardly satisfy their everyday needs. Many were forced to take on second jobs on the side. And here was I with all my plans, which quite obvi-ously alarmed the curators or even angered them. At one meeting with all the curators I promised to try to arrange stipends for them for training in modern museology, for further education and even perhaps abroad. I could see their skeptical expressions, which translated as "We'll believe it when we see it." In my seven years as director, I managed to send most of the curators and the restorers and photographers to continuing education courses at foreign museums, thanks to the assistance of many friends, colleagues, and sponsors. I could see how motivated and cheerful they were when they returned to their workplaces after those workshops, how good it had been for them to spend time with their foreign counterparts—most of them could only have dreamed of traveling on their own.

Trust takes time. At first my colleagues shied away from contact with me, as though afraid to knock on my door. But on my morning rounds I would chat with one or another of the curators. "We've been told that you don't want to receive anyone. That your receptionist has been instructed to turn everyone away, since you don't wish to be disturbed." I learned that my two secretaries had spread the rumor that I was snobbish and inept. I took the two women to task and explained to them that in the coming weeks I would put together a team of my own, and that they should look for other work. I couldn't have been prouder of my new office help: Fatma Alzahraa was responsible for scheduling all my appointments; Mona Abdel Nazier oversaw all research activities in the building; and Albert Girgis was the most energetic book-keeper I have ever met, a walking computer with an incredible memory for names, figures, management protocols, directives, and regulations. Albert reviewed all contracts for exhibitions abroad. In my seven years, the three of them were a tremendous support and made manageable the enormous flow of paperwork through the director's office. They called my attention to documents I would do better to read twice; anything they placed in front of me I knew I could sign without hesitation. Their two predecessors used their brief time in my office to forge my signature on inaccurate billings for overtime and honoraria. In addition, in my name they ordered from the antiquities service's replica department in Zamalek expensive copies of artifacts the museum supposedly needed to present to especially important visitors, guests of the state and diplomats. The replicas were nowhere to be found. I informed Zahi Hawass, and was amazed that the two women nevertheless continued to be employed in Zamalek.

I soon learned that the museum's fundamental problem was not the blatant lack of money. The more I rummaged through the files and made phone calls reminding people that our requests had not been met, the more I came to sympathize with my desperate predecessors. The Museums Department, especially, routinely procrastinated. In an interview with the Egyptian press I once explained that my most maddening obstacle was the Museums bureaucracy. The next day the department's angry director phoned me. How could I have said such a thing in public? I then enumerated my various requests gathering dust in his desk drawers. After that it was somewhat better for a time, but eventually everything resumed the old routine.

We arranged that every morning the curators would meet with me to discuss the day's schedule. The museum is huge, and without a fixed appointment I might have gone for weeks without seeing my staff. I now got to know each of them personally, was able to praise them, motivate them, correct them. A museum is only as good as its employees; that I had learned in Europe and the United States. I wanted to raise my colleagues to the standards I had come to know abroad.

Before the nine o'clock meeting I would make a tour through the still empty building. One morning I chose to have a look at the exterior as well. My gaze fell on the main portal, the beautifully carved doors, dating from

1902, with their lacy botanical ornaments and copper fittings, the Egyptian crown and once shiny gold stars. All had been covered up with thick layers of paint. I also studied the façade, the figures in their niches, the marble steps leading up to the portal—the once gleaming stone had turned dark beneath layers of grime. I put the restoration of the doors and scheduling a date with the cleaning firm on my to-do list.

When I asked who had been responsible for the paint that had to be scraped off the façade so laboriously, I was told that it had been the minister of culture Farouk Hosni's right-hand man and the chief architect of the antiquities administration. The two of them had also initiated the installation of the heavy marble slabs on the ground floor interior walls and statue bases, which didn't match the museum's decor. I asked the museum's architect why she hadn't prevented it. "We couldn't do anything to stop it. The two men are very powerful." I called on our family friend Klaus Heinen in Cologne for help. He was an architect, and came to Cairo at his own expense. Klaus confirmed my suspicion: The marble slabs were extremely heavy and posed a structural risk to the cellar vaulting. In addition, condensation building up behind the marble slabs was damaging the walls. I put the marble slabs on my to-do list—and can now jump ahead and report that they were removed during subsequent renovation measures, and that the two gentlemen, who had managed to make quick fortunes by awarding contracts to large companies, are now sitting in prison.

I was also unhappy with the situation on the east side of the museum. An ugly extension was serving as a group shelter for policemen on watch, and an unsightly concrete wall closed off the area from the street. The men would spend the night in filthy rooms, hang their laundry ouside, and carelessly throw out scraps of food. But what was worse were the ancient objects lying around the museum: parts of sphinxes, obelisks, statues, sarcophagi, reliefs, and even two tomb chambers. Everything was covered with sand and dust. I commissioned Mai Terade and two young colleagues, Wahid Edward and Wahid Girgis, to work with the restorers, inventory the blocks, clean them, and restore them. I asked Lutfi Hassan, the antiquities administration's chief restorer in Luxor, to choose the most beautiful objects for a sculpture garden. Lutfi and our workmen managed to create a delightful green circuit. But before that we tore down the ugly police barracks and created rooms fit for human occupation on the museum's north side. The concrete wall was removed, and in its place iron railings matching the historical design were installed. Now passersby were able to look into the inviting sculpture garden from the street. I also established a deadline by which the gardeners were to plant new trees and shrubs.

Tahrir Square is surely the busiest traffic circle on the African continent. The museum was buffeted by traffic pouring across the Nile bridges. The square was no showplace, especially since the view of the museum was obscured by an ugly construction fence around a huge space in front of the Nile Hilton—presumably the most expensive building site in Cairo, symptomatic of the public building sector's brazen corruption and turgid bureaucracy. But as well as the smog, sand was carried into the city from the desert by the wind, infiltrating the museum, its galleries and vestibules. Every morning squads of cleaning women worked their way through the building. I would watch their sloppy mopping and try not to lose my patience. They would push in front of them waves of dirty water that ran under the wooden display cases and cabinets and naturally invited mildew and damaged the wood. Thick layers of dust on cornices and pedestals should have been removed much more frequently with industrial vacuum cleaners. The cleaning staff would wipe the glass of the display cases with rags and cheap cleaning products and create more smears than transparency. I ordered microfiber cloths from Germany, and instructed the cleaning women and men to be more sparing with their water and to not use cleaning agents on the surfaces of statues. I was henceforth known as the 'German cleaning devil.'

The cleaning firm's boss scrimped everywhere he could, on cleaning products, on equipment, and on the wages of his workers, all of whom were uninsured—even though they were required to climb tall ladders and scaffolding. He was concerned mainly with making as much money as possible out of the cleaning contract. But he also had other tricks up his sleeve: His employees charged with cleaning the toilets were instructed to require a baksheesh from visitors and thereby collect a tidy sum each day. I instructed our security people to put a stop to that, but discovered that the head of the cleaning firm was in cahoots with the chief of police, with whom he shared his proceeds from the toilets. I then spoke with the cleaning people themselves, and was astonished to learn how many of them were well educated, even university graduates. One woman explained to me that she was a graduate engineer, but as a single mother couldn't find another job. They were young people whose parents had done all they could to see that their children were able to attend the university, and were now, in turn, obliged to accept any job, however poorly paid, to assure a future for their own children. Egypt's wealth—how contemptuously squandered it was under Mubarak. But at least I won one battle against cronyism. The cleaning firm was dismissed and the police chief transferred.

Sabah usually accompanied me on my rounds. We enjoyed strolling through the empty galleries in the early morning, calling each other's attention to things we might not have noticed before. The ground floor takes visitors on a journey through time, from prehistory down to the time of the Ptolemies, from the hand ax to the Narmer Palette, from the tiny statuette of Khufu down to the glowing alabaster head of Alexander the Great. The second floor is devoted to ensembles of finds and specific themes: Tutankhamun, Yuya and Tuya, the Tanis treasures, the exquisite jewelry from the princesses' tombs at Dahshur, and the filigree sheet-gold armbands of the priests of Serapis from Dush in the Western Desert. And then there are the precious papyri, coffins, canopic jars, musical instruments, medical and surgical instruments, and so on. On each circuit I would see something new, perhaps details I had never noticed on a diadem or necklace of Princess Khnumet or the wonderful panther heads, carefully embossed in sheet gold, on a beaded belt of Mereret. Again and again I was drawn to the Roman-era mummy portraits. Their naturalistic depictions show the deceased with wistful expressions. This style of encaustic painting, the use of wax and tempera pigments on thin wooden panels, replaced the centuries-old, stylized coffin paintings of the Egyptians. The museum owns an impressive collection of such paintings, which are perhaps equalled only by the frescoes in Pompeii. Each portrait holds the secret of a Mona Lisa.

I said to Sabah, "We simply have to have a space for special exhibits. We need to be able to interest visitors in objects that otherwise tend to get overlooked."

We wrote it down on our notepad. Months later we celebrated a first such show with *Fayum Portraits*. I had suggested giving Room 14 a new coat of paint that would serve as a suitable background for them, and procuring new display cases with modern lighting. I had been given the paint, but plans for the display cases are still lying in the drawers of the antiquities administration's Projects Department. For the exhibit, with Sabah and my American friend the book illustrator Biri Fay, I wrote a children's book that for the first time would appeal particularly to the youngest visitors. When Prince Charles and his wife Camilla, Duchess of Cornwall, visited the museum, the prince wanted to visit the special exhibit, as he remembered the portraits from an earlier visit. Happily, that meant good publicity and appreciative press notices.

It would have been logistically impossible to move from room to room with special exhibits. So with the help of Zeinab Tawfiq, curator of the Late Period Department, we cleared the ground-floor Room 44, the first gallery to the right of the atrium. *Fayum Portraits* was the first of thirty special exhibits we put together in that newly cleared space in those seven years. They not only appealed to the public, they also fulfilled another purpose. To each opening event we would invite ambassadors, cultural attachés, diplomats, foreign cultural institutes, and of course prominent Egyptians. The illustrious guests made for a festive atmosphere, and our staff would bring their colleagues and families. Press and television reporters would be there, so many Egyptians were attracted to the shows and left appreciative comments in the guest book. Such public attention was a boost for the curators. Most had felt neglected for years, earning miserable wages and working in miserable conditions, often without even a desk of their own. The special exhibits helped to improve their income with special honoraria, gave them a chance to publish scholarly essays in the exhibition catalogs, and finally allowed them to present their collections and knowledge in a new way. Since foreign excavation missions were invited to present their activities in the museum, curators came into contact with archaeologists, and together with their recent finds could display pieces from their own collections. That helped to spark the curators' creativity. Room 44 inspired us to be constantly on the lookout for new themes, to consider the collections from new points of view.

My favorite department was the one displayed in Rooms 3 and 8—the Amarna epoch, the era of Akhenaten and Nefertiti. They ruled for barely sixteen years, but more than anyone before they changed centuries of Egyptian tradition. They turned away from Egypt's polytheism, from the Amun city of Karnak (Thebes), and worshiped the old sun god Aten alone, in a cult that many religion scholars and cultural historians see as a precursor of monotheism. Around 1340 BC Akhenaten and Nefertiti unleashed a cultural revolution—and to some extent they did so in the year 2004 as well.

Many of the wonderful Amarna artifacts were poorly displayed. Ibrahim Abdel Gawad, the curator responsible for them, was reluctant to change anything. He had taken over the department that way from his predecessor, and planned to leave it that way. I couldn't accept such an attitude, and told him that the space needed to be redesigned.

Abdel Gawad responded, "If I were to act like you, I could leave my head at home!"

"I'll tell you what, Mr. Ibrahim, you can simply stay at home entirely. I need someone here who's committed to the department. Perhaps I should look for a young curator who could provide a fresh approach."

That gave Ibrahim Abdel Gawad something to think about, and suddenly he became one of the most committed curators. My colleagues had previously complained about his conservatism, but now he was bursting with ideas. First the walls were painted an 'Amarna' shade. Then we retrieved pieces of the shrine of Queen Tiye from a hidden wall niche and placed them next to the wooden coffin that was also found in KV 55. The gilt shrine was executed in the Amarna style, and bears the names of Amenhotep III, Queen Tiye, and Akhenaten. Piece by piece, we now placed things together that belonged together. The body of Akhenaten's coffin came to stand next to its lid, from which it had long been separated. At some point the coffin had disappeared from the Egyptian Museum, and in the 1990s it reappeared on the antiquities market. It was purchased by the State Collection of Egyptian Art in Munich and masterfully restored: The fragile wood, partially covered with gold foil, was treated, and the inlays of cobalt-blue, turquoise, and transparent glass and reddish chalcedony now shone as brightly as when they were new. The foil and intarsias form a beautiful feather pattern that can also be seen on Tutankhamun's middle coffin and viscera coffins. After it was restored, the coffin was returned to Egypt.

Ibrahim was incredibly industrious. Display cases were moved and rearranged, and in the newly won space the beautiful quartzite head of Nefertiti came to be bathed in new light. Her flawless face could now be fully appreciated. I always thought how wonderful it would be if only we could sometime place the colored bust from Berlin next to it. That void continues to be an open wound in the Egyptian psyche to this day. We feel we were tricked out of the bust, and cannot understand why we are not permitted to display the queen in Egypt too. We have sent Tutankhamun around the world so that everyone, including those who couldn't afford a plane ticket to Cairo, might be able to admire him face to face. Why couldn't the same thing be done with Nefertiti?

At the Ministry of Culture I asked whether I might propose an exchange of exhibitions with Berlin. We could send some of our more precious treasures, and in return borrow the Nefertiti and some of the models from the Thutmose workshop displayed in Berlin. But Ashraf al-Ashmawi, a ministry lawyer, explained, "Were we to apply for such a loan, it would be an indirect acknowledgment of Berlin's ownership rights, something we'll never do."

In the absence of legal recourse, only a diplomatic solution might be found. The two countries could agree that the bust is on permanent loan from Egypt to Berlin's Museum Island. Thus its continued display in the Neues Museum would be assured, yet the Egyptians' claim to its ownership formally acknowledged. But Berlin was highly unlikely to take such a step, even though at one time it had been prepared to give back the bust. In the 1920s the Egyptian Museum and the Prussian minister of culture agreed to exchange the Nefertiti for other equally unique objects from Cairo. Curators, directors, and lawyers had reviewed the division of finds from 1913, questioned witnesses like Borchardt's colleague Bruno Güterbock, and come to the conclusion that the bust should be returned, though Germany was not legally obliged to. The Egyptians' moral claim was respected. Why couldn't today's curators, directors, and Cultural Ministry rise to that same level of goodwill and at least place a note next to the Nefertiti display case that reads "On permanent loan from the Arab Republic of Egypt"?

That would be a nod to a former colony that shared its most priceless possessions with the world long before it was permitted to choose whether to do so of its own free will. Sometimes it makes sense to look at things from the perspective of the other party, the underdog, to understand that wounds of this sort never heal and will always put a strain on the two countries' relations. There are those who say, What would the Egyptian Museum do with the Nefertiti? The place is already overflowing with art treasures! True. But the same can be said of Europe's museums. Such abundance doesn't annul the Egyptians' right to see such an icon of their cultural heritage—90 percent of the populace can't afford a trip to Berlin. Just as all other museums do, we could guarantee the safety of the bust against theft, vandalism, and natural catastrophe. How many works of art in European and American museums have already been victimized in attacks by disturbed people? How many works of art were lost in night bombing raids on Berlin? Berlin explains that the Nefertiti is too fragile for such a trip. But people also transport nitroglycerin. There are always ways; one only has to want to find them.

Our rearrangements in the museum apparently came to the attention of the antiquities administration's chief architect, a man already well known to us. One morning he had six huge display cases deposited in the corridor outside the mummy gallery. They were so big they could easily have held the largest of coffins. The museum was in urgent need of new display cases, the man explained.

"I didn't order any vitrines," I countered, "and if I had, it would certainly not have been cases like these. They don't match our rooms and the historic interior decor." The chief architect grew nervous. But it was obvious to everyone that the old vitrines needed to be replaced. "Why didn't you ask me what sort of display cases I could use? What are they supposed to cost?"

He named a figure per piece that would buy a medium-sized apartment. An absurdly high price, and I could not shake the feeling that the chief architect was in cahoots with the marketer or manufacturer of the vitrines. "Take these crates away. They're blocking the hall for visitors."

The man left, grinding his teeth, and from that day on it was perfectly clear that he wanted to get rid of me as quickly as possible.

Display cases were indeed a problem. Some of them had come from the museum in Bulaq and were built in 1858. To me they were an essential feature of the museum's history. Other very simple vitrines had been added as needed. If a thief tried to open one of these, he could be stopped thanks to its surveillance camera. But there was no getting around the fact that we had to do something. We had the old vitrines rebuilt with new lighting and shatterproof glass, and ordered new cases that matched the old ones. Today the museum has more than sixty new vitrines made in Germany.

After the reworking of the Amarna Department, we took on the collection of Yuya and Tuya, Tutankhamun's great-grandparents. The museum owns the couples' complete tomb inventory: furniture, coffins, mummy masks, mummies. Here again curator Ibrahim Abdel Gawad had changed nothing since he arrived. The beds and the chariot were in precarious condition, also the coffins and the mummies, which, miraculously enough, are the best-preserved mummies in the museum. But Ibrahim and his team were proud of the new Amarna room, and willingly responded to my desire to restore the Yuya and Tuya collection as a next project. One object after another was taken to the laboratory and surrendered to Dr. Elham Abdel Rahman. The restorer began by studying the bed, and spent days trying to discover how the linen covering was woven and bonded to the wood. She experimented by weaving several trial pieces until she hit upon the ancient cabinetmaker's secret. The laboratory was highly motivated, and we also sent them the chariot and the coffins lined with silver plates. The restorers also analyzed and treated the mummies. Today most of those objects have been restored.

While all this was happening I had any number of strange requests to deal with in the office. A glance at the return address was usually enough to set off an alarm. The chief architect and Amal—Ali Fahmi's friend and later wife— sent me a list of objects the museum was to make available for an exhibit at a hotel in Sharm el-Sheikh. We never lent objects to hotels or travel agencies, yet the two insisted. The catalog and posters for the exhibit had already been printed and distributed. I wrote to the Supreme Council, explaining that a hotel can hardly meet the antiquities service's security requirements. Luckily, at just that time a report arrived from Sharm el-Sheikh's chief of police: He could not approve the exhibit for security reasons.

That was the beginning of more or less open hostilities toward me that in their acrimony and potential danger reached a first culmination in August 2005. For the jubilee year 2002 a special exhibit, *Hidden Treasures of the Egyptian Museum*, had been mounted in specially refurbished cellar rooms that could be reached only by way of a single entrance on the museum's left side. In the summer of 2005 a special exhibit titled *Giza through the Ages* was installed there, organized by Mahmud Mabruk, head of the Museums Department in the antiquities service; the chief architect; and Fahmi's fiancée Amal. The objects all came from antiquities depots in Giza: statues, steles, and smaller objects. I was shocked at how carelessly the chief architect and Amal were treating the pieces. They responded to my efforts to intervene by assuring me that they didn't have to take any criticism or guidance from me. I wrote to tell Zahi Hawass that I could assume no responsibility for that exhibit and the safety of its displays. They were not part of our collections, the organizers were not members of the museum's staff, and the exhibit was being held not in the main spaces of the museum but in an annex that we were unable to monitor. I remembered my predecessor Eldamaty's advice and kept a copy of my letter.

After the exhibit was dismantled, its displays were temporarily left in our cellar storerooms. At the time they were picked up, I was attending a congress in Italy. Sabah informed me that three small statues from the Giza exhibit were missing and that we would be held responsible. By then Sabah was already the head of the newly established Cellar Department. She and I knew that no one could have left the cellar with three statues. The museum is like a fortress, secured by hundreds of security personnel and police. The entrance to the cellar was under constant surveillance, and could only be opened by curators and police together. I spoke to the policeman who had overseen the transport of the objects into our depot. He explained to me that the three statues had never even arrived in our cellar, and had not been displayed. I sent his statements to the Supreme Council as protocol.

A few days later I read in the newspaper that the police had arrested the thief. A photograph pictured a smiling young man who appeared a few days later, once again smiling, under escort of the state's attorney and the police. We followed them into the cellar rooms. The thief was asked to show where he had taken the three statues and how he had managed to abscond with them. It was quite obvious that the 'thief' was improvising. In the cellar staircase he pointed to a piece of limestone left there from the renovation and explained that he had also wanted to steal that stone, but had had to leave it. The state's attorney could see perfectly well that all that was nonsense. But the young man smiled as though wishing to tell us, "Don't worry, nothing will happen to me." Then as he was being led away, he turned around once again and said in a loud voice, "And don't forget to pay my mother the money!" A short time later he was released. However the policeman who had testified that the objects had never been exhibited was beaten and disciplined.

But that was not the end of the incident. Zahi was unusually irritated, and attacked me in the press. It was I who should bear the responsibility because I had neglected my duty by attending a congress in Italy. Next day Zahi and various legal representatives were in my office. Zahi again accused me of being at fault. I replied, "It's you who bear responsibility for the exhibit, not I. I wrote you a report. I properly informed you and declined all responsibility." And I showed him a copy of my letter.

*

Again days passed, and then came a succinct notice from the state's attorney that the police had found the statues. But every day before that I had had to present myself to the Supreme Court for questioning. The psychological pressure on me and my family was enormous. Zahi telephoned, vehemently regretting that bringing me back from Germany was the greatest mistake of his life. Meanwhile, the chief architect and Fahmi's fiancée organized additional exhibits for the museum annex. I wrote to Zahi saying that he should kindly leave special exhibits up to us. We had the experience and know-how in dealing with valuable artifacts. From then on the two excluded me from all internal administrative communications. I either received no information about events, congresses, and lectures, or the invitations arrived too late.

Amal had every reason to hate me—I had blocked so many of her undertakings. There was the pianola episode, for example. One morning a restorer knocked on my door and asked to speak to me in confidence. It was about Amal. She was coming into the workshops when I was away from the museum and bringing objects from Fahmi's antiques store to the laboratory. The chief of police and the director of the laboratory knew about it. "If you'll come with me to the laboratory you can see the things in the corner."

It was strictly forbidden to bring in pieces from outside the museum, and access to the restoration workshop by outsiders was only with the director's permission. Amal's behavior was therefore actionable. I asked a few curators to accompany me to the laboratory. The director wasn't there, but a few of her closest associates were. I later learned that behind my back she had overheard everything I said by way of a cell phone. I photographed all the objects and wrote a protocol that I had signed by the curators. In one corner stood a pianola, a player piano in which one could easily have hidden objects. Amal was obviously having her husband's antiques restored in our workshop. The case was never investigated, either internally or by the police. The laboratory director and head of the museum police were disciplined. Amal was unmolested. She must have had good contacts. One of her associates confided to me, "Be on your guard. Amal despises you."

There were also comical interludes. Once a man stormed into my office, brandished his camera in front of me, and shouted that he would not be prevented from taking pictures in the museum. I assured him that taking photographs in the museum was allowed as an exception only with permission, and in this case I saw no reason to grant it. The man became pushy. No one could stop him.

"I'm a close relative of Dr. Zakaria Azmy, one of the most powerful men in Egypt!"

I explained that even so he wouldn't be allowed to take photographs. He then threatened to speak to the doctor.

"Which doctor was it you wish to speak to?"

"Dr. Zakaria Azmy!"

"Help yourself, here's the telephone. Call him. You can also call Hosni Mubarak." I stepped out and fetched one of our guards from the security service. "Please keep an eye on this man. If he takes any photographs, kindly escort him out of the museum."

It was a delightful scene, one that I warmly recall to this day. "You won't stay in office a day longer! Zakaria Azmy will have you dismissed!"

In April 2011, after the Revolution, Zakaria Azmy, Mubarak's last chief of staff, was accused of corruption and is now serving a seven-year prison sentence. According to the testimony of witnesses, between 2006 and 2011 he accepted gifts with a value of LE1.4 million.

Similarly droll was a call from the president's office. The famous singer Mohamed Mounir would be coming to the museum after visiting hours to record a song for President Mubarak. He would be bringing along musicians, dancers, and a camera team. The song was to figure prominently in the president's election campaign. I refused permission, and was rewarded with the usual hue and cry: How dare I refuse a request from the president. "The museum's security regulations forbid any dance or musical performances. Since I am responsible for security, I have no choice but to say no."

I also owe my happiest hours in the museum, and perhaps the most important legacy of my work there, to an attempted swindle. Only a few weeks after my arrival, in April 2004, my phone rang early one morning. My sister Safaa was greatly agitated.

"Have you read *al-Akhbar*?" she asked.

"No, I don't know what you're talking about."

"They report that a relief depiction of the god Hapi from the Hathor Temple in Dendera has disappeared from the museum's cellar."

Naturally I was shocked, but I immediately asked myself how that could be. How could anything disappear from the cellar? I hurried to my office, where people from the ministry and the antiquities administration were already waiting for me. The atmosphere was tense, and I tried to calm my colleagues. "If the relief is in the cellar, we'll find it."

For the first time I had the cellar's double doors opened, and what I saw alarmed me almost more than the news of the vanished relief. Behind the steel door I could squeeze down the cellar corridor only a few meters, for stacks of crates blocked my way. And I could only see for a short distance, for every second light bulb was either burnt out or unscrewed. I asked for a flashlight and shone it between the crates. But the corridors were filled with crates and boxes; tightly packed shelving along the walls reached nearly to the ceiling. Everywhere were swaths of cobwebs, dust, dirt, and fusty darkness. Finding a relief in that chaos would be like searching for the proverbial needle. One could only pray. I motioned to a staff member and asked him to open a crate. I have no idea why I pointed at precisely that one; I could have pointed to any of the dozens of others surrounding me—but in fact the relief in question was inside it. My colleagues eyed me furtively. They had witnessed a miracle.

I wanted to know how the newspaper had come to write that a relief was missing. I didn't know the writer of the article, but I phoned him and asked where he had gotten his supposed information. What had led him to put such a claim in print without proof? Someone had called him; he couldn't reveal the name. Privileged information.

"Why didn't you ask me for an explanation? Isn't it part of your professional ethics to give concerned parties an opportunity to comment?"

The journalist said something about freedom of the press, and we left it at that. But the reaction of the policemen in our guard unit was also astonishing: "If that guy shows up here again and wants to enter the museum, we'll simply arrest him. We'll say that he started a fight, accosted one of us, insulted one of us. He'll be in jail before he knows what happened." Aha? So a person is put behind bars so quickly? All it takes is three united policemen?

The next time I encountered the journalist at a reception, I thanked him. He was completely flummoxed. He hadn't expected that. "I thank you. If you hadn't written anything I wouldn't have visited the cellar so soon." We had meanwhile sent the relief back to Dendera, where it now stands in its original spot in the temple.

The Egyptian Museum's cellar is the stuff of legend. Now and again in the past scholars had been allowed down there if they were searching for a specific object in the residue of an excavation for their researches. For nearly one hundred years it served as the central storeroom for all the artifacts awarded to Egypt in the division of finds. At 10,500 square meters, or an area nearly the size of two football fields, the museum's catacombs had absorbed through all those years crates and boxes from every part of Egypt and from every archaeological mission—there was no record of how many lay down there, what was in them or lined up on all those kilometers of shelving. That was not unusual neglect on the part of the museum; for many decades that had been common practice in other major museums as well. It was only in the late 1970s that foreign and Egyptian excavation missions came to see the value of complete lists of finds.

From today's point of view, in the previous decades the work of archaeologists had been almost wantonly unscientific: They wrapped each little pot, every worked stone, every collection of shards, fragments, and unidentified objects in newspaper and bags, packed it all into wooden boxes, and sent it to the depot—without enclosing a complete inventory list. In their publications they would include descriptions and photographs of numerous objects, but fail to mention which of their boxes they might be found in. Outstanding objects were placed in our display rooms, but unspectacular finds ended up in the depot. Today we know that even the most unimposing object can provide important information—perhaps even be the missing piece from a total picture. The fragment of a roof frieze could belong to an ensemble that some other museum has been searching for for a long time. Nowadays scholars take complete documentation of finds for granted.

In the next few days Sabah and I made repeated forays into the unknown. The cellar hadn't been opened for a considerable time. Separate modern depots had long since been established in the Delta, in Saqqara, and in Luxor. It had been a long time since any new crates had arrived in the cellar—the storerooms were full, overfull, and it was a labyrinth, a vast storehouse. Letters were painted on the pillars for orientation, but even with a map of the cellar it was no simple matter to find one's way and always know in which of the many corridors and under which vault you were standing. With a flashlight we would squeeze past shelves filled with mummies and mummy coffins from all epochs of Egyptian history; then meter after meter of skulls from the cemeteries of Nubia; then ceramics of all kinds and ages, pots, bowls, cups, pitchers. In between we would see stacks of wooden planks—apparently remnants of a Nile barque—then stumps of columns, heavy steles, portions of temple architraves, sculptures, and reliefs, fragments of wall decorations from tombs and temples, some of them in colors, and everything under cobwebs and centimeters-thick layers of dust.

At least the crates bore the names of scholarly missions and indications of the excavation site and the date. There were crates from Howard Carter, from a time when he was still only dreaming of Tutankhamun. On other crates we could read in faded crayon: Deir al-Bahari 1914, Memphis 1923, Saqqara 1922, Tanis 1939. Many of the excavators' names are now known by every student of archaeology: Winlock, Carter, Lauer, Mahmud Hamza. On one shelf we happened upon notes from the Nubian expedition of the British archaeologist Walter Emery from the 1930s, black-and-white photographs of landscapes that had long since lain hundreds of meters beneath the surface of Lake Nasser, drawings and maps of the Nile bank near Abu Simbel. Did Emery's institute have any idea where his documents were?

From one crate lined with crumbling straw we pulled out fat-bellied jugs, vases found in 1922 by the American archaeologist Winlock in the Tomb of Meketre (Eleventh Dynasty) in Deir al-Bahari —the tomb has been sealed since 1922, since which time no one had seen either the grave or the vases. There were clay tablets from the Nile island of Elephantine, discovered in 1907 by the German Egyptologist Otto Rubensohn—and what messages did they carry?

"It's like being on an expedition," I said to Sabah.

"Yes, like an excavation," she responded. "As though all these things were waiting to be found a second time."

"In any case, it will be the largest inventory ever undertaken in the history of Egyptology, and you're going to direct it."

I wrote a report for Zahi Hawass, describing the situation in the cellar and the necessity of producing a reliable inventory. He agreed with me that the museum finally needed a modern database and approved the extra funds. We formed two teams, each consisting of three archaeologists, two restorers, and an archivist. Sabah, to whom the database project had already been entrusted, became head curator for the cellar and oversaw the inventory. Each object had to be examined and described, its condition noted, and a preliminary estimate made of its historical and scientific importance. Finally, everything was to be professionally cataloged and documented in photographs.

Sabah plunged into her work, and first that meant clearing out. She had truckloads of dust and debris removed from the cellar. Each morning she would descend in a white curator's smock, and by afternoon her smock, gloves, and breathing mask would be black. She would then sit at her computer until evening, entering photographs and object descriptions into the database. To me Sabah embodied all the noblest qualities of the Nubians: reliability, honesty, industry, and humor. I was extremely happy to be working with her.

After some four weeks we knew that there were roughly 2,000 crates. From samples we could estimate that they held some 40,000 separate objects, that is about a fourth of the museum's known holdings. Each time we opened a crate there was always the excitement of wondering what it might contain. It was as if its contents had never been excavated. We counted a large number of coffins, from the time of the Old Kingdom down to the period when Egypt was ruled by Greeks and Romans. I had been infected with find fever. Every time I discovered a new treasure, I would scream out loud for joy. Normally I had no problems with dust. But once I suffered a major allergic attack when dusting off a mummy's linen wrappings. The doctor wanted to banish me from the cellar, but that would have meant banishing me from my profession.

I couldn't always take part in the work, of course, but whenever Sabah made an extraordinary discovery she would call me. For example, together we opened the crates of the French Egyptologist and architect Jean-Philippe Lauer, who had excavated in the Step Pyramid at Saqqara in the 1930s. In one of them, without more detailed information about the find, we discovered a small box with little gold sheets from the mummy of Pharaoh Djoser, which was never found, even a gilt fragment of his foot. In Lauer's excavation report there is not a word about such gold finds. We also marveled at other treasures: children's mummies with gilt masks, two larger-than-lifesize wooden statues that are now displayed in the Imhotep Museum in Saqqara. There were soon so many beautiful pieces that we decided to display them in a special exhibit: *Masterpieces from the Cellar*.

Those days in the cellar were among the most delightful times I spent in the museum. We were completely undisturbed down there. The police would close the steel doors behind us, there was no cell phone reception, no disruption from outside. Sometimes Sabah and I could only think of ourselves as two funerary priestesses. In pharaonic times there were special priests who embalmed the dead, wrapped them as mummies, and guarded their tombs, thereby assuring that they could enjoy their treasures in the afterlife. Today it is our job to preserve all those mummies and coffins for the future. The priests' embalming rituals occupied them for a period of seventy days, and it takes today's conservators at least that long to conserve mummies for the future. I often had to think of my mother and her pious abhorrence of disturbing the dead. But weren't we motivated by an equal reverence? Our cellar was one huge cemetery, filled with hundreds of mortal remains. For science they are only footnotes to history. But they help us to answer the questions of the living. Where do we come from? Who are we? And where are we going? In our collections we find answers to the question of how we became who we are.

Today the greater part of the cellar has been cleared out, the finds distributed among regional depots in the places they came from. Some have been displayed in new museums, for example the Imhotep Museum in Saqqara, El Arish Museum in northern Sinai, and the Suez Museum. Offices and modern computer workplaces have been set up for the curators in some of the reclaimed cellar spaces.

We could easily have put together a second exhibit titled *Masterpieces from the Attic*—for the museum's top floor, inaccessible to the public, is a mirror image of the cellar. Complete coffin ensembles, that is to say multiple nesting mummy-shaped coffins, had been stored there. First the dust had to be cleaned off them by Somaya Abdel Samie, the curator of the Coffin

Department, with her assistants and workmen. They brought to light fantastic underworld scenes. Each coffin is unique, a world of its own.

I wrote a report suggesting that the top floor and its treasures be made accessible to the public, but the idea was rejected. I also proposed decorating portions of the catacombs as tombs, in which sarcophagi, coffins, and mummies could be displayed, explaining such themes as mummification and the realm and cult of the dead. The cellar ceiling could be painted to resemble a starry sky, and special lighting would create an unusual atmosphere. That too was rejected.

Even while making new discoveries in the museum's holdings every day, we would check to see whether the objects were also entered in our registers. That was a complicated business. Every scholar who for research purposes has ever looked for a specific object in the Egyptian Museum can appreciate my alarm when introduced to our registry. In 2004 there was no complete inventory of all the objects in the building. Instead, there were various parallel inventories about whose completeness no one could say anything reliable. There was the handwritten Journal d'Entrée, the museum's oldest register. Listed in it are all the objects that had come to the museum and been assigned an official inventory number over the course of the past hundred years. The oldest volumes of those heavy journals are in a worn state, with frayed, partially torn and mended pages on which here and there additions or corrections have been pasted. Groups of objects and complete collections to which, again, individual register numbers were assigned, were entered in the Catalogue Général. That register is in a more presentable condition. The so-called Temporary Register lists objects about which it was uncertain whether they would stay in the museum permanently or be forwarded to another one. A fourth register, begun in the 1950s, lists the holdings of the seven display departments, but even that one is incomplete. The inventory is a project for coming generations, and God only knows when the database of our entire holdings will become accessible on the Internet.

In the past, whenever Egyptian governments were in urgent need of funds they would send our art treasures on tour. Foreign exhibitions are a lucrative business—for many participants. The Egyptian lender profits, but so do the host museums and exhibition halls, transport firms, insurers, book authors, catalog printers, marketing agencies, travel organizations, and merchandisers. In addition to my job as director of the Egyptian Museum, I was also responsible for exhibitions abroad—often enough of objects from our own holdings. In my seven years no task was more onerous than that one. Loan contracts and their fine-print addenda had to be carefully read, and also the insurance policies and their liability exclusions. Finally the transport of all the listed objects had to be arranged, making sure that they were handled professionally and suitably placed in the host museum. After the close of the exhibition and the objects' return to Egypt, they had to be carefully examined for any damage. Each such event amounted to a logistical and legal suicide mission. Heavy objects recently raised from the sea in the port of Alexandria would disappear into the holds of giant transport planes, and I would pray that *Egypt's Sunken Treasures* would actually return in one piece. I insisted on contracting only the most professional art transport firms.

Treasures of Tutankhamun was surely Egypt's most legendary and financially successful blockbuster show. On its worldwide tour between 1972 and 1982, Tut's gold mask earned roughly $11 million. A million and a half visitors saw it in New York; in Cologne lines formed for weeks as more than a million visitors came. But a sculpture of the goddess Serket from the tomb treasure came back damaged. For that reason the government issued a travel ban for Tut. In 2004, however, that ban was lifted by Minister of Culture Farouk Hosni—Mubarak needed $500 million for his Grand Museum. This time it wasn't to be the gold mask, rather a series of equally irreplacable objects from the tomb treasure. I was in charge of the exhibition *Tutankhamun, the Golden Beyond*, which then toured around the world under various names. The 131 objects in *Tutankhamun and the Golden Age of the Pharaohs* were insured up to a total of $650 million; the 149 objects in *Tutankhamun: The Golden King and the Great Pharaohs* up to $550 million. Together with *Cleopatra's Sunken Treasures*, they brought in roughly $100 million. Blockbuster shows are big business—especially for insurers and their agents. The policies have to be bought by the borrower—that's part of the deal.

An exhibition organized by the antiquities service for Madrid was one of the first to be assigned to me. The Supreme Council usually sent selected journalists to openings of such events abroad. I was always surprised at how quickly many journalists would perform their duties so as to have more time for shopping and relaxing in their hotels. This time they had reason to complain, and phoned Zahi Hawass. They had landed at Madrid's airport, but there was no one there to greet them and take them to their hotel. That day all of Madrid was in a state of emergency. There had been a bomb attack in the city's subway, with many dead and wounded. The city was in shock. And Zahi managed to shock me as well. He made me appear before the antiquities service's investigative committee to account for the absence of taxis for the journalists. The hearing about my supposed dereliction of duty had gone on for three hours when I asked the judge whether they were kidding me. What could I have done about an act of violence? The judge kindly explained that he had been instructed to take his time, so that we could assure the journalists that I had been harshly questioned. It was pure chicanery. In the same way I was repeatedly called up before state's attorneys and investigative judges in connection with mere bagatelles. The judges were always friendly, and begged my understanding—we all had our jobs to do.

But back to business. A Danish firm that had organized a large exhibition with objects from the antiquities service even before I returned to Egypt from Germany wished to put together a new one. I refused. The owner invited me to come to Denmark. Perhaps we should first get to know each other. I also refused that offer. A short time later the man contacted me again. He sent a list of museums that were interested in his exhibition so long as a number of prominent objects from our holdings were included. I didn't trust the man, so I began to do my research and questioned my museum colleagues. It turned out that the man had offered some of the major museums in Europe, the United States, and East Asia a show of antiquities with objects he had supposedly already been promised—while in fact he was only now requesting them. He was attempting to play one of us off against the other. A dubious way to do business. Because of his government connections, the trick had obviously worked before; all that had been necessary was to generously bribe those connections, as he told me. A similar attempt was made by the owner of a large Egyptian insurance firm who was very eager to get into the exhibition business. Since he owned a number of large hotels, he invited me and my family to make use of one of them. We could holiday there as long as we wished—all inclusive of course. I struck him off our list of insurers.

Also remarkable was a request from the Pushkin Museum in Moscow. The Russians wanted an exhibition, but were prepared to pay neither loan fees nor insurance. Even so, we were ordered by the president's office to organize an exhibit for Russia. It had been arranged between Putin and Mubarak.

I explained to Zahi, "We have exhibitions in many different countries, and all of them have to pay. What could I tell them if it were to get around that we also make exhibitions available for nothing?"

Zahi replied that if that's the way Mubarak and Farouk Hosni wanted it, we had no choice. But as we were discussing it, Zahi was handed a letter from the Pushkin Museum. It demanded that we accept its conditions and pay for the insurance ourselves. It was then up to me, the already notorious nay-sayer, to write a sharply worded response.

"Egyptian exhibitions are permitted only under Egyptian conditions. In the present circumstances we have to turn down the project." I bore full political responsibility for the denial.

Quarrels among directors in the antiquities administration became increasingly heated. I disapproved of the most important political projects: the building of the Grand Museum in Giza and the so-called urban development project in Luxor. Hosni Mubarak had laid the cornerstone for the Grand Egyptian Museum in February 2002—for the seventh time, as comics groaned. The planning for the museum alone devoured millions. In 32,000 square meters the museum was supposed to eventually display 120,000 objects—roughly as many as the museum in Tahrir Square—and not only ancient art but a 'best of' from all Egypt's museums. It would have to be the "largest museum in the world," of course, for Mubarak wished to erect a monument to himself. In conferences with the Museums Department I argued against the views of the president's office, the Ministry of Culture, and the antiquities service. It was my conviction that we didn't need a new museum. If we could only tear down the ugly National Democratic Party building that stands between the Egyptian Museum and the Nile, there would be room on the grounds of the old museum for depots, workshops, and new exhibition spaces, and the cost would be far less. In fact money was not an issue. The building costs, at first estimated to run to $400 million, then $500 million, and by then $620 million, would be financed by an interest-free loan from Japan and by donated funds. The Japanese were great optimists; they were counting on Egypt's paying the money back over the next ten years. Egypt's new government is carrying on with Mubarak's plans, but it too is overconfident.

In such conferences the several museums wrangled about which one would house which star objects in the future. There was the new Grand Museum in Giza, which claimed the largest and most beautiful objects. Then there was the National Museum of Egyptian Civilization in Fustat. It also insisted on only the best and most beautiful pieces. And finally there was the museum in Tahrir Square, which owned most of the objects in question. We wrestled with each other for years.

"If you gut the museum," I explained, "it will be the end of it."

We quarreled loudly over the lists of holdings of the new museums, and naturally I fought for my own building. In December 2010, shortly before I left the museum, the Ministry of Culture presented me with the ultimatum that I was to provide it with a list of the hundred most prominent objects that were headed for the new museum. Mubarak wished to celebrate a so-called soft opening of the Grand Museum.

"But there isn't any museum yet," I explained to Zahi Hawass. "There are only construction sheds."

"They'll build a pavilion for the objects."

I told him I could present such a list at any time. On the set deadline I showed my selections in a PowerPoint presentation at the ministry before minister Farouk Hosni, Zahi Hawass, Mohamed Ghoneim (who was in charge of the Grand Museum project), and several other gentlemen. I can see from a few photos that were taken that the minister and Mohamed Ghoneim were by no means pleased.

"That's no list of bests!" Ghoneim shouted angrily. "That's not what we had in mind."

The young Egyptologist Mohamed Gamal announced, "We've put something together ourselves."

I could have predicted it: one hundred of the Egyptian Museum's masterworks. I protested. "Those are our objects, and will remain so."

The minister erupted in exasperation, "What do you mean 'our'? We all love the old museum, but now we're building a larger, modern museum, and we need these objects."

I rejected their list, and the minister ended the meeting. Mohamed Ghoneim took me aside. "You've just cut a poor figure in front of the minister. Zahi had already told him that's how Wafa El Saddik is!"

I assured Ghoneim, "I am the way I am. I prefer that to having to swallow an unacceptable list out of fear of the minister."

"We wanted to make you the first director of the Grand Museum after your retirement. But now you can forget that."

"That's fine too," I responded.

I could see the way one hand was wasting millions of pounds and the other taking them from defenseless people. In my seven years in the museum I encountered endless stories reminiscent of Victor Hugo's *Les Misérables*. The least of our workmen were paid no more than LE5 a day, less than $1. Our staff members in the lowest pay grades had neither social security nor health insurance. If their salaries weren't paid, they faced insoluble problems.

One day my eye was caught by Mohamed, one of our security people. He looked especially pale and weak, and I asked him whether he was ill and needed help. He then burst out that his three-year-old son had cancer. I recommended that he take the child to Children's Cancer Hospital 57357; there every child had the right to get treatment. He replied that he had been turned away. In order to pay for treatment at another clinic, he had sold everything he owned, even his furniture. He simply no longer knew how he was going to feed his three other children. I had a few friends with a social conscience, among them Doria, who had so often helped me before. And this time, as well, she paid for the child's treatment. A few weeks later Mohamed placed a sheet of paper in front of me for my signature. It was a request to be transferred to his hometown, Sohag. His son had died, and in her sadness his wife could no longer stand living in Cairo.

Another of our security men who also worked nights as a park guard had been unable to buy food for his family for two days. I was forever having such conversations. I went to Zahi and explained that we had to raise the low wages. These people were drained and unable to concentrate, none of them could live on the salary from their job. They all had a hard time simply existing.

"The Supreme Council has no financial leeway," Zahi explained. "Long-term budgets have been set that allow for new museum building, for the allée of sphinxes between the Luxor and Karnak temples, and for restoration projects."

"If we were to raise tourist admission prices everywhere in Egypt by only a pound," I suggested, "we could set up a relief fund."

Zahi asked me to submit a proposal, which he would pass along to the ministry. With roughly ten thousand visitors to the museum each day, equal receipts in Giza, Karnak, and the Valley of the Kings, in addition to a few thousand entrance tickets for other museums, a sizable sum could be accrued each month. But the ministry rejected the idea. I refused to give up, and proposed diverting a portion of the proceeds from exhibitions abroad into the fund. Zahi agreed to that, and after that a small relief fund was established within the antiquities administration. Sadly, the Revolution has for now blocked that source of income. Zahi also mandated that foreign missions would themselves have to pay the inspectors assigned to oversee their excavations. I opposed that, for it would mean that inspectors would be dependent on the very people they were supposed to monitor.

One day my secretary Fatma approached me trembling. There was a dead man lying in front of the museum. Albert explained that one of the cleaning men had wanted to work on the building's façade and had fallen. Dr. Sohir, the museum's doctor, was already outside with the man, who was still alive but needed to be taken to the hospital, for he was bleeding internally. I proposed taking our ambulance, but the head of our police cadre forbade it. The ambulance was only for tourists. I was stunned, and ran to the ambulance myself and saw to it that the man was loaded into it. After twenty minutes the driver phoned me: The hospital didn't want to accept him because he was going to die anyway. I told him to drive to the university clinic. But they wouldn't take the poor man either—he had no health insurance. They would need advance payment. I called the director of the military hospital, a magnificent, highly influential officer who finally saw to it that the man received treatment. A week later he was back on his feet. The director of the museum's cleaning firm was reluctant to report the incident. The man was moonlighting with him and was not insured.

One of our curators injured his spine lifting something in the cellar. On my return from a business trip I learned that he had been lying at home, unable to walk, for a week. The hospital refused to treat him because he had neither health insurance nor cash. Again Madam Doria covered the cost of the operation. The punch line was a letter to the museum from our central administration: The curator had to be let go because he was failing to come to work regularly.

My commitment was talked about. So many people came to me that I would often go home exhausted. Azmy would say, "You're not Mother Teresa!"

True, but I am my mother's daughter. And the older I got the more I noticed that the seed of her education was bearing fruit in me: I couldn't stand by and do nothing.

But we also had serious problems in the museum. An alarmingly high number of still very young colleagues had cancer, and others were losing their babies in the first weeks of pregnancy. Five colleagues had died of cancer. I couldn't rid myself of the suspicion that it had something to do with our x-ray machines. There was one at the entry gate, another in front of the main portal, and a third at the entrance to the administrative offices. Employees had to pass through all three of them several times a day. I wrote to tell the administration that I considered one machine at the main portal sufficient, but the Projects Department wanted to add yet another at the entrance to the cellar. I refused and began to suspect that somebody must be making money from those barriers. It was impossible that our people should be exposed to the radiation forty to fifty times a day, especially since the monitoring policemen didn't even look up when the machines beeped. I asked the chief of police to remove the machine at the entrance to the offices. Since he would not accept responsibility for that, I had it taken away by one of our workmen. I thought particularly of two popular female staff members who worked closely together and had no choice but to pass through the monitors several times a day. Both had been diagnosed with cancer. There were no responses to my reports. After I retired, the machine was put back at the entrance to the administrative offices.

The museum was staffed mainly by women, who—as in other countries—bore the double burden of a profession and a family, especially during fasting time. They needed to cook for their families before sunset, as the children were hungry to break their fast. Many of their families lived on the far outskirts of the city—also on account of their poor wages—and buses took a long time in the holiday evening traffic. I therefore suggested that we close at 3:00 p.m. instead of 6:30 p.m. during Ramadan, a change that was accepted. I also asked the travel agencies to inform their clients promptly of the revised operating hours. But when we closed the portals at 3:00 p.m., the Ministry of

Culture regularly telephoned that the museum had to stay open. I referred to the approved new arrangement, although the guard personnel had to stay. For travel operations with good connections to the Mubarak family the museum was opened. My women were infuriated.

Along with all these activities, I was also required to greet our state guests. The museum was an obligatory part of any such visit. Whether presidents, kings, or ministers—everyone wanted to see Tutankhamun face to face. There were brief but interesting encounters. There was the ex-king Gyanendra of Nepal, for example, who considered himself a god, and whom his wife and entourage could only follow at an appropriate distance. There was Che Guevara's daughter, a very nice doctor who told me that her father had also studied medicine and would have liked to become a doctor had fate not willed otherwise. I guided Prince Charles, Mohammad Khatami of Iran, Queen Rania, Raúl Castro, Luiz Inácio Lula da Silva, Wen Jiabao, and Dmitry Medvedev. The latter's chief of protocol explained to me that the Russian president had only an hour, as he had to meet Gamal Mubarak immediately afterward. You mean Hosni Mubarak, I said. No, Gamal. Who else did I think was ruling Egypt! Then when I met the president in Rome I understood. Hosni Mubarak was a tired old man.

I lived in two different worlds. Here economic misery, there the affluence of foreign diplomats. Every week I received three, four, sometimes as many as seven invitations. After a day at the museum I would rest a little, then dress for the genteel ambassadors' homes. It was not uncommon for me to be the guest of honor and serve as the party's prominent decoration. Many invitations I couldn't decline, but many others Azmy and I fully enjoyed, for we got to meet interesting people from all over the world, and also very wealthy Egyptians who would then invite us to their own homes. There we would see a degree of wealth we had never encountered, not even in the richest oil countries. Then the next day I would see our guards and gardeners. More than 40 percent of our countrymen live in abject poverty. "This cannot continue," one of the museum's workmen said to me. On principle I did not attend any festivities paid for by the antiquities administration. For example, there was the *iftar* feast during Ramadan. Every year it was held in a five-star hotel for directors, journalists, actors, and people who had nothing whatever to do with archaeology. Every bite stuck in my craw.

I was also invited to the Danish ambassador's residence, and I told him about the Lego exhibit I had visited with my children in Cologne in 1993: *The Secret of the Pharaohs*. I told him about my dream of setting up a children's museum in our cleared-out cellar, where children could be exposed to the culture, history, and archaeology of ancient Egypt in a way that they could understand. I showed him my earlier correspondence with Lego, and he promised to speak with the Danish enterprise. I became a little overzealous, which is normally not my style.

"I would be delighted if Lego would present the exhibit to us not as a loan but as a gift—a gift to the children of Egypt."

The ambassador laughed, but he liked the idea. Only a week later he wrote that Lego was agreeable and that the embassy would cover the transportation costs. Months later we set up the exhibit in empty cellar rooms beneath the museum's west side. Colleagues and friends came from all over, including our Cologne CATS society, and helped with the construction: committed curators from the museum, the American Egyptologist and artist Biri Fay, the director of the Roemer- und Pelizaeus-Museum Hildesheim, Regine Schulz, the museum educator Ros Eavis-Oliveira from Portugal, the American Janice Kamrin, who was then directing our database project. She brought along her son Umar and some of his schoolmates so that I might see from them what interested and excited children most. They wanted a "homey" museum, they said. So we bathed the rooms in warm light, built in play and reading corners, had the height of the display cases reduced, and the labels worded for children. Needless to say, the spaces were handicapped-accessible, and we offered special programs for blind children. At the entrance, the children were greeted by an imposing sphinx made of 47,500 plastic blocks.

We looked for intriguing ancient objects, which we naturally displayed in secure vitrines. The children were supposed to be able to compare the Lego deities with the originals. Each room was devoted to a special theme, bread baking and beer brewing, for example, everyday life along the Nile. There was a four-thousand-year-old loaf of bread, nearby a thirty-three-hundred-year-old paint box. In another vitrine a harpist made of Legos plucked his instrument to soft music in the background. There was also a large map made entirely of Legos. There were displays about papyrus and the art of writing, about the cosmology of the gods, the world of the pharaohs and their families, and about life after death. And hanging on a wall was Tutankhamun's gold mask built from 25,500 Lego bricks. On January 18, 2010, Prince Henrik of Denmark opened Egypt's first archaeological children's museum. At the end of my career I had realized my dream. I was allowed to hire three kindergarten teachers.

My dearest wish had also been to set up a media center with hearing devices for blind children in the new Children's Museum of the Egyptian Museum in Cairo (CMEMC). Upstairs we created a special circuit for the blind. They were able to touch selected stone sculptures and other objects. Since we had no money for texts in Braille, we trained blind adults to serve as guides to accompany the children through the museum. I always tried to stay nearby for a few minutes, waiting to see the smiles that always appeared once the children's fingertips softly explored the hieroglyphs. There were many days when I needed those smiles. They came from another world.

Some people at the Ministry of Culture made some of my days absolute hell. I had been warned, but I felt that I knew them better from our early days, hoped that the time we had spent together at the Supreme Council would serve as a bond between us. But I underestimated the impetuous temperament of the man heading the service, his compulsive need to be respected, his unpredictable temper. He would dress down people in front of others. The most difficult days were those of the board and the Permanent Committee meetings. Some people very much enjoyed criticizing me and trying to find loopholes in the management of the museum by any means, based on arrogance and ignorance. When I responded to their points I discovered that the critics had virtually no knowledge of the topic under discussion: Their sole aim was to make themselves appear important through unjustified criticism.

It is important to say, however, that despite the many difficulties I experienced in dealing with Zahi, during my years as director of the museum he made it easy for me to achieve many of my ideas for its development.

By promoting himself, Egyptian archaeology, and ancient sites, Zahi did a great deal for the tourism industry. He got the slow-moving machinery of the antiquities service to function somewhat better, founded museums, procured cooperative ventures and funds, retrieved stolen art treasures, and upheld the moral right of former colonial countries to their cultural heritage. I only wish that he hadn't devoted his energy to Mubarak's Grand Museum.

Mutual friends have joked by asking me how I was able to stand him for so long. But I had a museum to run; my personal feelings didn't matter. Whenever he was extra vehement on the telephone, I would say to myself, It's about the issue, not you. And in fact we were generally able to agree. Zahi accepted more of my suggestions than he declined, he helped the museum more than he damaged it—he only needed to be guided. Also, despite all our major battles, he regularly renewed my contract. Maybe he didn't like me at the end of my tenure, but he also knew that as director I was of use to him. But I also had the feeling that he wouldn't permit anyone else to appear in focus. One day the producer of an American television series came to my office, a translator at his side. I told the producer that he could feel free to speak to me directly.

The man was astonished. "Zahi Hawass told me you don't speak any English." I was sad about the end of my tenure. I hadn't had enough time. So many vitrine labels were still missing. How much of all the work we had done would visitors notice? To most of them it would only be obvious what had not been done, and of course that was a great deal. At the beginning my colleagues were wary of me and my activism, but I was able to win some of them over. Two curators who insisted on keeping everything as it had been were promoted to directors after I left—an act of revenge by the system that I could have predicted. When I left I explained to my colleagues that what I would miss most were the investigative judges and state's attorneys. That was the first time that we were able to laugh about them.

My laughter left me barely six weeks later, when a group of men broke into the Egyptian Museum. To this day we don't know anything about the burglars and why the thefts were not announced immediately, why for weeks the museum's directors and the antiquities service were unable to provide a list of the stolen artifacts to the Egyptian police, the customs and border control authorities, Interpol, and UNESCO.

Terrible things took place in that early phase of political upheaval. There was a security vacuum, for the police and security services left archaeological sites and depots unguarded. That allowed for plundering and in some places complete destruction of excavation sites. In both Saqqara and Abusir, storerooms and excavation sites had already been plundered in January. But a temporary high point was reached at el-Hibeh in central Egypt. There, with

a bulldozer, a band of apparently known criminals plundered the huge excavation site—a largely intact city mound that was settled from the eleventh
century BC down into Greco-Roman times. The police closed their eyes, the
antiquities service refused to listen, although on-site archaeologists repeatedly begged it for help. In other places farmers plowed sites being studied.
It was not only the poor digging in the hope of finding treasure—pure greed
was also tempting educated people.

On March 3, 2011, Zahi Hawass resigned from his post at the ministry,
saying that he was no longer able to protect archaeological sites. In early April
there was a raid on the storerooms of the Austrian mission in Pi-Ramesse,
Ramses II's ancient capital, today the village of Qantir on the eastern edge of
the Nile Delta. General Abdel Rahim Hassan, the chief of the tourist and antiquities police, announced that criminals were becoming increasingly bolder,
were now even daring to enter exposed areas like the pyramid plateau. The
number of stolen artifacts identified ran into the thousands. On top of all this,
official information was impossibly confusing: In March 2011 the Ministry
of Antiquities announced that roughly eight hundred artifacts had been stolen
since February. In April the same ministry declared it had no reliable figures.
In February 2012 the new minister of antiquities, Mohamed Ibrahim Ali, maintained that 2 percent of all the historical artifacts stored in the country's depots
had been stolen, thanks to inadequate precautions since the Tahrir Square Revolution—at the same time, he conceded that roughly 35 percent of all the stored
objects were undocumented. How does that jibe? We don't know how many
objects we have, but it is certain that 2 percent are missing? Only 2 percent?
That would still mean hundreds of thousands of objects. The only thing that
was clear was the complete lack of reliable information. I have no idea why.

It hurts me deeply to have left my post in such a situation. Whenever I
saw my museum on the television screen, my heart bled. It was painful seeing
my country in such a state. But I took care not to join the chorus of those who
were now loudly calling for law and order. Weren't those calling loudest for
the return of authority and state power the very ones who had deliberately
fomented the chaos? If the prisons hadn't been opened, if the police hadn't
withdrawn to allow brutal gangs of thugs to get to work? How many of those
now presenting themselves as the solution were yesterday still part of the
problem?

What was my place? What could I do? I tried to draw international attention to my country's endangered art treasures. Illegal trade in antiquities was rampant. It was closely tied to organized crime, which was also profiting from money laundering and trade in drugs and weapons. I gave lectures and distributed documents with lists of objects that only a short time before had been entrusted to my safe-keeping in the museum. I spoke with museum colleagues from Libya, Jordan, Syria, Iraq, Lebanon—everywhere the same fear of plundering and destruction of the region's cultural heritage. Our people were fighting for political self-determination while their cultural past was being destroyed with grenades and bulldozers. In lectures, interviews, and conversation I tried to make it clear that the more we lose sight of where we came from, the more uncertain it is where we're heading.

9

THE SMILES OF THE BLIND

Clusters of young people were standing in front of the Antiquities Ministry in Zamalek. Graduate Egyptologists blocked the entrance, demanding work and reform of the ponderous, plodding antiquities administration. The year before it had been the same: a crowd of people blocking the portal steps. Students had the minister, Mohamed Ibrahim Ali, trapped in a conference room and were chanting "We want work!"

I had an appointment with the minister and slowly worked my way toward him. I reached for the microphone and asked if I might speak. "You should give the new minister some time so that he can get to work on your requests. It cannot be done overnight. If only we're patient we'll manage the new beginning!"

They were still standing there. Their patience was truly being tried. It wasn't only the ministry; the whole country was short of money. The pyramid plateau in Giza and the temple complexes in Luxor and in the oases were empty; so were hotels, shops, excursion boats. On the Corniche, Luxor's road along the bank of the Nile, rail-thin horses stood in front of their carriages. The coachmen scarcely had money for their oats.

222   The Smiles of the Blind

So much has happened since the start of the Tahrir Revolution in January 2011. We have a new president, a new constitution, new parties, new coalitions. For the first time in our history we were allowed to vote, and—no matter which way we voted—we're dissatisfied with the result. The country is politically divided. The only thing that unites people is their dissatisfaction. Everyone I talk to is disappointed, rich and poor, intellectuals and working people. Whether taxi drivers, neighbors, or friends, they all complain: no work, no income, no prospects. And they ask, is this what we made a revolution for?

Everything is in short supply—most of all patience. The Egyptians took to the streets for bread, freedom, and social justice. They hoped that if only the billions that Mubarak and his clique had stashed abroad were to flow back into the country the economy would rapidly improve. That didn't happen. On the contrary, the economic situation only worsened. The British journal the *Economist* reports that Egypt is in eighth place on the list of countries that have had to experience a drastic reduction in their living standard since 2011. Moreover, the foreign media focus almost exclusively on the gloomy side of the crisis, and to my mind their dramatizing the situation only intensifies the negative trend. There are, and always will be, conflicts between the Muslim Brotherhood and its opponents. But these are played out in the country's inner cities—not on the pyramid plateau, not in the Valley of the Kings, not on the beaches of Hurghada, nor in the oasis of Siwa. Tourists are not affected by them, and Egypt's economy cannot recover as long as tourists stay away. The longer they do, the more difficult the internal political situation will become. Prices are rising, the value of our currency sinking. People feel helpless.

In the library of the Egyptian Museum I met a young inspector. She was desperate. She didn't know how long she could continue to support herself on her small salary, whether she could even continue working for the antiquities service. She would have liked to work further on her master's degree and go on for a doctorate. But did that make any sense when even the best academic credentials didn't guarantee even a minimal existence? It is the same wherever I go, in the museum, in the ministry, or in Tahrir Square. I tell young people: You are Egypt's future. You brought about this marvelous Revolution. You'll be rewarded for your sacrifice. You mustn't give up! I am convinced of this—but the people I talk to are less and less inclined to agree with me.

I watch the exodus of our educated young people. Three of my most industrious colleagues in the museum are already in America. Others have taken unpaid leave and are either sitting frustrated at home or searching for a higher-paying position. It is precisely the intellectuals and the well educated who are leaving the country. And what are we to do without these people? The literacy rate is sinking lower and lower as children and young people are neglected. The son of the doorman in our apartment building, Mohamed, is nine years old. He wants to quit school and collect garbage. I tell him that school is more important; he needs to learn and get a good education.

"But my best friends have already left school. They're working as garbage collectors or selling newspapers or begging on the street. At least they make a little money."

A nine-year-old who already sees no sense in further schooling. A young Egyptologist who would like to improve her academic qualifications, but feels that it makes no sense financially. I have spent half my life working for better schooling and higher academic standards at our universities. I tried to convince my colleagues in the antiquities service that the museum is a learning place too, and at the same time a place for social integration. Up to that time it had been visited almost exclusively by tourists. When I became director in 2004, Egyptians made up precisely 4 percent of its visitors, but by 2010 they were at least 10 percent. More and more school classes and groups of blind or handicapped people were passing through the rooms and galleries. They, especially disadvantaged children, enjoyed the educational workshops. But it was clear how little they knew about their country's history and how enthusiastic they were learning about it. For a long time Egypt's pharaonic, 'heathen' heritage was ignored by the society's Islamic majority. It saw the ancient sites as mainly a source of income. But true appreciation needn't cease when the receipts dry up.

I had to experience bitter setbacks. The children's museum in the cellar of the Egyptian Museum was opened to great public acclaim—and was closed again shortly after my departure. The idea of museum education was still foreign to the new (old) people in charge. Yet today I am more than ever convinced that we need not only one children's museum, but many, as they are based on a profoundly democratic idea: that in any who are encouraged to become creatively engaged with their history and its monuments, who are inspired to create their own art, to play and to dream, a seed is planted, one that will lead them to freely develop themselves and their abilities. Art is freedom. Creative thought and activity are liberating. Only this sort of freedom makes genuine art possible.

One of the most striking manifestations of the Arab Spring was the appearance of wall paintings and graffiti, with the simultaneous disappearance of the regime's obligatory propaganda images. Everywhere people could admire colorful wall bulletins, cartoons, caricatures, and picture stories that had materialized in ugly side streets, on garage walls, and the façades of high-rises. They constituted a people's gallery and—to the degree that they have survived—they commemorate the Revolution. I am not a fan of ordinary graffiti; often enough they are disgusting scrawls, but faced with the Tahrir graffiti I was filled with admiration. In those pictures and similar sculptures I could recognize the creative impulse our museum education workshops had hoped to awaken. So I am certain that the Arab Spring will ultimately make possible a future for the children's museum. Especially since we now need such museums more than ever.

I grew up in the founding years of the Socialist Republic of Egypt. People boisterously celebrated their national self-determination—the Arab nation itself and pride in it were values in themselves. But socialism and pan-Arabism were political myths that were exposed as such even during Nasser's lifetime. Egypt's 'socialism'—just as in the former Soviet republics—encouraged a military–industrial complex whose cadres form a state within the state to this day: rich generals, high-placed brutes fattened with state contracts. The myth was dead long before Nasser was.

Under Sadat there was widespread disappointment and disillusionment. He recognized this, so played the 'Islamic card'—as an antidote to the ever more aggressive protests of the Nasserites and Leftists. The 'pious leader' promoted the Islamization of public life. He declared that sharia, Islamic law, was to be a part of Egyptian jurisprudence. Also for the first time it was incorporated into the new constitution. Nasser had had the Muslim Brotherhood arrested, but Sadat courted it and condoned its massive support by Saudi money. Today Sadat seems like a sorcerer's apprentice, a man who became the victim of the very people he had conjured up.

Under Mubarak Egypt came to see the face of the card. Officially, Egypt was a secular state. Its middle and upper classes pursued a western lifestyle.

But among the vast majority of Egyptians left behind in poverty, the Muslim Brotherhood's conservative Islamism had long since become accepted. The pendulum had already swung back in the late 1980s—through the whole Islamic world.

For Egyptians the issue of self-respect after their long humiliation as a colony played a major role. After the political and moral failures of Nasser, Sadat, and Mubarak, to simple, pious Egyptians Islam seems to be the only uncompromised ethical and moral authority. Since the 1980s a conservative Islam financed by Saudi Arabia and the Emirates had gained a foothold. It was to them that the Muslim Brotherhood owed its financial and organizational backing and success. But the views of imams are increasingly being perceived more and more as inimical to progress, out of touch with everyday life, and patronizing. The Islamism of the Muslim Brotherhood and Salafists will also be revealed as a political myth. The Muslim Brothers will also prove disappointing to many. I wonder what political trump card will be played next.

One of the biggest positive surprises about the otherwise disappointing constitutional referendum were the long lines of women in front of polling places. In interviews, they explained, "It's about Egypt's future, it's about our children and grandchildren. The women were demonstrating, We're here! We're not weak!" Even though the constitution was accepted by the majority of voters, the numbers reveal another truth: Only a third of all eligible voters took part in the referendum.

Since Nasser, women have had the same constitutionally guaranteed civil rights as men, and since 1956 they have had the right to vote. We are equally entitled in all political, social, cultural, and economic areas. In fact, during the 1950s and '60s the education of girls and young women improved greatly. Many women worked, and they gradually came to occupy responsible positions in public life. To Islamists women are men's inferiors, primarily wives, mothers, and homemakers. Most reactionary are the Salafists. In their view, unmarried couples can't even be seen together in public. In June 2012 a young man in Suez was killed by the Salafists simply because he dared to take a walk with his fiancée. But the more drastically the Salafists limit women's rights, the greater the resistance to them will be. Resistance is also urgently needed, for radical Islamists are iconoclasts and enemies of culture.

If they should ever rule the country, we would truly have to fear for Egypt's ancient heritage. This is another reason why I am counting on women. They are standing with their backs to the wall. They have to defend themselves and pass their defiance along to their daughters and sons.

Thanks to a prevailing moral vacuum, our societies—not only Egypt's—are becoming increasingly defined by selfishness and inequality. In Egypt, moreover, after years of paternalism the idea of the authoritarian state is blocking our way to democracy. Everyone suffers from it: our constitutional judges and parliamentarians, the Muslim Brotherhood, the president. There is little sense of compromise, little respect for those with different opinions or of a different faith. Such is the legacy of decades of dictatorship. This is why we have become what we are.

What do we want to be tomorrow? It is the job of politics to organize a unified society, to see to the distribution of wealth, to help the weak and disadvantaged. I feel that Germany can serve as a model for us, for in my opinion it still has the greatest concern for social justice. We would do well to look to it politicallly—just as I learned a great deal about modern museum management in Germany and Austria. Egypt stands only at the beginning of the path I hope it will take in this direction, but without neglecting its own goals and visions.

My career landed me between cultures, and over the years I have increasingly considered myself a bridge builder. For that firm bridgeheads are needed. Only the person firmly anchored on both sides can help others to come together. I will continue to work to see that reciprocal interest in the two countries' respective cultures remains so strong that their peoples wish to get to know each other. To that end I will be delighted if readers of this book accept my invitation to Egypt. Journey up the Nile, meet the people, marvel at the wonders that await you. Help us to preserve this unique cultural heritage and create a democratic society. We need friends, support, and encouragement, especially in these difficult times of self-discovery. Perhaps we will meet each other somewhere in the halls and galleries of the Egyptian Museum, in front of one of its marvelous statues. Perhaps you'll have the good fortune of being able to watch blind children exploring hieroglyphs with their fingertips. You should see their smiles!

INDEX

227